THE *ART* OF UNDERSTANDING YOUR BUILDING'S PERSONALITY

DISCOVER
HOW
BUILDINGS
ARE
PEOPLE
TOO!

Wayne P. Saya

ARCHWAY
PUBLISHING

Archway Publishing books may be ordered through booksellers or by contacting:

Archway Publishing
1663 Liberty Drive
Bloomington, IN 47403
www.archwaypublishing.com
1 (888) 242-5904

Because of the dynamic nature of the Internet, any web addresses or
links contained in this book may have changed since publication and
may no longer be valid. The views expressed in this work are solely those
of the author and do not necessarily reflect the views of the publisher,
and the publisher hereby disclaims any responsibility for them.

Any people depicted in stock imagery provided by Getty Images are
models, and such images are being used for illustrative purposes only.
Certain stock imagery © Getty Images.

Wayne P. Saya and WP Saya & Associates, LLC - all rights
reserved SUSTAP, LLC Certification for Facilities-Profiler and
Facilities-Profiling are a separately protected enterprise.

Cover Artwork: 1994 — Monica Williams, Maryland USA - Wayne P. Saya
Copyright Registration Number / Date:VA0000671560 / 1994-08-17 — Art
Reproduction Title: The Art of Understanding Your Building's Personality.

Vintage 1863 US Capitol photo courtesy Library of Congress - Negative
pressure building graphic courtesy of Building Science Corporation,
Westwood, MA - Personal Photographs courtesy of Wayne and Nancy
Saya – Custom graphics prepared by WP Saya & Associates, LLC

ISBN: 978-1-4808-8732-9 (sc)
ISBN: 978-1-4808-8731-2 (hc)
ISBN: 978-1-4808-8733-6 (e)

Library of Congress Control Number: 2020902476

Print information available on the last page.

Archway Publishing rev. date: 05/08/2020

CONTENTS

DEDICATION

For almost two decades my children have been aware that I had written a manuscript, a book about buildings that required some updated materials and one or two more chapters. Year after year—Dad! when are you finishing your book? And then there were the comments from Nancy, my better-half—You know your father? He'll just take his time like he does with everything. Well, I'm semi-retired now, and with a number of recent science-related findings it was now time to complete a project I had started decades ago. This is for you my children, and my wife Nancy, who I call Tweety.

There are a couple of industries that I think should be mentioned, the first being commercial real estate. I wanted to reveal some helpful antidotes that I hope can help in the day-to-day operation of your buildings and built-environments. Unlike the hospitality industry, large and hi-rise commercial real estate relies heavily upon your understanding of your facility's operations and engineering along with the structures you operate. With that in mind I hope these writings as seen through my eyes relieve at least some of your confusion. For my friends within hospitality—I hope you can take comfort in reading some interesting times I had within the industry, and my attempts to uncomplicate the complicated. I'm sure you can identify with some issues regarding your profit margins—as well. During these times of uncertainty with airborne viruses and contagions', having a diverse understanding of the structures you use for shelter and protection—I have always believed is helpful.

"A real friend is one who walks in when the rest of the world walks out."[1] ... There are a number of well-respected professionals in both commercial real estate and integrated facilities management which have contributed to the success of our trade-craft and industry. Michael Rogers over at EMCOR Government Services (EGS) and Roger Frischkorn of Cushman & Wakefield Secured Services, both out of Washington, DC—thank you for the years of loyalty and friendship. Steven Sakach, Dan Packa, and Ed Clark, Jr,—my retirement compadres and great prior work-relations through the years. Roger Peterson over at Aramark, my apologies for my over-zealousness regarding the Army-Navy rivalry. Sergio Vasquez, difficult to keep track of your travel. Bill Koran and Terrence McManus, the best energy guys west of the Mississippi.

To the friends over at ASHRAE, you're second-to-non in the industry. Daisy Gallagher—thank you for a great Foreword, and Virginia Gibson (Sis) for your years of continued friendship and your service to the Navy League.

Dale Downer and my friends within the US Department of State-OBO, William (Bill) McMillian at (SFL-TAP), and FEMA/HPSF—you know who you are. COL (Ret) Dom Garzone—a simple thank you! and Les Gable, I hear you're loving jets in Pensacola—also a simple thank you!

. . . . I always look forward to our gatherings.

---

[1] A quote from early American columnist, Walter Winchell.

FOREWORD

I am thrilled to write this foreword, not only because Wayne Saya is a friend and a colleague, but because he brilliantly encapsulates the complexities of civil, mechanical, and electrical engineering as an exercise on how buildings function and behave, how they operate, and how to understand their operation all in a delivery that makes the complicated sound simple. He exposes the anatomy of a building in a way never before realized and has taken off the blanket of secrecy in what makes a building tick. It is because of this simplistic style, that all levels of professionals from experts to those who know little of the workings of the buildings they manage can enjoy the true nature of buildings. As a member of the Washington, DC business community for more than two decades, I interact with policymakers and other influencers and Wayne is known as an advocate and voice on behalf of the build industry. The 114th U.S. Congress recognized him in the Congressional Record which states, "…. His continued advocacy is a critical tool for engineers, mechanics, and buildings that might not otherwise have a say." I have also interacted with Wayne on several business projects, his passion for buildings would have you think they are truly awake or as he likes to say "buildings are people too." In the late 1980's, Wayne was recruited by Siegfried (Sigi) H. Brauer, one of the founding partners of the Ritz-Carlton, as Chief Engineer for its Boston property. During this period, besides learning the company's financial and management program, Wayne helped Boston's engineering director to realign the mechanical operation of this vintage hotel. In less than a year's time, Sigi transferred him to the Washington, DC property as Executive Engineering

Director overseeing a multi-million-dollar renovation on behalf of the Ritz-Carlton. I met Wayne close to a decade ago, when he was the Executive Director of a DC-based national facilities engineering organization. I found him to have a strong grasp when it came to writing technical engineering documents which he has done for a number of the nation's leading facility and property management companies. Wayne was employed by companies within the past forty-plus years utilizing his expertise as technical services director and senior vice president positions, helping to position accounts such as the U.S. Government Accountability Office (GAO) and the International Monetary Fund (IMF) in Washington, DC, along with high-rise office towers. Wayne as an electronics' design engineer was an early pioneer. He is also a US Patent holder in alarm systems design. He is a licensed Department of Public Safety HVAC technician, an internationally Certified Plant Engineer (CPE) and Certified Professional Maintenance Manager (CPMM). He has also instructed at Fort Bragg. In my long-standing career, I have had the privilege to serve and continue to serve in several capacities, as Board Advisor, Strategist and Chief Program Officer for government and industry on numerous national and global projects in the build industry. Having worked directly with executives in engineering, real estate, construction management and military, civilian and industry officers on projects such as the launch of a global energy-efficient insulating building technology, serving as lead executive on the World Green Energy Symposium, the executive architect of social, economic justification analysis, lead architect of economic summits and author of sustainable and economic plans, provides me with a deep appreciation for Wayne Saya's book "The Art of Understanding Your Building's Personality." Wayne's writing style is genius. He manages to interject the Cartesian method approach of Rene Descartes and other like-minded seventeenth century thinkers then converts you into the belief that buildings communicate with you and once again challenges you back by incorporating the disciplines of chemistry and biology with the science of subatomic energy and leaves you with the realm of possibility of living breathing buildings. Wayne also educates the reader in how buildings deliver a wide-open avenue for epidemic-type of outbreaks within small towns and major cities, a wake-up call when reviewing our most recent pandemics. He renders it all, simplistically for everyone from facility maintenance engineers, asset managers, or the manager of buildings or facilities. He takes you through the structure and mechanics of a building, what makes it work and run as he compares it to the essence of breathing. In between, the pages are filled with lessons learned and details on his close affiliation with Sigi, who had a great impact on Wayne's life and a source of inspiration for this book. The relationship between Wayne and Sigi alone is enough to read this book. It exemplifies a trust the two had with each other rarely seen in today's culture. Wayne points out that many property managers still use a Rolodex style approach and rely too much on third party contractors. They undercut the health of their own building in place of making their bottom-line profit margins. If property and hotel managers implemented this new knowledge in the operation of their buildings, they would certainly operate them much differently. This will also increase their profit margins from the energy savings derived from a more efficiently-run facility. This book was cleverly designed to provide buildings with a voice. In the "The Art of Understanding Your Building's Personality," the focus is on changing the paradigm, a culture that believes predictive and preventive maintenance is strictly a cost center when these programs should be looked as a profit center. One of the key phrases used within the Utility Management vs. Energy Conservation Chapter specifies "if you operate your building properly, energy efficiency happens automatically." When I asked Wayne why now, he told me he started the book back in the mid- 90's and Sigi's sudden death hit him hard so he put it down. He picked up the manuscript again once he started instructing at Fort Bragg. Watching the faces of the military students, he said brought him enjoyment that had been lost shortly after Sigi's sudden passing. Once he retired, Wayne decided to take on some of his writings and previous short publications and merge them together in this book. I believe deeply in the importance of providing access to careers through training for those in the military transitioning to civilian life. Wayne and I also share this same commitment and have both advocated to Congress for legislation on this measure. Wayne took his experience one step further, using his electronic design engineering experience, he merged it with a decades'- long facilities engineering background, and combined both into teachings he developed for career US Government and Military professionals transitioning to civilian life. This book will also serve as a great tool for those in the military transitioning to civilian life interested in learning more about the build industry. There are so many touch points throughout the book. It is heartwarming, engaging, educational, informative and prolific. Wayne asks you to reflect, "Do you know your Building's Personality?" What would Descartes do? What would Sigi do? Join me and discover why "Buildings are People Too!"

INTRODUCTION

Of the three or four career opportunities I had as a young adult, I started in electronic design engineering, but ended in facilities engineering. It certainly wasn't the profession I chose, but the one where I based my career in. After a stint working with government associates, where I enjoy friends from that time to this day, my facilities engineering career started as an assistant chief engineer within office buildings in Boston, Massachusetts USA while next trying out the maintenance and engineering trade within the hospitality industry. At the time I had no ambition making this my career path, but at the time it was easy. I understood the mechanicals and electrical systems. It was fun and it allowed me to look at buildings the very way I looked at the intelligence of electronic circuitry. However, I can assure you I wasn't a facilities geek obsessed with the built environment, you know, those having such strong ties to their buildings that they believed in neutron bomb remedies – kind of a kill the people save the buildings intellect? I was a young guy first wanting to be a hockey player and ended up talking to buildings. Hey, I didn't start the conversation, they did! I'm told as long as I don't actually hear them talk-back, I'm OK. So far so good. But I do get a bit perplexed when I feel a sense of their communication, the kind I'm certain you too will begin feeling as we take this journey together toward the understanding of buildings.

In time I entered facilities management, where I was no longer cooped up in an office working on intelligent electronic designs that would end up under review with companies and think-tanks such as Arthur D Little in Cambridge USA, and others, staring at monostable multivibration circuits for the variety of frequency-hopping communication systems. I was fortunate having excelled within the electronics field while receiving a couple of US Patents for my efforts, one of which I was advised went directly to Uncle Sam. A couple of early college-age mistakes had me seeking a break from the tedious experimentation of electronics and some hardships the craft produced. I had reached a level in electronic design where I couldn't shut off the thinking of circuits. I felt like a computer receiving downloads, and I just wanted them to stop. The change to facilities engineering replaced those downloads of complex circuits with a fun distraction. At the time I had perceived this distraction would be a temporary break. Instead of understanding the artificial intelligence of timing circuits and advanced frequency hopping techniques, I got to enjoy the functional workings of a building. But then I started to envision a whole lot more, some of which I will try my best to put into words within the following pages.

I became interested in electronics through Dad, who showed me how to use a soldiering iron at the age of five. I remember those days on Philips street on Beacon Hill in Boston.

Dad was Ralph Saya, my hero, and outside with family members such as aunts and uncles, our last name was spelled differently. The original spelling was Saija. Dad had explained that when he received his paper driver's license in the mail, the i and the j together was mistaken by the motor vehicle registry as a y. At the age of seventeen, Dad did not want to reveal the mistake for fear of his license being held up for an unknown period, where everything went through the U.S. mail, so the spelling of my Sicilian surname and the name of my own foundation was changed in 1934, more than thirty years before I was born. It's coincidental how the structures we now build go through the very name changes, although for different reasons.

The Boston Post

There is no strength in exaggeration. Even the truth is weakened by being expressed too stron[g]

WEDNESDAY, JUNE 9, 1948

THIRTY-SIX PAGES—THREE CENTS

WBZ-TV Debut
Scheduled Tonight

Sets Within 40-Mile Radius to Get Video

Post's "Views and News" Scheduled by Station

BY HOWARD FITZPATRICK

ADMITS TAKING WOMAN'S $9750

Man Allegedly Promised Mother to Get Son Out of Jail, but Bet Cash on Races, Police Say

NOW 97 TELEVISION LICENSES IN NATION

FAVOR NO TAX FOR GARAGE

Senators for Hub Commission Provision, 18-8

PALESTINE TRUCE SET FOR FRIDAY

Ask Arabs and Jews to Reply Today to Terms

PROPERTY MAN IN TV HAS WOES

RED SOX HALTED BY INDIANS, 2-0

WBZ-TV On The Air!

Ralph Saya at Cinema Incorporated one year before WBZ-TV started broadcasting from Boston, Massachusetts USA (1947)

Dad was an early pioneer in television, starting the film department around 1950 at the second NBC television station in the country, WBZ-TV in Boston, a number of years after the first commercial TV station, WNBT-TV started airing in New York. But Dad also shared that the New York station started airing a short period before WBZ was opened. All TV stations east of the Mississippi started with the W for Westinghouse, and later stations west of the Mississippi started with a K for Kaiser, or I think that's how Dad explained it. Before 1946 commercial broadcasting was done only east of the Mississippi. Both stations were owned by Westinghouse Electric, which was owned by the Radio Corporation of America (RCA) at the time. This is why the W.B. in WBZ stood for Westinghouse Broadcasting. Dad told us it was a couple of executives from RCA that tried recruiting him first in 1948, but it wasn't until around 1950 that he had realized that the TV experiment was working in Boston, so he sent a letter to a Mr. Sarnoff in New Jersey, where he later received a phone call while in his Boston office of Cinema Incorporated, and was ultimately offered the film position in Boston. The stories and memorabilia of Dad's adventures within television, his Hollywood connections helping early films edit for TV, and his film inspection equipment designs while helping Harwald of Chicago, would need its own book to describe.

WBZ-TV annual gathering of retired film department members – rear left: Roy, Jack, Lou Bortone (retired art director) & Joe – front: Ralph Saya (2007)

Anyway, Dad was one that had life in general figured out. He nurtured my understanding of electronics, having me write multiplication tables along with ohm's law equations on napkins as homework after school. It was done on folded napkins that forced me to write slowly in order to avoid ripping the napkin, which by design provided me with a better memory-retention of what I was writing. I was also required to write out certain elements from the periodic table that were color-coded so that I would choose and understand conductivity and the nature of the various conductive metals. Dad was my friend and my hero and I was his buddy, just as I too now have a buddy that now watches over me and our country. Dad and I shared this special bond until a month after his ninety-fourth birthday, on the morning of Thanksgiving Day, of 2011.

Wayne, Jr. standing watch over sleeping Wayne, Sr. (1998). In 2017 Junior graduated the United States Naval Academy, Annapolis, Maryland, as a US Naval officer.

On my own, I went deeper than just learning these atomic numbers and their associations. I became amazed when I had learned that everything on earth, from paper to dirt, to water from the faucet are made of live atoms. The pages of the books I read had a different atomic number of live atoms associated with them while the ink on the pages had a different atomic number of live atoms. Dad use to tell me that if I put on a special pair of glasses, I would be able to see all of the different atomic structures moving within the concrete of the sidewalks to the leaves on the trees. Of course, no such thing as a special pair of glasses existed, but to me, it was all real and magical. I remember it was from that day forward I would treat everything, from the chair I sat on to the pillow on my bed as though they were alive, because internally they are! I even remember I was around ten years of age when Dad came walking into the kitchen as my eyes were watering. He had asked, *Hey buddy what's with the glassy eyes?* I remember telling him I had broken an antique hand-painted dish. You see, I had believed the atoms within this hand-painted stoneware were now damaged to a point where certain atoms were killed and disappeared forever. Dad cleared that up right away. He explained in so many words that nothing ever dies. As a young facilities engineer, I remembered those words spoken a decade earlier by Dad.

The concept for this book started around 1989. I was preparing an electronic repair for a timing circuit to a third-generation building alarm system. It was an 'Autocall' brand system, and this circuit was visibly burnt up. At that time, I explained to the east Cambridge, Massachusetts USA building owner that part of the building's brain had fried. As a young professional, it was rather cool and enjoyable to identify the building as having a brain. Two years later while chief engineer for CW Whitter and later Whittier Partners, a Boston, Massachusetts real estate company, now CB Richard Ellis, I was overseeing work on a vintage Buffalo Forge air-handling-unit, I was engaged in a conversation regarding this old ventilation system, explaining to vice president Dan Ward, that his building was having difficulty breathing. It was during this conversation that I first remember coining the phrase of Building Personality Profiling.

I would use this term yet again in 1992 when I needed an avenue, a method that I could anchor the understanding of buildings too. It was during this time that I introduced the Cartesian approach to Sigi Brauer, whom you will meet in Chapter One. I would use the Building Personality name as a part of the Ritz-Carlton's energy management program that Ritz had submitted as a part of their

Malcolm Baldridge quality award submission. When the company had learned I had used this phraseology with my prior employer, management advised they probably would not pursue the name or concept after Malcolm Baldridge. They didn't. Although saddened for sure, it was not the end of the program where it has been alive and well since those Whittier days.

Chapter 2 is where the Cartesian approach lives and where your building's art of understanding starts. This is the chapter specifically designed to change your mindset. This is the method I used with Sigi and a pathway for understanding that he enjoyed, although we only reached a certain level together. The chapter does not get into rigorous origins or the beginnings of various theories. This is not an engineering textbook that attempts to apply various complex models. Chapter 2 is an exercise that is designed to forever remind your brain to think differently about a building.

I tried to be a bit meticulous when describing technical issues, using plain language. If in the unlikely event you get a bit confused with some of my overviews on Descartes explanations or don't understand a particular method of understanding, skip it, and keep reading. Come back to the part later, because some of these descriptions are reworded in different ways throughout the book. I remember when I was translating Descartes several methodologies to that of our building, I would occasionally go back to his seventeenth-century style of writing for it to sink in. Fortunately, I have fixed some of those parts to make it easier reading for you, but take your time with chapter 2 to allow the concepts to sink in. This is your pathway to a new discipline.

I've been told that there is a chapter or story that will provide a different enjoyment, that may cause some of you to go directly to that particular chapter. With this in mind, I would suggest and somewhat urge you not to skip or circumvent any chapter without going back. Aware of your building's personality will change your intellectual perception, your view in society's model of how things work as it did with me. There's a lot to digest.

Where some aspects revealed within the following chapters may appear surprising, being attentive to these writings and being aware of them may appear to be the same thing, but Science has found these two are in fact separate. Your brain can pay attention to something without you being aware of it. So, although you may believe what you are reading may be forgotten because of its mild complexity, your mind may very well use this information to understand and associate antidotes within the following easier to read chapters.

The information and antidotes contained within the following pages are shifting a paradigm, allowing a building to be more understandable to owners and asset managers, where prior to this understanding, asset management and facilities engineering have at times been at odds according to the technical and engineering language barriers. The intent here is to expand your mind's understanding of your building as you walk through its various parts. You will start to visually and thoughtfully understand its operation in ways not before realized.

I will take you through the structure and mechanics of a building, the very essence of what makes it breathe, and to some, directly, what makes it work and keeps it running. First, you will travel with me through time and space. No, this is not a science physics novel, but a journey where you will have to learn to understand your building. After all, as building owners, managers, and real estate professionals, how well do you reliably know the structures you own and oversee? You are executives and professionals of business, not seasoned facility engineers.

I can tell you that the qualified facilities engineer knows much, but how much? What does the facilities engineer really practice when caring for your property? What does he really know that you do not? He is the building's advocate, the voice of an edifice that by itself cannot speak our language, yet is translated in engineering terms by its human advocate. It is with these terms and practices that require translation into an understandable explanation.

First, I must warn you - the building owner - that I will expose your building to your property management team, giving them a format to explain which body part of your building needs capital maintenance or upgrade funding. In-turn, property management should know building owners will have a clear more concise understanding of the needs of their property after you provide your request for operational or capital funding. The Beneficiary should be the building, but as always, this too depends on economics.

Natural life——mechanical life. —Nature——synthetic nature. What distinguishes these two from a higher superiority? Are we the organic creation of a superior mechanical force? I think not! Yet, think of how we have created the very extension and blanket of protection for ourselves by replicating our own human structure, our body. Unconsciously or otherwise, we have created buildings in our own image. Oh, how all becomes relative as you will soon discover, for relativity just never stops playing a significant role in our continuing evolution and communication toward the understanding of your building's personality. Understanding the personality of your building is clearly an art.

I have written this model as a proactive and in some respects an interactive exercise for learning and understanding how your building functions and behaves. How it operates and how you can understand its operation. The use of the building is not at issue. From high rise office buildings and the hospitality industry to the mechanicals incorporated in hospitals to industrial manufacturing plants, buildings are all built similarly. Some are taller or longer and contain different parts, similar to a person borne with a higher level of intelligence or a dissimilar thermal envelope of skin.

The languages of the various engineering disciplines, such as mechanical, electrical, and electronics, are replaced with a combination of straight, clear and concise interpretations, using a Cartesian method, an approach that uses a philosophical and scientific system of René Descartes that incorporates like-minded thinkers of the Renaissance period, merging these giants of history with those of our modern-day engineers.

Descartes, Albert Einstein, Max Planck and dozens more, separated by centuries and recognized through their physics, believed there was some type of intelligence beyond their understanding that provided instruction for nature. These were geniuses in their field. Rock stars in today's world.

One important fact to keep in mind, this isn't a book about

religion or religious beliefs. It's about the understanding of the structures we design, build, and maintain. Connotations and quotes presented from the giants of physics past and present that reflect God or origins of unknown intelligence should be reflected upon and interpreted by you the reader. For me to delete these passages during a particular discussion would leave a question, a blank as to what these giants of physics were actually thinking and talking about. In the end, your unique understanding will be the engine driving this book of Understanding. Where science or creation lead us will be up to you.

These conversions will also provide a revealing look into how buildings communicate with you, whether you are the facility maintenance engineer, the asset manager, or simply the person or group who owns or manages the building or facilities.

But how do you provide a realistic and easy-to-understand explanation of your building that incorporates so many major categories and topics, while simultaneously comprised within a variety of professional disciplines? All it would take is one substantial oversight or mistake while merging specific categories such as electrical engineering with basic human anatomy, and the understanding offered turns into basic fiction. It had to be done accurately.

Reflecting upon a number of my experiences throughout the decades and around the globe, I've shared some of these accounts within the built environment profession while sharing with you my understanding and reasoning behind each one. I've enjoyed a variety of interactions with structures and facilities taller than the Empire State building and lower than a dozen floors underground, in the basement. I looked at each encounter methodically, believing a less-complicated remedy was achievable, and for the most part what simply worked well for me. I never counted the times that associates would advise me to try this or try that. For me, to guess was never an option.

Thinking in simple terms, I understood that the method of categorizing books in a library is typically by subject. So, how are the subjects of mechanical, electrical, and civil engineering with the principal disciplines of chemistry and biology, all merged with the science of sub-atomic energy, categorized? Don't worry, it's far less complicated than it sounds. The goal was to maintain a focus on the main subject, the building. Several technical foundations had to be prepared for each subject matter to be successful in providing a context for the areas of each described category. But I think to stay on the main subject, the building, was the most challenging when providing the varying explanations. The number of details within the variety of subject-matters constantly required a necessity-check. Consequently, the determining factor was whether a questionable sentence or paragraph would benefit the goal of changing our current mindset. Time was taken to understand each of the topics, and in my case, well over twenty years for a project that will most likely never be completed in my lifetime. However, this was not the only reason for the time and delay in completing this manuscript.

I could not write the manuscript without providing all methods a building uses to communicate with its caretakers and occupants, where within chapter 4 you will learn the reason there is more than artificial intelligent systems. Without including all methods of such communication, your understanding becomes incomplete, an attempt to force-feed the reader with a partial explanation, side- stepping a major component of a building's originality. It's like Coca Cola®; once you change the recipe, it's no longer the Real Thing! Frankly, I just did not believe society as a whole was ready to hear the evidence, so I routinely procrastinated, I took my time. Chapter 4 is a rather revealing and scientifically proven means of communication our structures offer, so rather than offer additional experiences that surrounded my-own understanding, I included the real thing.

Next, the traditional method for offering such a multi-category program, or in this case, understanding, is typically through the use of a tutorial. However, realizing the dynamics of the systems within each category, and the complications of intertwining these categories, offered a real dilemma in confusing the reader. I needed to include the true story that precipitated the development of the

Cartesian approach I used for the straightforward examination of our building. An uncomplicated way of understanding the building was key, so un-complicating the complicated was a necessary approach.

When I reflect upon the various experiences I've enjoyed throughout my career, I realized I needed a process and procedure that was based upon a causal analysis. Namely:

- The true story behind the program
- the system used for creating the program
- a variety of antidotes and experiences explaining the program
- and finally, information previously unknown but revealed through science and technology to understand a major yet real component of the program. You see, buildings are people too!

Skeletal-frame of the dome covering the US Capitol during construction in 1863, was originally inspired by the east front of the Louvre, as well as the Paris Pantheon.

Big Al

It was just over two-hundred years before Schauberger's publication— whom I'll introduce to you later–where in 1863 a story began about a young unknown soldier from the American civil war who came to view construction of a larger Dome under construction upon the United States Capitol building, where he wrote: *It seemed—in utter defiance of the rebellion. Then as never before I felt that my first loyalty was to that Dome—rather than that of any other State.* This was a soldier's emotional feeling of loyalty to an architectural structure—a building. This was an organic human in admiration of his material counterpart—a human structure admiring a material structure. Could this have been a photonic connection experienced by this soldier?

I remember a while back during a visit to our nation's capital, as I walked the Washington Mall in front of the Smithsonian castle and staring, while lost in thought, at the very Dome that the young civil war soldier had once vowed loyalty. It was a wonderful sight where on this humid day in 1994 I could see a helicopter returning Thomas Crawford's nineteen-foot Statue of Freedom from a lengthy restoration and placing her back upon the pinnacle of this skeletal framed structure, where she had stood since the very day that the young soldier had expressed his humanistic emotions.

During this visual encounter, I imagined being fingered by the past where, in an instant, my memory played all of the surrounding sights as a quickly passing vermilion-colored blur and the Dome was centered directly ahead, within a transforming circular picture of blue, as though I had gone beyond the speed of light and started to revert back in time. Although my wrist-watch had not changed to an instant of slow-to-rapid reverse, in a flash I was imagining Einstein's special relativity lapsing me into history, with a consciousness of finding myself standing beside that young soldier, while simultaneously enjoying the experience of witnessing the Dome's completion all over again. Nonetheless, in that same visual moment, the reality of this event had me in the present, witnessing this Dome's present-day reality and future.

This brief hypnotic reflection with time dilation encouraged me to cross the Mall and a short walk down constitution avenue to the Albert Einstein memorial on the grounds of the National Academy of Science and Engineering. Standing along-side of me was my three-year-old, Melynee, who had curiously asked, *what's he daddy? That's Al Einstein, sweetheart,* I answered. Looking up at Einstein's lost-in-thought expression she proudly proclaimed with hands in the air, *He's Big Al daddy!* To this day and within these writings I refer to Albert Einstein as Big Al.

Picture of Wayne, Sr. holding daughter Melynee in front of the Albert Einstein memorial on the grounds of the National Academy of Science, Washington, DC (1996)

Whether recalling an emotional remark of a young civil war soldier in his admiration of the Dome of the United States Capitol or retrieving from our own memories such emotional utterances about a similar man-made site, buildings surely have personalities of their own. Nevertheless, it is the personality of one who first envisions the material building. Yet, no matter what vision man may have for his designs, the building's own temperament ultimately takes over and overwhelms its creator, providing evidence of a hidden singular personality.

A sixteenth-century philosopher and mathematician created the concept—later, building and facility profilers developed the rules. Now building owners, managers, and real estate professionals can understand and practice the facility profiler's best-kept trade secrets.

CHAPTER 1

The Builder of Empires is Called Back to Nature
—Remembering Sigi Brauer

Strange is our situation here on earth. Each of us comes for a short visit, not knowing why, yet sometimes seeming to divine a purpose.[2]

——Albert Einstein

To Big Al, it was enough... to wonder... at the secrets. More than occasionally each year I would receive a phone call that would light up my day. He was the only icon I knew, and he was calling me. Mr. Wayne—this is Sigi, in that strong firm German accent, that came only with a self-confidence found nowhere else. Siegfried H. Brauer was his name, Sigi to his friends – Mr. Brauer to everyone else. But this day was different. This call was not from Sigi. I recall it was Tuesday, September 4, 2001, and it was

Siegfried H. Brauer, Circa 1992

---

[2] Albert Einstein Archives, The Hebrew University of Jerusalem, from The speech entitled, "My Credo," for the German League for Human Rights, 1932, AEA 27-067.

a close friend, Scott, telephoning me about Sigi. In a low calm and deliberate voice, I was told Sigi was gone, his life taken in a car accident the previous Saturday, on a road near Lake Shore Park in the New Hampshire Lakes Region, just over an hour from my home in Nashua. I stared at the ceiling until I realized there was, in fact, someone on the phone. Sigi was still working on the Turner Hill project, and there was the major air conditioning issue confronting Trinity Place in Boston—with the impending closure of the North Winds Energy Plant. What about the trip to Miraval in Arizona? He was the monarch building another empire! My mind was racing for an explanation. The epitome of self-sustaining coolness, a founding officer of the modern Ritz-Carlton Hotel Company, I don't understand how nature could have reclaimed the builder of empires? *Wayne, I am told it was instant—he knew nothing of what had happened.* This was a statement to comfort me, that Sigi's body had been spared pain, while his celestial soul, using Descartes words, carried into an unknown level of spirit. Within an instant and as unpredictable as quantum mechanics, his body had been turned-off, separated from a spirit known by much more than many. I felt lost where there was not a thing I could do about it. I was in unfamiliar territory, instead of interpreting his building engineering, I was selfishly trying to interpret the loss of a friend, while later in a hollow sense attempting to interpret his loss to an entire industry. If it were Sigi calling I could somehow fix it, no-matter what he threw at me, no matter the impossibility his problem or vision entailed, it was Sigi asking, my friend, and the one who made it known I would receive his call after everyone else. This was not because I knew all of his answers or because I was this brilliant technician. It was because of a comfort level I always tried to provide him without gloating. *Mr. Wayne—I don't call you frequently because you are already here.* This was Sigi's explaining his reasoning for typically seeking me out last. I think he believed my previous explanations stored within his memory provided him with a skill, a thought process from lessons learned, and to a point he could locate the answers to most questions he sought within his world. As regret would have it, the realization was factual, it was someone else on the phone speaking about Sigi, and for the first time I could not explain to Sigi the problem he now possessed.

It was not until I was within Sigi's shared beach-house at his funeral on Lake Winnipesauke that it hit me. Sigi once wagered he would give me something, I would not have a clue how to fix. This wasn't fair! You just can't leave without giving me an opportunity, a question that was solvable! I have thought of this final effort for a while. Sigi knew the body as a machine since those days when we shared those rather lengthy explanations of Rene' Descartes. Those Ritz note pad pages I would send him and in-turn handed back to me after our meetings, letting him know the issue was discussed. Sigi disliked a cluttered desk. Sigi had to know deep down I would not let this unexpected challenge go unanswered. I would also expect he had too much confidence to know his legacy was well-secured with his well-known reputation. With all we had been discussing and projects still incomplete before his departure, I consider this as an unfinished assignment. So here we go.

Meeting with the Hotelier

Frank Sibilia and Wayne Saya in West Palm Beach, Florida, during the pre-opening of the (then) Ritz-Carlton Hotel (1992)

Around March of 1992, I received a telephone call from Boston's engineering director, Paul Saccone, a Massachusetts Maritime Academy alumnus and local acquaintance within the Boston, Massachusetts, facilities engineering community. Paul had replaced veteran facilities engineer Frank Sibilia, who was sent to open the soon-to-be Ritz-Carlton in West Palm Beach, Florida. Frank had a career of opening hotels, and he was Sigi's encyclopedia for the Boston property. Frank explained that it was his dream transfer, to retire In Florida while working within a comfortable position. As one Topic would lead to another, I learned that the blind employment adds I had earlier responded to were generated by a national luxury hotel chain, the Ritz-Carlton. Paul was calling to inform me he had received my inquiry, but I had never believed the ad was for a Boston hotel. With varying thoughts, along with a strong hesitation toward avoiding a return to the hospitality industry, I was asked incidentally if I would meet with someone very important with this hotel company. With a sense of curiosity, I had questioned why? I was happy where I was and having a wonderful time within my sandbox of buildings in downtown Boston. *Just meet with this guy,* Paul calmly suggested, where I may like what I hear. *Sure, OK, why not?* Little did I know I would meet with a force stronger than electromagnetism, and more elusive than gravitons.

I was cocky, confident, and curious when the day came, not realizing I would arrive at an environment I was not remotely expecting. Yet, I simultaneously maintained a professional sense of cockiness and humor. In taking liberties of paraphrasing from time to time, I will attempt to bring out a sampling of the many conversations I have had with Sigi and others.

First, Sigi had this strong yet calmly commanding German accent, using a European etiquette or form of address when speaking to members of his staff, such as Mr. Wayne. Second, his W would sound like a V. *So, Mr. Vayne, what makes you think I vould accept you as a Ritz-Carlton employee?* At that moment and with my current position secure, my cockiness had me believe this would be an enjoyable time. Why? because I was not aware this was a defined true to word interview, I was only to meet this guy, and I was not looking for a hotel to replace several high-rise buildings. I was, in fact, comfortable within the position I held with a major Boston real estate partnership, so my answer—*Mr. Brauer, if I may, and with all due respect, what has you believing I would accept a position with your hotel?* Sigi hit me with a warm smile, as though he too was about to have fun, and what was to be a twenty-minute discussion ended in just over an hour. After all, was said and done, to this day I cannot imagine anyone of us not having a sense of pleasure from this meeting, and I believe the two of us truly enjoyed each other's openness and boldness. I cannot speak for Sigi, but I had a great time. I was pleased with myself, and that's how he nailed me. He wanted me to come back for more. Because of the length of the interview, he perceived and in-turn knew I sought after challenges. As an example, when I explained to him how hotels, in general, were not interested in operating buildings properly, but only interested in their respective bottom line profit margins, a statement I believe true to this day, Sigi instantly replied: *so why wouldn't you want such a challenge? Prove to me how I am doing all of these things wrong.* This was a man who had no noticeable ego to bruise but a sense of position while surrounding himself with those who supported his weaknesses. He was the successful statesman behind the mahogany desk with not a thread or a hair out of place, sporting a selectively assembled support team, and a larger-than-life photo of himself hanging on the wall of his professionally appointed office, picturing him at the finish line of the Boston Marathon. He was a closer and one so comfortable in his own skin. There was also one clear and unequivocal thing that is now and forever penetrated within my memory since his passing - during this meeting, Sigi explained: *Mr. Wayne, do you want to know why I am so successful—I will tell you, and I want you to learn from me—I am going to tell you a secret— I maintain the mystique—perception is reality—and providing personal respect.* Sigi required perception studies from each of his hotels. Each of his General Managers were required to do these studies with their Executive Committee members. Sigi continued by explaining to me that the service and attention he provides to such a beautiful building, its aesthetics, and guests, should match the attention we would offer a beautiful person. *When you walk in the doors of this establishment, you will always see your personal elevator operator ready to take you to your floor.* When I did ask what was so overly special about this? Sigi replied in certain words—*when a guest comes in the original hotel, I do not want them doing any work, not even as much as pushing an elevator button, and this automatically provides the guest with a personal escort to their floor, and another means of providing them with a fond farewell—but also know and remember—when I am no longer here, hotel employees will no longer operate the elevators.* It was not unexpected, and with an overwhelming sadness, with Sigi's absence these last hotel elevators in Boston, operated by ladies and gentlemen serving ladies and gentlemen, became automated with the dawn of this renovated Boston landmark. A substantial amenity of a by-gone era was now forever gone.

Sigi believed that each person is responsible for the tasks assigned to him or her. Any reasoning for a failure belongs exclusively to the person who failed. Let's say that the reason I had not completed an assignment or task successfully was that the General Manager who assigned the task adamantly refused my request for a specific purchase or process to remedy the task. This would be my failure because it was my responsibility to convince the GM why my request was required to accomplish his assigned task. This was vintage Sigi.

Sigi was an institution and truly enjoyed rearranging a building's budget to maintain that Building's Persona, its' beauty, its' aura, what I would later identify as a component of its' original personality. He would always merge this beauty with what he called, a building's character, a building's dignity, a proper welcome for his guests. With the new owners of the Ritz-Carlton Hotel Company, Marriott brought some great hospitality experience, but in my opinion, a naïve approach to this globally recognized luxury brand. Would you permit an original part of your body to be replaced with a non-original non-organic part? In maintaining the beauty of the aesthetics of its vertical transportation, I think it's safe to say that Sigi's vision of how a building that services a luxury client, should operate by favoring the building and the architect's intent, while also favoring its' beauty. Two to three employees now could be cut in favor of elevator automation. Sigi would always say that the guest is not always right, but remember they are never wrong. With this in mind, Sigi was not always right, but he was rarely wrong.

I understood Sigi's appreciative view of a building's aesthetic beauty went mostly against the philosophies of both Rene Descartes and Alexander Gottlieb Baumgarten, a German philosopher from 1714 to 1762. Where I believed Sigi's philosophy to be his unique method of success, Descartes had explained his rejection of such aesthetic cognition by claiming it comprises value judgments that are not methodical but merely subjective or personal. This is where I would love to have seen Sigi and Descartes sparring it out in a room.

I have read that Germans are the only race of people who use the word aesthetic(s) to designate what most identify as the critique of taste, and although Baumgarten would agree with Sigi, he also believed such critical judging of beauty should remain rational up to the level of science. While I am not a particular scholar of Baumgarten's philosophical writings, bringing such an observation where science has recognized aesthetic beauty as pointless and therefore not realistic. Regardless, Sigi remained adamant in his view that his critique of taste overrules a true science of sensibility. Sigi had a way of convincing you why he was right, regardless of how long the debate or conversation, and he had the patience to do so as our first meeting revealed. Nothing needed to make sense, it only needed to be right. In the end, it did not matter to Sigi how his views were perceived by others but only that his philosophy toward the success of his buildings and in-turn the company was followed, where his loyalty to the boss was unwavering.

Earlier when believing I would be speaking with some special executive of a high-end hotel company and its offerings, I came out of a meeting surprisingly comfortable, mesmerized having met with one of the most down to earth yet statesmen like personalities I had ever encountered. From Building Personality Profiling to customer interaction, the outlook of working within this culture was not as significant as the prospect of working with this commanding and unique personality. A few days later when I received a telephone call advising that I had been accepted for an appointment with this company? yes, an appointment, I too accepted, but not without an appropriate amount of sadness. Within the past five years, I had developed an attachment to the buildings I had traveled and maintained. I would miss Dan Ward and his allowing me the opportunity to speak about his buildings in a way typically heard only when speaking about friends. I very much enjoyed the environment I was in and knew I would be in for an unfamiliar change and challenge.

Sigi's Challenge

When I arrived at my new workplace, it came complete with a toy box filled with opportunities. For instance: Sigi used his utility savings, his hidden savings account, or slush fund if you will, to use for his special projects, or for just merely making his profit margin. I recognized where I had come from, they could not use the utility bills associated with the commercial real estate industry as hidden profit centers similar to that of the hospitality industry. On the other hand, utility budgets of hotels were incorporated within the owner's profit margin. After realigning and changing the hotel's high energy use machines and equipment, Sigi recognized hidden profits were developing. The utilities budget for the year was already etched in stone before my arrival, so any utility savings above the previous year's numbers, or above those of his budget were Sigi's to use, or as he would put it, properly belonging to the building. I built a graphic for Paul and Sigi that provided them with a means of understanding the approach I used for maintaining an equilibrium toward the building's labor and line item operational expenses, with the utility costs which were the last to affect the bottom-line profit margin.

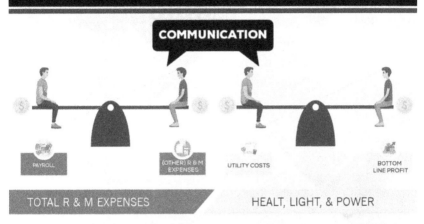

HIDEN PROFIT CENTER

COMMUNICATION

PAYROLL · (OTHER) R & M EXPENSES · UTILITY COSTS · BOTTOM LINE PROFIT

TOTAL R & M EXPENSES · HEALT, LIGHT, & POWER

A building in balance - Balancing the hidden profit center payroll had to balance with the 'other expenses' that typically were third-party contractors performing work, where in-house labor was not performing. If the contracted labor expenses became higher than the in-house labor, an evaluation would be conducted to determine whether it was less expensive to increase the in-house labor in order to reduce the contracted labor.

With some facility budgets, the utilities budget is fixed. When this fixed budget is showing a supplement, these additional funds can be transferred to the operational side of the budget to be used as either profit or for any operational repairs or projects. The in-house payroll can have an impact on utility expenses through the operation of HVAC&R systems, and this is the reason the entire operational budget needs to be in balance.

Around four or five months later, I remember being asked by Paul to meet with Sigi. Sigi wanted me to provide a number of projected savings that incorporated New England's seasonal weather changes. This would undoubtedly have me using some technical language that I knew Sigi was not disciplined in. This was such a unique question because of the variables involved with changes I had already made with the hotel's mechanicals. Not actually taking his question seriously, I explained to Sigi I wouldn't know where to begin? I will paraphrase using his reserved and methodical style, without the ability to show his confident and reassuring smile—Sigi calmly asked whom I was serving? I guessed at the answer, believing he was looking for recognition. In fact, he was setting me up for success as he would later put it. In-turn, I advised Sigi I was serving him. *Wrong answer Mr. Wayne! We are ladies and gentlemen serving ladies and gentlemen. Your efforts are providing me with the resources I need to service our guests. You are serving our guests!* Sigi went on to explain how the employee culture of this company merges with its external customers, its guests. Next, I was asked: *what in my engineering associates as nicely as ladies and gentlemen serving ladies and gentlemen?* For around ten minutes, Sigi allowed me to entertain him with a graceful analogy of electromagnetism and its role in motorized systems. *See, the information I seek is there. I trust you—I understood everything you just explained... go and walk around, let Paul know you want to leave your office early and be with your family. You should know that you are empowered to do this. Make-believe you are me, and how you would understand while sitting in my seat. I want you to pretend that I am stupid, and you need to make me understand using simple language.* Without realizing, Sigi was applying the theory of Einstein's relativity. Although Sigi was oblivious to the concept, this was something I could work with. This was something I understood. I was to create an antidote relative to his needs and wants.

Sigi was a true visionary, and by extension needed to understand. *Do you have a vision, Mr. Wayne?* I could explain the individual components and the repairs and change I effected, but why was this system built differently than the way I was changing it? Yes, he was aware of the changes that were made to the hotel's mechanicals, but this was not enough for him, it was not enough to know what repairs or modifications were performed. Sigi had to understand the underlying reason that provoked my thinking, anyone's thinking, but why the change was necessary and not necessarily how it was accomplished. He wanted to understand engineering without years of education and experience. Sigi didn't care that a specific twenty- five gallon per minute pump using a fifteen-horsepower motor was required, or that this system required only a pump. After all, and thinking like a visionary, there were additional facilities, buildings within his portfolio that could benefit.

Leaving early as Sigi suggested and heading back to the car and the St George condo on Revere Beach, I lost all thought of Sigi's assignment. I met my wife Nancy, whom I call Tweety, and we walked to the beach. I was with nature on this cool day. I remember the winds started picking up. It was nature's air-handling unit as I had once described to Dan Ward during my earlier CW Whittier days. It then hit me. I was on Sigi's time. The downtown high-rise office buildings were no more. I was to explain an air-handling unit relative to what? A cooling tower is relative to what? What was the air-handling unit providing? Nancy looked at me ever so strangely. Is the ocean an enormous cooling tower? No! What am I doing? What is Sigi looking for? The wind had now picked up to a point where we crossed the street and back to the Condo. Let's start again—an air-handling-unit is relative to what? It was providing air to the building. Again, relative to what? Relative to a person receiving air to survive. A person receiving air, a building receiving air the same way. Of course! The building is breathing. Sure, why not! I am now starting to remember, who was that French mathematician and philosopher? He thought of the human body as a machine. Descartes! Rene' Descartes! That's his name! Descartes view of the human body was exclusive and a revelation of the unknown during the sixteenth century. Descartes uniquely combines the imagery of man-made structures such as clocks, fountains, and mills with natural elements like rivers and trees to explain the functions of each part of the body. To Descartes, the natural and the mechanical are both similar in their process. In line with Descartes thinking, nature, and synthetic nature, or the biological make-up and skeletal structure of man corresponding with the electromechanical make-up and structure of a building.

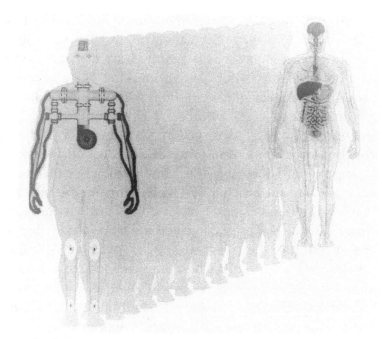

Birth of the Organic Human to the Descartes Mechanical Man
(Coloring page for Wayne Saya, Jr)

I met with Sigi the next day. While realizing I was offering him the building as a body, as a mechanical slave, Sigi asked: *so what are the pipes? what do they do?* I answered something to the effect: *Are you talking about the veins and arteries that provide comfort cooling and heating? or the plumbing track that leads to the bowels of the building?* I will never forget the mild excitement shown on his face. Sigi provided a look as though the rules had now been changed and the rule book was now being rewritten. I could see from his lack of focus that his mind was envisioning issues beyond my reach, and in time our perennial conversations would last well after our time together at Ritz. From this point in time, I used the human body to caricature the building. In-turn, buildings were becoming more and more exposed to humanity's structural and mechanical extension for us. Sigi had pushed me to think more outside the box, and freedom to experience a non-distractive environment for thinking freely. As an independent thinker and visionary,

Sigi encouraged a self-directing management team, so long as that independence provided equilibrium between his product, the building, and the owner's profit margin. Sigi gave me time off, I was off the clock, as much as management and my immediate boss would allow. However, I am certain Paul was in the loop at all times, where his relationship with Sigi was certainly much closer during this period. I was working on my own to resolve the issue of communicating the engineer's language to a layperson. Sigi understood that complex issues required creating a sanctuary for the mind. However, needless to say, results were expected.

The Malcolm Baldridge Days

What can you say about an environment with an idealistic culture, combined with a group of visionaries that had a stubbornness for achievement, and an owner, Mr. Bill Johnson, willing to give these visionaries the freedom and money to use for achieving such a vision. Sigi made it clear he was not the conductor, the ringleader, where that title belonged to the one, he called the boss, Horst Schulze. In-turn, while playing pool at a hotel opening with Sigi in Barcelona, Spain, I overheard Horst refer to Bill Johnson as the boss! Each visionary had their own boss. Nonetheless, Sigi was recognized as a catalyst for his region's success and a major contributing factor to the company's achievements. Ironically, you won't see Sigi's name within most articles or documents where the Ritz-Carlton founders are mentioned. Sigi was a founding officer, the man behind the curtain, having Horst's ear while protecting his boss and friends. A neighborhood friend of Horst from an old German township, Sigi was the northern regional vice president, with Joe Freni, whom history recognizes as one of the original founders of the modern Ritz-Carlton Hotel Company, the regional VP for the southern part of the country. It was also clear, and frankly, to my surprise that Sigi did not embrace the processes and procedures of achieving the Malcolm Baldridge National Quality Award. Sigi believed in a single vision, his vision, the one that had achieved much success. But the boss, his boss, and inseparable friend wanted the industry recognition of such an award and the purported increase in corporate profits that was said to be gained from such recognition. *Always remember Mr. Wayne, your bosses' priorities are your priorities.* I would later hear this same phrase from Paul, revealing it was an expression not only directed at me but a Sigi-philosophy and standing order for the position I filled.

The U.S. Malcolm Baldrige award was and still claims recognition around the world as the premier foundation for the promotion of performance excellence in all sectors of the economy. Its goal is to inspire organizations to achieve excellence within their industry through their positioning of the latest innovative management practices.

During this period at the end of 1991 and entering 1992, Paul and I worked on the Energy Management program that was scheduled to be placed within the hotel's library for the Malcolm Baldridge inspectors. Because of my specific facilities engineering background, I was assigned by Paul to create a draft that the two of us would later collaborate to complete. Later, we received a visit from the company's vice president of engineering, Phil Kebb, where we went over the draft, and where issues were strategized while adding specific language unique to all hotels. Phil was the person behind bringing in a Servidyne® manual energy tracking and trending program to the company. This was a paper program back in the day when energy tracking and trending was in its infancy and just coming into the hospitality industry. Computerized building automation was also in its infancy. The engineering director from each property would telephone into Servidyne® with their energy numbers each month. It was our building's EKG and EEG program rolled into one and each month they placed the results of all hotels within a master binder for the monthly corporate meeting.

I had learned shortly thereafter that Phil had come up to Boston from the Atlanta corporate office to provide input to make this document acceptable to all the hotels within the Ritz-Carlton portfolio, and specifically to meet the deadline for incorporating into this award. Just picture and imagine, in 1992, the energy management program for The Ritz-Carlton Hotel Company was placed on a designated shelf within the corporate office library just days before the Malcolm Baldridge inspectors arrived. Exciting times. This was the skill and tenacity of a culture and drive to succeed regardless of the task. However, it was not unprincipled. We put together the goals and achievements throughout the year into a multi-paged Utility Management Plan that incorporated a number of Process sheets for each of the engineering disciplines. I had coined these process sheets, Building Personality Process Sheets. The final product was inserted inside each hotel's binder at the corporate office library in Atlanta, Georgia. Looking at the original plan today, I am reminded of those carefree days, when empowerment meant succeeding. When the inspectors arrived at the corporate office, Phil was said to be prepared to explain the successes of the Utility Management Plan through the eyes of the manuscript and in-turn the successes provided within each property's binder, while the inspectors were unaware these successes were accomplished before the Utility Management Plan was written. One had to be in Atlanta to see how the Engineering Management Plan was actually presented. Nonetheless, Boston's engineering binder was said to be available with all of the other Ritz-Carlton properties within the corporate office library, designed for the inspectors to visually see and review the successes experienced at this and other selected property sites. As the principal author, I followed Pat's direction to incorporate our program into steps that designated each responsible party. As a Total Quality Management (TQM) initiative the program had to be crafted into steps while efforting to show continuity at each hotel and throughout the company. It was a mutual effort the three of us I think we're proud of. I know I was. Why? The inspectors were due at the corporate office within days and the written program needed completion. Rather than have the energy program create a building's success in Utility Management, the program was initially crafted in such a way where the individual processes were built around the successes of the Servidyne® results. We needed to make sure all hotel sites fit into the model successfully, and that we had results to show. Therefore, the program steps were designed from the Servidyne® data. This was Sigi's and the Boss's self-directed and engineered work-environment, empowerment shown in its most unique and open form. It wasn't as much as a secret formula toward winning the award as much as it was a do-or-die scenario where their never-say-never philosophy was like a drug—you wanted more. A culture and a belief that was highly addictive. Although other departments faced similar deadlines, there complications or circumstances made each department unique to themselves and all with similar deadlines as experienced with engineering. I remember attending a meeting with the TQM manager, Pat, whom I had overheard explaining how the housekeeping policy was placed on the shelves just hours before the Malcolm Baldridge inspectors arrived. Exciting times for sure.

I also remember a time back in those days when Marriott Hotels and Resorts made an attempt or two to win this most prestigious quality award, but with no success. I also remember in 1992 being asked to brief one of Marriott's Boston engineering directors from the Marriott Long Wharf, a local friend of mine, George, on the programs we at Ritz-Carlton incorporated within our engineering presentation.

In 1995 Marriott purchased a forty-nine percent stake in the Ritz-Carlton. As a bonus, the Malcolm Baldridge award came with the sale, wherein 1998, they purchased an additional fifty percent stake in the company, giving them ninety-nine percent ownership of the Ritz-Carlton. An unfair talk within the industry was: If you cannot win the Malcolm Baldridge award, just buy it, but this was just callous. You see, the Baldridge award is much easier to win with under a thirty to forty hotel portfolio, and even then, the expense is extremely high. With Marriott (at the time) well in the hundreds of properties and resorts, coordinating an effort of that magnitude was epic. Failing the designated percentage of inspections within each class determined success or failure, so even attempting such an award with hundreds and now thousands of properties would be monumental and more than likely cost-prohibitive. I would suggest this may be the reason the Ritz-Carlton is currently the only hotel company ever to win this prestigious award, along with the aesthetic understanding of a group of European visionaries having a *Wision*.

Cooling the Cooling Tower

A short time into my employment at the Boston Ritz-Carlton, I had conducted a Facility Condition Assessment review to determine the effectiveness of the individual HVAC and heating systems of this vintage property. One of my findings determined that the second of two chilled water chillers for cooling the hotel would need to be activated when outdoor temperatures reached sixty degrees Fahrenheit. This was because the age of the systems within this property did not incorporate a way for outdoor air alone to cool the interior building with the volume or cubic-feet-per-minute (cfm) of lung capacity air needed. A second issue was the building incorporating a two-pipe system—indicating only the chilled water for cooling or hot water for heating could circulate through the building at one time, where these two systems shared the same piping system.

The issue I had confronted, Once the outdoor ambient air temperature reached sixty degrees Fahrenheit, by 11:30 AM the building would require start-up of the second chiller. This was because the condenser water temperature within the cooling tower (assigned to this chiller) would become too high to maintain chiller efficiency. When this situation occurred, the chiller would no longer have the ability to maintain its chilled water temperature setting, because the condenser water no longer had the efficiency to remove heat from the chilled waterside. Remember, the basic principle of air conditioning cooling is to remove heat, and what it leaves is cold.

Ironically, during the shoulder seasons (Spring and Fall) the hotel would only need to operate the second chiller for around five hours, or until about 4:00 PM when the day started cooling-down, so during these two, six-week periods, the hotel would operate a second chiller for only four-and-a-half to five hours each day, causing the electrical demand and usage cost to spike an additional $6,000 plus each month. This added cost accumulated to four months—a third of the year, and not good because it cut into Sigi's slush fund. Paul warned me I may be called to Sigi's office, and I was. *Mr. Wayne, what is the issue with cooling my building? Sigi, your building is hot and wants to sweat, but the cooling tower assigned to this chiller has reached its limit, so the second chiller with a second cooling tower needs to be operated. OK—Good—I understand. So, what have you decided for fixing the first chiller to allow my building to sweat more?* Yes, it was Sigi's building.

Sigi did not believe that an issue that rose to a problem could not be resolved. His core belief was simply derived from Baumgarten's philosophy as described earlier. It was Sigi plain and simple, and if you wanted to stay in his respected graces, above that of his good graces, you would solve the problem. Otherwise, you were merely a good employee he would keep for operational necessity. So, here I believed I had an answer that would satisfy his need, I advised him he would need a larger cooling tower, the size of which I would need to calculate. Good—go out and use your intelligence and come back to me to explain how you will do this using your budget. Foremost, this was not my budget, it was Paul's, and there was no capital expense designated for a new cooling tower, which Sigi I'm sure had known. Earlier, Sigi had explained during his executive committee meeting, that all departments would need to become leaner. Paul later advised me this was because Bill Johnson was using the hotel as collateral for opening another hotel, and this would not be the first time the Boston property subsidized other hotel purchases and openings.

Let's cut to the chase, after determining the additional BTU's (British Thermal Units) of cooling required for these five hours, I recognized there was a second cooling tower on the roof not being used unless they operated the second chiller. I simply tied the two cooling towers together using appropriately sized PVC piping along with a small Taco® circulation pump to circulate water from one cooling tower to the other. Sigi now had an additional twelve-hundred BTU's of cooling by expanding the building's major sweat gland, its cooling towers.

Warned by Paul that Sigi did not like gloating, Paul merely advised Sigi that the building's cooling had been resolved. This would need to be in place until such time as ownership elected to upgrade the roof-top cooling towers. Later during the week while passing Sigi in the hotel lobby, I said hello using a simple nod of my head. Sigi looked and gave that look of satisfaction with a warm smile, stopping briefly to say he was taking off for a few days to see Wolf in West Palm Beach—some memorable moments are always etched in your memory. You received his warm and unflinching respect so long as your ability and aptitude provided the additional means for making him and by extension the hotel successful. As Sigi pronounced on many occasions, my job was the same as his, to make my boss successful, and by remembering the boss's priorities were my priorities.

As the weeks passed, we added additional upgrades and procedures to make the primary cooling tower more efficient. When it was noticed the cooling tower fan-bearing grease leaked out faster than normal, the bearings would be replaced, creating a noticeably elevated RPM speed for the cooling tower fan, a simple case of providing a medical check-up on our body's efficiency to cool itself, preventive maintenance for the building. The heat from the condenser water (cooling tower) was now being exhausted faster - a good thing. Remembering it is our job to keep the operating wattage as low as practicable, we want to keep the chiller as efficient as possible because heat is watts—watts is power—and power is your electric bill. Therefore, a lawn sprinkler pump was connected to an industrial water hose that was connected to the rooftop water supply. The hose was next placed into the water basin of the cooling tower for thirty minutes to an hour to cool down the cooling tower (condenser) water temperature. The overflow of the cooling tower water basin allowed the excess hot water to drain while we introduced cooler water using the hose. Typically, we lowered the basin water temperature around five to ten degrees before activating the second cooling tower. We put a cool cloth on the forehead of the building to help cool it down. This procedure kept the cooling tower fan from operating sooner, maintaining a more efficient chiller operation that used less electricity, less wattage, fewer calories.

Empowerment and Realignment of the Building's Energy

In 1992, Sigi sent me to the Ritz-Carlton, Washington, DC., as his engineering director and renovation liaison between Bechtel Construction company and the new hotel manager, Cheryl O, a Ritz-Carlton and industry superstar with an elite Saint Michael's College pedigree. Cheryl was being transferred from the Ritz-Carlton, Cleveland, Ohio, to the DC property. Mark Uhl was the engineering director in Cleveland, a little on Mark later. I will just say that Cheryl was an amazing and extremely capable GM that knew how to handle herself within a German culture alpha male-dominated company, although I can't say that Chery accepted their various male behaviors. As a private Roman Catholic college grad, she knew how to handle herself, and the boys knew it!

The hotel was about to engage in a fifteen-million-dollar operation (renovation) that included replacement of one of the two steam boilers. But they chose Bechtel as the General Contractor, a behemoth in global engineering, construction, and project management. This was a company that builds country infrastructures, airports, chemical plants, and nuclear power plants, and not your typical company that would take on a single mid-size hotel renovation. It was the equivalent of hiring the captain of a nuclear aircraft carrier to captain a rowboat. The reason—during this period, Bechtel was working on major infrastructure projects within Saudi Arabia and virtually reshaping this middle-east region, and the owner of this hotel was Saudi billionaire Sheikh Abdul Aziz bin Ibrahim, the brother of (then) King Fahd's 'main' wife. The Sheikh also owned Ritz-Carlton hotels in Aspen, Colorado; Houston, Texas and New York City. Needless to say, Royalty has its privileges. If the Sheikh wants to use a behemoth to renovate his latest acquisition tent, who were we to say no!

The Sheikh purchased the hotel in 1989 from an owner other than the Ritz-Carlton Hotel Company. I am sure the hotel was in rough shape at the time the Sheikh purchased the property, because when I arrived three years later in 1992 it was in rough shape, least of which was the vintage hideous yellow Victorian caricature wall- covering. They advised me that for the past three years or so Ritz- Carlton management had been trying to secure funds from the Sheikh to renovate the property, and they had recently secured the funding, with a visible emotion of relief. The atmosphere was tense, and I was confused at the reason until I was briefed.

The Sheikh was not happy, and this was not a good thing by any standard. Namely, for the past three years, Ritz-Carlton was not making the profit margins they had agreed to. From the meetings I had attended, this was because, at the time of the contract signing, Ritz-Carlton legal believed the renovation was to take place within a reasonable time after their purchase and signing of the new management agreement, so the Ritz-Carlton legal people too were not happy. The Sheikh believed the renovation was merely a paragraph within the contractual agreement that outlined the profit margins, and they too were right. As shown by many Arab scholars, a cardinal evil is to be put to shame in one's tent or street or village or tribe. This property was one of the Sheik's tents. Sigi was sending Cheryl and me to a property owned by a not-so-happy Sheikh. It did not matter the hotel was maintaining antiquated and stained, peeling wallpaper within the corridors and guest rooms, furniture dated from the 60s, and carpet curling and rippling. Asking for a premium price for such a lack of luxury could not be done, and Cheryl's new team could not accomplish the profit margins without such pricing. Sigi believed the way out was to take care of the Sheikh similar to the way we cared for our guests. That was all we were to worry about. Horst's concerns were not our worry. The DC hotel had a job to do, and that was all we were to focus on. It was a careful dance. Sigi had explained in so many words that his boss was dealing with royalty who believed in the written letter of the contract and from a middle-eastern culture that knew how to deal with (what they had perceived to be) deception. There was no room for honest oversight or mitigating circumstances. The owner may be late with the renovation, but we signed the contract, and a verbal understanding in any form was not worth the paper it's written on. The job was clear, they empowered me to work with Dave from Bechtel to help push the renovation through while working with Cheryl whose job it was to operate the hotel, overseeing the renovation, and make each annual profit margin. No pressure. David was Bechtel's highly detailed and well-qualified project manager.

With the renovation now in high gear, I noticed that the volume of paperwork performed by Bechtel is creating some significant delays. Specifically, approvals for routine change orders (caused by unforeseen conditions during the bid process) and the delivery process for new equipment and pre-fabricated exterior construction materials. The issue was Bechtel's project management process that required a piece of paper for every significant and insignificant detail—not a process but detail. I felt bad for David but frustrated with the process. This was because Bechtel's mandatory clerical processes and procedures had been designed specifically for building nuclear power and chemical plants and such, to achieve technical excellence for meeting world-class quality and safety standards while optimizing schedules, and regularly adjusting critical supply chain deliveries. Realistically, Bechtel was creating a thirty-volume Encyclopedia Britannica set, when all that would have been needed was less than a dozen three-ring binders.

One day, I witnessed a delivery truck arriving at the hotel and carrying the new furnace and boiler system. There was just one problem, It was a steam boiler, and not the forced hot water boiler I had requested as a change more than a month prior. Those facility professionals who know the advantage of going directly to a hot water heating source for hydronic heating, in place of using a heat exchanger, already get it. But those who don't were the ones seeking to understand. If ever there was an incident that would test the muscle of Ritz-Carlton employee empowerment, this was it. I refused the delivery of the boiler. David came out with guns blazing while explaining how I was not the project manager. Regardless of how much I privately believed he was right, I countered by explaining how all engineering conducted within this building was approved by me. I didn't want to pay additional thousands of dollars each month for natural gas during the Fall and Winter seasons by having steam heat the hot water that provided heat to the hotel. I wanted the hot water heated directly. After all, the hotel had to produce a twenty-three percent profit margin and replacing the old steam boiler with a forced hot water boiler would provide for significant savings in utility costs. The move would allow this boiler to remain offline during Summer months and become the lead boiler during the heating season where hot water would directly feed the hydronic heating system, in place of having a steam boiler heat the water first through a heat exchanger. Within minutes, Cheryl was out on the sidewalk. The phones were ringing from DC to Sigi's office in Boston, and the VP of Engineering in Atlanta was even called to ask whether what I was doing made sense. After all the phone calls and discussions, three hours later the truck left without delivering the boiler. Cheryl sided with my decision and trusted that this was the choice the hotel needed to be successful. Six months later, the Washington DC property went from the last place on the Servidyne® energy tracking and trending score to knocking Paul and Boston out of first place. Don't misunderstand me, the Boston property sliding into second place was not a leadership issue, but that of Paul's staff and its' understanding of the building's revised procedures incorporated for the all-around HVAC operation I had put in place before I had left for DC. Using Sigi's philosophy this was my failure, and he was right. Besides, we based Boston numbers upon his existing antiquated equipment and the band-aids installed before my departure. Whereas, the DC property was benefiting from a new forced hot water boiler and furnace along with a new operational program. Yes, I had an unfair advantage.

The cooling side was different. Each major machine brand at the time (Carrier, York, and Trane) had their own special and unique characteristics. What I liked about the Boston Ritz' old

R-12 Carrier model centrifugal chillers, were that they provided an ability for staff to manually control the machines demand-setting. The demand regulates the speed of how fast your chiller can reach the desired chilled water temperature. When the operating engineer needed to get to a lower chilled water temperature faster, he or she would demand the chiller to do that with the turn of the manual demand control. A seasoned facility profiler should frown on this procedure because instantaneously raising the demand automatically raised the demand and usage portions of the electric bill. Therefore, and in place of this emergency procedure, you created a synergy with your building, aware in advance of your climate and what your building would need and in-turn want in order to control its energy output. If you were not within a climate you were familiar with, you would use the heating and cooling degree days established within your region. This was the nice feature of the report developed by Phil Kebb and Servidyne®, where the heating and cooling degree days were incorporated within the monthly report.

With the Boston property, there was only so much you could teach another maintenance staff member in the needs and wants of the building. Most of the time I had believed those which received my instruction were acting more robotic, just following instructions, because regardless of how much you repeated the reasons for why you were performing certain and specific tasks, knowing your building is something you just can't teach. You had to know how the building would react with any given weather situation, how the outdoor temperature and humidity influenced the indoor climate, or how much your building's thermal envelope (skin) could protect or maintain an indoor environment you were creating, and so on. While the typical trained facilities engineer used the demand load calculations and more, the personality of the building (and by extension the building itself) would tell me what systems required adjustment. It was a dynamic you as the operator felt tied to. You knew the R-Rating of your building's insulation, or its ability to keep the heat or cold out would require a certain pre-adjustment because you and the building are one.

You didn't require the ASHRAE calculations to inform you of what your building would do or how it would react. You just knew. It was the equivalent of climbing without a rope —without a calculator—free calculating. The better you perform using your ability to read the building's needs and wants, the better you get at free calculating. In the end, your energy numbers showed it. The more freedom you develop without the use of calculations, the better you become at free calculating. Free calculating is a major component for knowing the personality of your building.

Free-Calculating

Free calculating - it's like autopilot, an unconscious function that has enabled me to perform tasks quickly and correctly with minimal conscious thought. During my experience in Boston, I was Keenly yet consciously aware that by reducing the water temperature sensor controlling the fan operation of the cooling tower, I could save twenty-five hp × twelve hours each day during an off/on operation, where each horsepower represents around 746 watts-per-hour. Next, around five cents for every 1,000 watts-per-hour, times an estimated eight hours of operation per day, times thirty days representing the month. You get the picture. Your experience level knows of how your building's thermal envelope responds from seven in the morning to three in the afternoon. You're free-calculating that it's mid-August in New England USA and New York where the feed-water temperature to your chiller's condenser loop is around ten to fifteen degrees warmer than during the Spring and Fall seasons, and about fifteen to twenty degrees warmer than Winter. The number of variables flowing through your human-computer tells you within reason the number of calories—measured in wattage—your building will be consuming to perform its energy run. You're asked during your ten o'clock meeting if you can donate toward the budget this month because of an emergency, an unexpected projected budget shortfall. Of course, your answer is yes. Sigi once commented: *Silence doesn't change the world, my friend. You create a line in the earth for people to follow.* You're a team player and this is a legitimate emergency request from the lady boss who is known to be truthful. You instantly make several free-calculating assessments. You frown on the direction you're about to take, but you're also aware this is a one-time deal. To start, you instruct your crew to remove all air filters from all of your air-handling-units for the month. This will provide a previously calculated savings of $950 in energy usage, where your blower motor will now have less resistance to operate. You're also aware this is a one-time annual offering because, without filters, you'll be bearing the in-house labor for cleaning the coils properly at the end of the month, pursuant to this lack of protection, and a procedure that weakens the fins of each coil after each mild acid cleaning, not to mention the biological crud this coil will inherit that will also require your crew to clean. I won't get into air-quality. Facility engineers are aware they're providing this calculation without their safety harness—their computer, so, a missed calculation can be disastrous. Therefore, only those experienced with an all-around functionality of their building that is produced with minimal conscious thought should attempt this type of off-the-cuff calculation and consequent risk. Sure, there are those facility pros that will offer an arbitrary approval to take a portion of their budget for emergencies without realizing the consequences or damages caused. These are the occurrences that cause suspicions within our craft.

After years of neglect and deferred maintenance, the DC area building had a voice. Ritz-Carlton was the building's advocate, its mouthpiece. The building could now radiate alongside its neighboring upscale counterparts within the popular upscale neighborhood of Embassy Row with pride and as an equal. While having these discussions with Sigi, he would equate this nature-merge with him riding his all-terrain vehicle within the New Hampshire Lakes Region of Lake Winnipesaukee. He called the lake his ocean. You could tell by the tone of his voice he loved nature and the escape it afforded him away from the calamities of Boston and the stresses of his position. With a straight and near serious face he offered a surprisingly rare look into his private life, where he boasted about a group of friends, he apparently would travel locally within the Lakes region using all-terrain recreational vehicles. While mentioning a couple by name, I got the impression he was very close to this group, where he explained using certain details and nomenclature of the thrill and certain dangers of the sport. It was therefore clear these friends were closer to him than the professional relationship we shared. But this was Sigi. If you knew him you were keenly aware that he was a naturalist and one serious about his health and the health of the environment.

Once, while the two of us were discussing the values of vitamin and mineral supplements, I shared with him the regimen of supplements I took daily. In-turn, displaying the competitor he was, he pulled three vitamin-looking pills from his pocket, challenging me to identify what they were. The only one I could recognize was the co-enzyme Q10 because it was the same type I too had been taking. Without saying a word and with a simple grin, he returned the pills to his pocket. I could only identify one. No more was to be said. The short answer—Sigi won! That was Sigi.

Illustrating a Free-Calculating Methodology

As an example of the measurement of efficiency and the need to develop the use of a free-calculating methodology, there was a restaurant Sigi had asked me to look at, post Ritz-Carlton. It was a friend of his, which meant this was more than likely a freebie. I wasn't particularly fond of Sigi offering me off to help his friends, because, during this particular period, Sigi's company was additional work against a full-time position I enjoyed as a member of the facilities management team of Tufts University in Boston. Regardless, there was always, and I mean always an underlying reason for the actions Sigi took. Where Sigi was expanding his Brauer Management company, it was a small enough request that hopefully wouldn't take up too much of my time, and thankfully it didn't.

This will be quick... The restaurant was not doing well in cooling two floors of the restaurant seating area, especially during this particular time while the city of Boston was experiencing a ninety- five-degree heatwave. There were two, twenty-ton semi-hermetic compressors. As a thought experiment, let's take the airflow of the 30,000 CFMs labeled on the air-handling-unit and use it to calculate the amount of refrigeration it will take to cool the ninety- five-degree outside air down to sixty degrees Fahrenheit. Not to worry, there's no math to figure here. I have found through the years that *this is typically the initial procedure a professional engineer would use*, to validate the air-distribution against the chiller system. **Let's start** using a standard one-hundred percent relative humidity model with the total heat content of twenty-six-and-one-half BTU/pound because of the ninety-five-degree temperature. Next, we'll use a seventy-eight-degree Fahrenheit wet-bulb (humidity) with an incoming air heat content of about forty-one and a half BTU/pound. Using the ASHRAE model we'll assume the density of the incoming air was around a typical .070 per-cubic-foot for this regional climate condition. After a physical calculation of 562.5 pounds/minute times the exhaust and incoming heat content (41.5 minus 26.5), we arrive at 8437.5 BTUs/Min. When we next calculate 1-ton of refrigeration (12,000 BTUs/Hour) as 200 BTU's per minute, we take the calculated 8437.5 BTUs/Min and divide by the 200 BTU/Min and reach around 42.2 tons/hr of cooling currently being delivered for this restaurant, **and here lies the problem.** After measuring the total square feet of the ground level and second-floor dining areas, the cooling capacity required was about 45-tons of cooling. That's more than 30,000 BTUs or two and one-half tons of cooling short.

Now let's use one of many free-calculating scenarios - I would know that the existing chiller system did not have the ability to properly cool the restaurant. How? An industry estimate provides between 400-500 square feet per 12,000 BTUs (1 ton) of cooling for a commercial application. Using the two × four ceiling tiles to measure the total square footage of the two floors, taken with the current forty tons of cooling, *I calculated about two-and-one-half tons of cooling short from the standard*. Next, I would use the approximate forty-five-ton cooling requirement I just obtained from this floor measurement exercise and address the existing system without going through the professional engineering calculations earlier demonstrated. I was now aware of how much this system could perform and the limitations of its components just through its operation. Also, Sigi's friend needed a quick and inexpensive solution.

Here, the quick and easy solution is to reduce the ninety- five degree outdoor fresh-air by reducing the exhaust air. In this case and from experience, closing the outdoor fresh-air damper from twenty-five percent to ten percent would create additional chiller capacity that would be more than sufficient to make up well over two-and-one-half tons of cooling that were missing. If we were to calculate, it would show an additional availability of about twenty- five tons of savings in cooling, or 42.2 tons of cooling minus 16.9 (0.4 x 42.2) tons, equal 25.3 tons of cooling saved. The calculations I estimated without performing these calculations were around twenty tons of savings, so I was in the ballpark. This savings frees up chiller capacity to provide far more cooling than we needed. I also knew that this calculation was based upon ninety-five-degree outdoor air, where, as the outdoor temperature moves lower, so does the savings in tons of cooling we can access. It was, for this reason, I reduced the outdoor air by a high fifteen percent. The second reason and more important, I didn't want to merely recover this restaurant from experiencing its warm temperatures, I wanted to drop this temperature down fast, really fast, and I didn't know the heat transfer condition of the cooling coils. What I did know was that these coils didn't look that great. Having access to this kind of additional cooling provided me with that option and insurance policy. After the restaurant was quickly brought to a satisfactory temperature, the ten percent outdoor air intake was thereafter raised to twenty percent which provided for sufficient air-conditioning recovery time and short-term solution.

I had learned a short while later that an original but antiquated fifty-ton single compressor chiller system was replaced with the dual twenty-ton cooling compressor units. This would account for this system's inability to cool the restaurant and the anomaly found between the total square feet of the restaurant and the existing forty tons of cooling.

Free-Calculating is not a whimsical guess. It's not an educated guess. It's not a guess. It's an art derived from your prior knowledge, education, and years of experience as a student of nature. You have been operating your building–synthetic nature—using true nature as your guide. You knew the winds from the north were present, but the accompanying cool air was not cool enough. Deductive reasoning best describes a free-calculating decision-making process.

Sigi's Philosophy 101

Boston's director of engineering, Paul, was a talented tactician and skills that have served him well to this day. Sigi trusted and used him in several ways, one of which was to educate me in the Sigi philosophy, while aiding me through several political hurdles I would face within the company. The decision I made to refuse delivery of the steam boiler was essentially based upon an earlier conversation I had had with Paul. Namely, the level of trust Sigi was granting his exec's required accountability at the highest level. If I believed I needed to make a decision that was within my purview, and such a decision was correct and would benefit the company, the decision was to be made without hesitation. However, if (as a director and executive of the hotel) such a decision proved to be wrong, the level of such failure would determine whether I was capable of maintaining such trust and position. Similarly, if my decision was deemed to be correct, and I chose to play it safe by staying quiet, I would later need to explain why my leadership as a director should continue. This was Sigi's leadership 101, and with his directors under the

Malcolm Baldridge rules, he reserved and used the management empowerment card to the highest level. Fortunately, I was beyond comfortable regarding the boiler change-out and the results it would provide, as the utility savings would later attest. Cheryl later advised me... *hey bud, you know you challenged the Sheikh's project manager, right?* Not realizing at the time, the consequence was more than just the restocking fee for a boiler purchase, but in fact, reached a level of the Sheikh's management contract - Ritz-Carlton's competency to manage the property. My blind answer to Cheryl—*yup!*

You have to be extremely comfortable with a hint of arrogant confidence to possess an ability that allows you to look at your boss, or even a building owner or manager straight in the eye to tell them what you think. I have learned through the years that it provides them with a sense of comfort, where they are unaware that there building is essentially yours, and that it is in fact in good hands. Every designer or builder that creates a building is not perfect, and by extension neither is the building. Simply put, pretend to believe that *those who think they know everything are annoying to us who do!* Once you pass through the entrance of that building, it is you that becomes its mouthpiece, you are its advocate, the voice of a mechanical environment and artificial entity.

To me, it wasn't a challenge to David's project management or competency but rather a disagreement of the mechanical engineering specification, and a firm need to modernize the design of the building's primary heating energy source. It was my understanding that the mechanical engineer was not hired to redesign the mechanical operation of the building, but merely to replace the existing antiquated boiler. I understood that the modern steam boiler selected met the energy efficiency upgrade, and the engineering was sound, but I needed more if I was to contribute significantly toward a successful profit margin, while (hopefully) play a role toward healing the wounds between the hotel owner and Ritz-Carlton, for this property anyway.

Wayne P. Saya

The Last Straw

Sigi was an early riser, and each time he came to visit the Washington, DC, hotel, I knew I too had to get up earlier than usual for a jog. Now that wasn't because Sigi forced his execs to jog with him in the early morning hours. It was something I did to show my appreciation for his visit to the hotel while trying to show him I too could keep up. Back then and probably today it would be called kiss-assing, and this would be correct. Regardless, Sigi had ten years over me but would always finish minutes ahead of my time. From the view I had from the cheap seats, Sigi liked his Nordic-Trac and his jogging, and liked to have either completed before his day began. I remember having only three of these early jogging sessions, but one, in particular, stood out. Running from the Massachusetts avenue hotel up to the Washington monument and back, and with the DC lobby renovation in full swing, we had breakfast at a Marriott across the street and less than a block away. Incidentally, Sigi never paid. While discussing some small talk about the Aspen, Colorado property, another hotel owned by his Royal Highness the Sheikh, the topic came up regarding the constant static electric shocks felt when touching the brass railings while walking down the stairs to the ballroom. The Aspen air was extremely dry; the carpet was an expensive high- end cotton blend, and the railings a polished brass. Combined they caused havoc when one touched any metal fixture or stairway railing. Sigi also wanted to understand with language easy to understand, why it was necessary to operate the air continuously for all the downstairs lower-level function rooms to eliminate these uncomfortable shock- hazards. I explained that during the hotel opening, we found several rooftop air-handling-units with malfunctioning humidification systems.

Involved with this hotel opening was the engineering director from the Cleveland Ritz-Carlton, Mark Uhl, whom after his Ritz days became the senior director of facilities and engineering at the Rock and Roll Hall of Fame and Museum, in Cleveland, Ohio USA. Today, with Mark and I semi-retired, we enjoy a professional long-distance friendship.

Mark and I located a defective float actuator similar to a Copes feedwater regulator within a roof-top mounted air-handling-unit. This design was to activate a water feed system that, in-turn, would fill a pan that was located in front of a circular blower within this air-handler. There was also a heating element inside the pan that was not activating. This heated water system was designed to provide hot water vapor to mix with the air that supplied these lower-level rooms, in-turn keeping the air from becoming too dry. It was this arid dry Aspen air and malfunctioning humidifier that was causing the static shocks experienced by staff and guests. Those brass railings and doorknobs felt far more than tickle from the static shock. By design, keeping these air-handlers operating, maintained an essential humidified air. In time, we worked on these and other issues out. As facility profilers, we knew directly what the issue was and the equipment that was the culprit of this electrical static. What we didn't know was whether the air-distribution system incorporated an appropriately sized supplemental humidification system. It would not have been unusual to find an undersized system or even a system that was not commissioned for operation, where this was a brand-new building and we were a part of the opening team. It was truly a relief to find a malfunctioning system, where these systems can be corrected. My experience in finding undersized or oversized mechanical systems are not good, because there is little you can do until the system, what-ever it may be, is upgraded or replaced with a proper-sized unit. If this had been the case at the Aspen Ritz, guests and staff would have suffered through a very uncomfortable period. During this particular 1992 hotel opening, I remember Mark had inquired as to why, during the design stage, a lower level water feature was not incorporated within this hotel, where one was installed on the ground floor. Because of this arid-dry Winter-season climate, buildings in the Aspen region have been notorious for providing hotel guests and homeowners with a facetiously-talked-about shock therapy program.

Mark Uhl and Wayne Saya at Snowmass Mountain, Aspen, Colorado, during the opening countdown of the new Ritz-Carlton Hotel (1992)

Mark Uhl and Wayne Saya, 24 years later at the Rock & Roll Hall of Fame, Cleveland, Ohio (2016)

Later the following week, Sigi telephoned to inform me I was going to their hotel in Dearborn, Michigan. *Mr. Wayne, the engineer in Michigan thinks the way to practice energy savings is to shut off the air-conditioning chiller.* Sigi would always make it clear I was not to make my counterpart at any other property feel challenged. My job was to make friends and offer advice while reporting my findings to the GM of the hotel and him. During this same phone call, Sigi asked me to explain why the energy bills were so different between the Dearborn hotel and the Phoenix hotel, where both buildings were virtually identical in design. With a slow, hesitant voice I advised Sigi I could only explain if he had a straw from a fast-food restaurant such as a McDonald's or a Burger King. After a short pause that seemed to last an eternity, whoever was sitting in front of Sigi within his office at the time drew the short straw, because I barely heard Sigi over the telephone send this person off to bring him a straw. *Mr. Wayne, I will call you back.* This was code for—don't go anywhere. A short time later Sigi telephoned back and we continued the conversation. At first, I remember being a bit spirited with Sigi when describing the importance of pressure energy while providing its definition. Namely, pressure energy is the energy contained in each unit of a fluid due to the effects of thermal kinetic motions of the atoms, lessened by the attractive forces of the fluid molecules on each other, or words to this effect. A mouth full for sure. In-turn I explained that by using the straw it would be easier to show him, rather than explain, how energy works in a building, where this particular demonstration would allow him to easier understand other issues, such as the increase and decrease of static pressure produced by an air-handling-unit. I had chosen the thick straw from a fast-food chain because they are designed to be used for thick ice cream shakes, allowing one to breathe through one with little effort. I asked Sigi to breathe in and out normally just using the straw. The DC director of Ritz-Carlton security, Scott, was in my office at the time and quietly restraining himself. I next asked Sigi to pinch the middle of the straw slowly, imitating some closed or partially restricted air dampers while continuing to breathe at the same pace. I explained as he was experiencing a need to work harder to achieve the same earlier volume of air, he was the energy source, similar to a motor where this energy source doesn't know the difference in the size of the ducts that supply air to the building, but only the effect. If the diffusers or air ducts of certain rooms are closed more or less than others, the motor will operate harder or easier, the same as you are now working harder to push and pull air through a restricted straw. The harder it was to push and pull air through the straw, the more calories you burn to accomplish the task. We measure a calorie to a motor in watts. 1 calorie per hour equals 0.00116222222 watts. Both are equal units of measure, one for biological nature, and one for synthetic or imitation nature. I coined it synthetic nature because our building is using a motor and air-handling- unit to imitate the lungs of the building. Where Sigi entrusted me and our conversations as personal, I had not gone into detail that air-handling-units typically suck or pull air through their filters and not push air through, a detail not necessarily important for the point I was trying to make. I was also hesitant in exposing Scott to Sigi being instructed to suck through a straw. Understand, Sigi had an aura that created this mystique about him, and rightfully so. When Sigi permitted the lowering of this vail that exposed him as one of us, a sense of happiness was generated to a point of playful and benign laughter. It was nothing meant as hurtful or derogatory. The honesty and professionalism entrusted us with remained steady.

Because Sigi was not one to use a straw, this was the last straw I knew Sigi to use. It was the art of understanding and dozens of talks I would enjoy with the Monarch of hotels.

The Barcelona Birth Defect

Late afternoon one day and with no cell phones back in the day, I received a message on my pocket pager from my office to call Sigi. Upon calling, Sigi advised I would be going to Barcelona, Spain, as a member of the opening team of the Hotel Arts. In-turn, I went to the General Manager, Cheryl, to see if this was a trip I could skip. She laughed. *Really? You're going to tell Sigi you can't go?* Cheryl laughed again. I went.

**Wayne Saya, Natalio, Jeff, Paul Saccone, January 1993
at Hotel Arts Opening Countdown, Barcelona, Spain.**

From January 6th to the 20th, 1993, the Hotel Arts in Barcelona, Spain, and the opening of this hotel under The Ritz-Carlton management, was a time not easily forgotten. The Hotel Arts was the first beachfront hotel in the two-thousand-year history of Barcelona. This was a forty-four-story exposed steel tower and at the time had bragging rights as the tallest building in Spain, where today it stands as around number eleven. The hotel did not carry the name of Ritz-Carlton, where Mr. Johnson owned the rights only to this name in the United States, except for the Chicago property. I remember the flight seated in the economy coach section as a long one, with a brief stop in Portugal. For this hotel, they directed my assignments at the facilities HVAC systems and the Laundry equipment and operation. However, the new vice president of engineering for Ritz—Ed, a fella with a somewhat strong southern accent recently hired from Hyatt, pulled me fairly quickly from these assignments, where I was directed to the main lobby of the hotel and shown the rear of the front desk and computer terminal screen that displayed a state-of-art building automation system BAS. Specifically, this area of the front desk could not provide proper access for staff to perform certain and specific intelligent functions, due to a design error in the location of its monitor, its computer and storage of this building's artificial intelligence. I was the surgeon assigned to correct this building's birth defect, a temporary relocation, and repair until the powers that be could make a permanent correction that would most likely require a later permanent installation. This type of pre- opening modification was typical within hospitality maintenance and engineering, but especially within hotel openings, where there is usually some system or piece of equipment that served a higher or more practical purpose elsewhere. This is usually because the design and construction phase rarely offer the operational side an opportunity to take part in the design phase of the project. Tell me I'm wrong! After all, they hired us to just make it work and keep it running, although I recall refusing the delivery of a steam boiler in DC—a tactic developed out of the empowerment culture. I can make a hundred guesses for the reason they installed this computer terminal in a mistaken wrong location, but the bottom line is that a significant piece of this building's brain required an emergency relocation. The Ritz-Carlton was not remotely prepared for such an overseas emergency construction change-order of this magnitude, nor should they have been. In-turn, I was asked to perform the surgery in less than twenty-four hours because the hotel was opening the following day. No pressure!

The computer terminal was hard-piped in three-quarter inch conduit, starting from a counter at the front desk to a rear employee corridor about thirty feet from where it sat, and interconnected from the front desk to the ceiling of a staff corridor, incorporating several four-inch by four-inch metallic junction boxes. The only tools I had were a couple of screwdrivers, two different sized pliers, and a pair of sheet metal shears I would use as wire cutters. My job, should I decide to accept it, was to relocate this terminal behind the front desk about forty or fifty feet away, if you measured following the piping.

There was a fourteen or sixteen-gauge multi-wire harness of wiring, where the thickness of one of these wires was close to the thickness of a typical U.S. household extension cord, only I recall these wires were individual and color-coded. Beginning from the rear of the computer terminal there must have been, if memory serves me correctly, anywhere from a dozen to sixteen separate wires connected to an apparatus that fed into the rear of the computer terminal. With the tools at hand, no electrical tape, and no replacement piping or tools to install such piping, the only way to relocate this terminal was to remove about 35-40 feet of multiple wires housed within a fixed ceiling-mounted piping network, while finding a way to relocate this wiring to a new rear location. First, however, I needed to disconnect each of these crimped wires to the rear of an apparatus, that was fed securely into a terminal, next relocating this terminal to a room behind the front desk. You're mindful that any wrong connection, any severed wire, even a piece of bare wire exposed that touched any of the ceiling-mounted conduit piping can cause a malfunction, a short, a stroke from failure in the system, and the building's inability to think, to perform the functions properly as designed. I knew what it required and what to expect, but I wasn't sure those who assigned me to the project were aware of such ramifications?

After it had taken the first day just to remove the wiring from the inside of (what had to have been) an estimated 35-40 feet of piping, the entire rear corridor of the front desk area looked like a major construction area. It was a fun project with dozens of ceiling tiles removed and about forty feet of multi-colored wiring spaghetti'd all over the floor is a sight you just had to imagine, and oh, the Ritz hierarchy was immediately advised of this condition. The time was approaching midnight, and I was exhausted, so this wiring just stayed on the corridor floor behind the front desk overnight, with the first guests checking in the coming day. I have to admit I giggled a bit to myself aware there would be concerned people wondering about the morning's opening.

That evening, I had no less than three Ritz engineering staff come to my room, explaining how Ritz executive management was wondering what the heck was going on. Even Ed sent the engineering director from Phoenix, Jeff, up to ask if everything was

OK. After assuring Jeff that all was under control, I merely advised in a facetious way how I had been in surgery all day and was going to bed. This was Barcelona, so virtually everyone but I would be out on the town until daylight. It was my birthday, so I enjoyed the remainder of the day relaxing in one of the hotel rooms that came complete with a multi-spray shower and a Grundig stereo system.

In the morning, I passed Sigi, where he stopped for a moment. *Mr. Wayne, I hear your name last night and this morning. How are you doing? Doing great Sigi—I'll have the project done by this afternoon.* After showing his patented grin and smile, he started walking away while turning around in mid-stride to say something to the effect: *Make sure you get a chance to get out and enjoy the city.* Sigi showed not the slightest bit of concern, the epitome of coolness, while I hoped silently that no hiccups developed. I finished early that afternoon. With no electrical tape, I tied the wiring into a long harness, using scotch tape and wire-ties to wrap the wires together every two feet or so, and using additional pieces of wire from the maintenance shop to hang this multi-wire harness from the ceiling. This was because the conduit piping was no longer going in the direction as the new terminal location, so, this piping would remain abandoned while still affixed to the ceiling. I then fished this wiring behind a wall of Sheetrock at the area where the terminal had been relocated, punching through the sheetrock wall to where the terminal would permanently sit. I think it is safe to say this job would have been a clear and unequivocal code violation back in the U.S., regardless that a majority of the wiring was low voltage. However, I was comfortable knowing that this high-voltage wiring, which carried low voltage and low amperage current, was safe for this temporary application. It was these types of details Ritz relied upon when directing a change, where a significant component of their training, even back during this era, was safety oriented.

As I fired up the system, I still had that sense of hope that everything would be OK. Let's face it, how many times have you performed a project or function that you believed went smoothly, only to learn later something was not working. It happens.

Fortunately, in this case, and for me the system woke up, a bit slow at first similar to a reboot, and I will say unexpected. Within a longer period than a few seconds, the building's artificial intelligence was awake and back in operation, and the lump in my throat disappeared. No troubleshooting required.

This was a necessity for guest satisfaction, and no number of warnings against this surgical procedure, other than safety-related, mattered. I was also comforted with a statement from Ed, that this rather radical procedure would be addressed at a later time. Our job was directed toward the guest, and any later permanent installation was not a detail within our worry.

On the day the opening team was headed back to America, I was told that our opening team leadership was informed that this level of relocation was not possible without a major change-order and within the time frame provided. They were not wrong. I accomplished the job by cheating with style while most likely voiding certain parts of the hotel's BAS warranty. In-turn, I learned Sigi requested Ed to offer me the job. Sigi was aware I possessed an electronic engineering background along with an HVAC degree and experience. He also had a good beat on my character, as socially awkward it was at times. Dating back to my initial interview, Sigi knew that I enjoyed a challenge. Although hearing this news put more than a smile on my face, it actually said more. It revealed a never-ending tenacity Sigi and this group of modern Ritz-Carlton founders possessed when dealing with people that used the word No! This word was just not within their vocabulary. You make your bosses priorities your priorities. I was merely one of many that were brought in to surround Sigi and his boss Horst, along with Ed, Joe, Herve, Wolf, and Marcus, of the modern Ritz-Carlton Hotel Company, to make them successful.

Trinity and End of an Era

Shortly after Sigi left Ritz-Carlton Management, he brought his bottled water and his name to work his Brauer Management brand. Of all the conversations and phone-calls we shared, our last project became quite an emotional rollercoaster for his Trinity Place building, and for me.

Trinity Place is a ninety-seven-unit luxury condominium residences in the Copley Square section of Boston. Sigi's company, Brauer Management, managed it. Sigi had his own luxury unit within this high-rise building. Sigi had just finished walking me through several areas throughout the Trinity property, regarding several issues that had been testing his patience. However, one issue was on the top of his list. While we would need at least another walkthrough, I had enough information to start a review of two issues he was having. Even though one of these issues was a review of a composite membrane waterproofing, applied as a component of the waterproofing system under the garage slab, the issue concerning him and his client was this building's inability to cool its luxury condo units and public spaces during the Summer seasons. *Mr. Wayne, I just need to know who is responsible to fix this problem.* This was a problem where several who's who of Boston and New England had residences within this high-rise establishment. I got the impression Sigi was not interested in how to fix the problem as much as it was who was responsible, a definite change in Sigi's management style from the Ritz days. Sigi knew it was not him or the Condo Association. My answer? *Sigi, your building is not feeling all that well, so we'll find the problem and let you know who should make it better.* And there it was, that half-smile and his patented look of self-confidence. You could tell that Sigi honestly enjoyed looking at the building as a living body. He was tired of the runaround and hiding of accountability that the engineering language provided. You could see in his face how he was now looking forward to discussing the building's problem where soon the builders and contractors would no longer have the ability to keep him from the discussion.

The larger issue; all written and implied warranties for the HVAC of the Trinity Place residences are for a period of one year, and unless Brauer Management or the Trinity Place Condominium Trust elected to take control of these warranties, the sub-Contractors hired to maintain these systems are responsible for their performance. Where this responsibility includes the entire HVAC system, Sigi was compelled to rely upon sub-contractors that were repeatedly explaining month after month, how all equipment installed was operating as designed. My job, should I decide to accept it, was to locate the reason the building was not providing sufficient cooling to satisfy the occupants and public spaces.

When performance is the issue, meaning, all systems are apparently working as designed, but not performing according to their specification, the problem typically falls upon, what I like to call, the nuts, bolts, and screws, of the system. Here, the chilled water is circulated by equipment that by design should be functioning properly.

I received the call toward the end of August after most of the summer and calm tempers were leaving. Don't ask. Fortunately, for me anyway, during the problem period, the city had been experiencing a heatwave. Also, during this period, Trinity Place had a contract in place to purchase chilled water from a company now no longer in Boston but formerly known as Northwind utilities. Please remember this was over twenty-five years ago. The reason for this purchase was because they developed the building dependent upon local public utilities to supply its hot water and chilled water for heating and air-conditioning the building. The building did not own or incorporate an in-house boiler/furnace or air-conditioning chiller.

To me, the issue was purely academic, since no residences of this brand-new building had the ability to cool. Either the design engineer made a grave mistake by selecting undersized equipment? not likely. The contractors installed the wrong-size piping through value-engineering? I very much doubt it, or the chilled water temperature was too low? Taking the path of least resistance, I checked the Northwind contract with Trinity Place, which showed that Trinity was contracted to purchase an average of 33- to 36-degree chilled water from Northwind.

The temperatures of the chilled water supplied to the building are predetermined within the Northwind contract agreement, and this chilled water temperature, along with the hot water temperature supplied to the residences and public areas, are established at the start-up of the building by the company that installed the Heating, Ventilation, & Air-Conditioning controls package. Invensys was the controls company, a nationally recognized and very reputable company sub-contracted via the mechanical engineer, and commissioned to design and install the heating and cooling controls for the Trinity Place condominium residences. Having the building's chilled water specification now in hand, I recognized someone had raised the chilled water temperature coming into the building to an average 46 to 48-degrees, using the Trinity building's own heat exchanger bundle. With these temperatures, there was no chance the building had the ability to cool down. So, why was this rather easy find made so complicated?

As a rule, it is extremely difficult to force any sub-contractor to change any of the engineering temperature parameters established by the mechanical engineer or controls company, because of liability. However, through the mechanical engineer, the sub-contractor will be more open to follow requests for changes to pressures and temperatures. The problem next developed into a calamity when the controls company called upon Northwind to lower the chilled water temperatures. In-turn, Northwind would validate that the temperatures were adjusted, and this information would get circulated repeatedly to all concerned. Remember, the warranties were on the equipment, not Northwind's performance, and the equipment was in good working order. Northwind was a public utility. Have you ever been successful trying to get information from a public utility? The equipment contractors continually complained it was Northwind, but when I had telephoned Northwind on behalf of Sigi, their representative casually shifted the burden on the contractor. Ironically, the conversation convinced me that Northwind was not intentionally trying to deceive me. Nonetheless, it was at this point that I suspected it was Northwind and not the contractor because the equipment was operating as designed. Meanwhile, Sigi depends on his warranty contractors to provide him with the temperature information required for the building to perform. This is a standard operating procedure, where building managers depend on their engineering support to possess or get this engineering-related information. Besides this, the condominium trust too was depending upon their management company, Sigi, to fix the problem. A real cluster bomb.

Through additional inquiries and friends in the industry, we confirmed that the Northwind chilled water plant oversold their chilled water. They had too many customers and their chiller equipment could not keep up with demand. They could not meet the contract temperatures for their customers. At this point, I did not believe it mattered how many adjustments they made at the building, where I suspected the Northwind plant could not provide the level of temperatures sufficient to cool the building. My next chore was to have an engineer adjust the chilled water supply valve to increase the amount of chilled water entering the building and in-turn determine if this adjustment would reduce the chilled water temperature at least to a level that would help. It was at this point when I received the call from Scott regarding Sigi.

I completed the project by submitting a rather detailed report to Tim and Chris at Trinity Place. The cover of the Brauer Management report used in October of 2001 is the same copyrighted cover used for this book, but without my name on the bottom.

When nature decided it was time to take Sigi's energy from our physical world, I was driving home after a long day. I thought of Rudolf Clausius and William Thomson's first law of thermodynamics; where all biological organisms require energy to survive. Energy exists in many different forms and can be transferred from place to place or changed between different forms, but it cannot be created or destroyed. Sigi is still with us, we just can't see him. This is my answer to Sigi and one that I am sure he has heard.

Our bodies are of such complexity of structure, the motions we perform are so numerous and involved, and the external impressions on our sense organs to such a degree delicate and elusive that it is hard for the average person to grasp this fact. And yet nothing is more convincing to the trained investigator than the mechanistic theory of life which had been, in a measure, understood and propounded by Descartes three hundred years ago. [3]

—Nikola Tesla, circa 1919

---

[3] Nikola Tesla and Ben Johnson - Nikola Tesla's autobiography: My Inventions was first published as a 6-part series in the Electrical Experimenter Magazine, Par 16, Experimenter Publishing Company, February-June and October, 1919. The piece was again published in book form as My Inventions: The Autobiography of Nikola Tesla, Hart Brothers, Williston, 1983.

CHAPTER 2
Mechanics of a Living Edifice

*Nature is unique, simple, continuous, uninterrupted,
resting upon a single primary principal and unified in its
laws. Whence all the rest right down to the most specific
are permanently drawn in an undivided linkage and
most wise order—buildings are humanistic machines,
synthetically created environments of nature.*

—Wayne Saya

Interpreting the mechanics of a building, any building—how
a building operates—how it breathes, thinks, and ultimately
survives is an art only facility profilers truly understand.
Misunderstood by most is the method of operation that defines
its personality. Yes, every building has its own distinct and
individual personality, its own way of letting us know that we are
again entering the realm of yet another self-sustaining sheltered
environment. This is artificial nature in its finest figure, yet there
is another form of nature that is not artificial, that of human nature
and the mechanical structure of the human body. To understand
the artificial environments we build, it is important to understand
where our environment comes from? How the environment was
born? How much are we truly aware of our body's mechanics,
fluid dynamics, our body's structure, our body as nature's perfect
temple, and how skillful we are as humans in the structures we
build? Most importantly, do we respect how our buildings are
truly conceived and maintained?

Nature's hierarchy is straightforward, where all life starts with the atom, and in time to a cell, eventually reaching the level of an ecosystem and finally to a biosphere or environment—our environment. This is the stepped progression of nature and in-turn, the artificial environments we live, work and play in. However, our study of nature's sub-atomic marvels and miracles has led us to quantum physics, a theory that places our environment within an unpredictable arena, but nature is far from being unpredictable as you will soon understand. This is where big Al's energy and matter equation becomes somewhat distorted. Matter becomes energy in his equation that leads to the conclusion that everything is energy, but energy is also Matter? Meanwhile, our life sciences are stuck in neutral with a mechanistic view of life, of nature. This is where Rene Descartes Cartesian approach comes into play, where his mechanistic view of nature was used to develop our model for the understanding of our buildings. The Cartesian Method, later developed by like-minded seventeenth-century thinkers as a means to view the mind as being wholly separate from the corporeal body, is derived from the philosophical and scientific system of René Descartes.

I have found the beginning of our human understanding of how we shelter within an intelligent environment, our created environment, a building that appears to date back to the Mayan peoples. This was a culture with customs and habits along with evidence of this period, that reveals their knowledge and understanding of caves used as shelters provided by the earth that incorporated natural ventilation. Air naturally inhaled into and exhaled out of caves. This was the Mayan shelter, integrating atmospheric pressure or natural pressure energy. A rhythmic vibration of air sustaining its inhabitants. Yes, everything is energy, and this environment may very well have been the first human interaction with a naturally sustained and intelligent environment—the first true nature-merge. This was perceived as our earth breathing and seen as proof of the earth being an animate and responsive being. This is nature's energy by design, where man's energy started with the invention of the wheel, a motion that causes heat, noise, and inefficiency, and the means and method of how we create the very ventilation entering our buildings today. We generate our power using everything round, fan wheels, car wheels, pump wheels, generators, all fossil fuel generation of heat-producing power. Today's technology is all about our mechanical generator creating heat to make power. Nature is the exact opposite, a natural motion that acts on a body moving in a circular path, directed toward the center around which the body is moving, like the wind, the circular rise of plants and vegetation, or a spiral tornado. Spirals are a basic form of motion in nature, used to cool and condense as opposed to technologies dedicated to the imbalances of heat and cold.

Beginning of the Human-Modeled Structure

Mayan Cave – The Breath of the Earth
Photo by Aaron Roth

This is also where our earth first provided us with a biosphere, a shelter, our ventilated environment. These Mayan caves enter thousands of feet into the earth's basement where, without such earth sustaining oxygen provided into these caves, the Mayan civilization could not have survived.

So, what is this pressure energy? Better still how do we measure such energy? The least complicated I can offer using simple terms would be to envision a measurement of one-inch of water within a column of water—a water column—equal to a pressure of approximately $1/28^{th}$ per-pound per-square-inch (psi). This is the design of a test instrument that has been used in the HVAC industry for quite some time, containing a very sensitive diaphragm that can respond to changes in pressure. One such type is the Magnehelic® brand pressure-gauge.

A pressure gauge that measures the static pressure of a ventilation or HVAC system. You will typically find these pressure gauges attached to the side of an air-handling-unit (AHU) of any medium, large, or high-rise facility.

Nature is independently unique where all civilizations never know what the actual weather will be or when a regional climate will change direction, or even whether a tornado will touch down at any given time. You can say that these Mayan caves were civilization's first experience with a ventilated environment using nature's static pressure, where these caves experienced many fresh-air exchanges daily, accomplished by a pulse that is in rhythm and vibration with our biosphere, our environment, our earth.

The Mayans believed that their caves were important to a level described as the nexus of wind, rain, and earth, they eventually described as the *breath of the earth*. Then unconsciously or otherwise, we evolved, as ancient engineering developed to build our independent life-sustaining intelligent shelters. Shelters beyond those simply designed buildings, and some produced by one of my favorite ancient engineers. His name was Imhotep, the earliest architect known to have probably designed and supervised the construction of the Step Pyramid of Djoser, in Egypt around 2630-2611 BC.

In biological terms, we can look at the early intelligent cave as the start of an intelligent structure, a cell developed into a biosphere and introduction of life for the first perfect structured environment. If you were to change the structural material from biological to inanimate, next removing our humanity, our consciousness, and what Rene Descartes described as a moving force, what remains is a material duplication of us, of a people housing a human operation within a duplication of itself, our self.

Introducing Rene Descartes - Unfiltered

To understand the movements and functionality of a building, your building, any building, you will need to be officially introduced to and indoctrinated into the world of René Descartes, 1596–1650. Descartes invented the Cartesian coordinate system, or dualism, along with analytical geometry while preparing the foundation for the development of calculus.

Not too long ago I was watching a movie about three brilliant women who worked for the United States NASA Space program, one of whom, Katherine Johnson, was identified as using analytical geometry as one math component to calculate the trajectory of the first American manned space flight. In reality and outside of the scriptwriters of Hollywood, California, Johnson along with engineer Ted Skopinski worked through key calculations that were produced within a published technical report. It was this report that Hollywood developed into this scene that may very well become an integral part of pop culture. By now you probably recognized this film as the 2016 box office movie, *Hidden Figures*. What you probably didn't realize was where analytical geometry came from. You guessed it, Rene Descartes developed this math along with Pierre de Fermat, a fellow French mathematician. As I sat watching I reflected upon how Descartes would have acted if he had known of the importance his math would play within twentieth-century manned space flights.

More to the point and the principal reason I had raised this particular subject, the non-exactness of our math, including Descartes math, later derived into a quantum mechanical conclusion. This is a principal component of why the artificial intelligence used within our buildings was developed into reactionary programs. But please understand, just because there are differential equations that cannot be solved exactly due to changing winds and waterway currents, among other reasons, mathematicians were required to figure out alternative ways to estimate answers for certain and specific situations, like landing coordinates for our space program. As Katherine Johnson's character proved, the use of ancient math called Euler's method, named after Leonhard Euler, a Swiss mathematician who lived from 1707–1783, was a requirement to complete an answer, however incomplete. His method was one of the many techniques applied to differential equations. This was because Euler's method confronts equations that just can't be solved exactly. You may have missed it, but during a scene of the movie where Katherine Johnson's character was calculating the landing equation on the chalkboard, while she was at the map pointing out the landing area, she explained: *Give-or-take twenty square miles.*

Ultimately, this give-or-take method provides for a very close estimate. I think this would have been a method I would have preferred when mimicking the intelligence of our buildings, because real-time weather information could be used to plug-and-play the controls of our building's automation system. Unfortunately, it does not. Our present-day computer programs do not use this close approximation, but rather a fuzzy style of programming.

Artificial Intelligence, computers, were developed from humans by humans. We were the original computer. The first known use of the word 'computer' is shown in 1613 within a book called The Yong Mans Gleanings, by English writer Richard Braithwaite. Spoken in old English, Braithwaite explained how computers were people, yes, we were called computers, who carried out calculations and computations, and the term carried through until we passed the torch to our electronic counterparts. It was these non-human electronic brains where our human reactions to our weather and our human condition were downloaded into artificial computing, we now call fuzzy logic, and are now the intelligence that operates our structures and facilities.

When it comes to the human building, Cartesian dualism describes that every human has a soul and a body but that the two are not the same. They are completely separate. Commonly regarded as the father of modern western philosophy, Descartes was also a leading scientist. This unique understanding and methodology—his way of thinking in the mechanical world of biology and mechanics—will be important for your own foundation of understanding in the operations and intelligence of our human building. We will be traveling directly into your intelligent structure, using Descartes unfiltered works to grasp the relationship of how our human biological construction mimic's that of a building's operation. The Descartes scope of understanding has been fashioned to interconnect your cognitive functions systematically with facilities-related processes. These interrelated functions encompass reasoning, memory, attention, and related terms and lead directly to the realization of information in how our mechanical world functions, and in-turn, how our buildings truly operate.

Wayne P. Saya

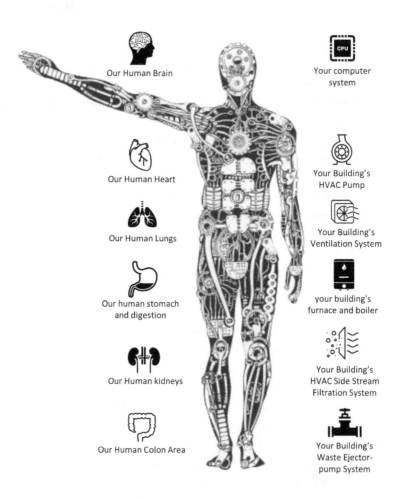

Our Human Brain

Your computer system

Our Human Heart

Your Building's HVAC Pump

Our Human Lungs

Your Building's Ventilation System

Our human stomach and digestion

your building's furnace and boiler

Our Human kidneys

Your Building's HVAC Side Stream Filtration System

Our Human Colon Area

Your Building's Waste Ejector-pump System

Descartes human as a machine methodology merged with the humanistic systems of a building.

Although Descartes did not use or mention a building or sheltered structure within his teachings, it is his understanding of our human structure and its non-biological mechanics he visualized. Where Descartes pictured a human as a machine, we are elevating his vision to a new level by envisioning the building, our structural machine as a human. More closely, the dynamic builds, even more, when we realize we work and shelter inside this human-machine. We have duplicated our self to sustain and shelter ourselves.

In 1910 a study of medical education within America was authored by Abraham Flexner for the Carnegie and Rockefeller Foundations that was to learn which medical schools would be interested in promoting scientific medicine. When the American Medical Association adopted the contents of the Flexner survey, they recommended that financial support and grants be awarded only to medical schools committed to scientific research based upon the Cartesian model. The Cartesian method is a scientific system and philosophy rooted in the works of Rene' Descartes. All therapeutic medicines and programs that did not follow the Cartesian model were considered unscientific and not eligible for future financial support. It was for this reason only a fifth of the existing schools during this period survived, while the eighty-percent that did not survive adhered to what was known as the *vitalist doctrine*. This was a doctrine that asserts "man assist but nature heals". The types of healing recognized by this doctrine were holistic types such as homeopathy, naturopathy, and herbal type remedies. Ultimately the eighty-percent were forced out of mainstream medicine due to the lack of financial support, and the Cartesian model became the standard. I never once believed that Descartes vision incorporated the abandonment of alternative remedies in place of one-hundred percent pure research. The doctor was now the exclusive expert in the knowledge of our health and diseases. Our body was considered a sophisticated and complex machine that could be understood only by an expert physician. When looking at it from this vantage-point I suppose I could understand the reasoning behind the engineering aspects, or what was under the hood.

From an architectural, mechanical and electrical engineering perspective, predictive and preventive maintenance that is derived from a facilities engineering site should not be disenfranchised from self-diagnostics or predictive and preventive maintenance. Not promoting the ability for a person to apply predictive or preventive therapies and natural herbal supplements through self-help naturalistic remedies were not something I clearly understood.

However, in the later twentieth century, a revival of exercise programs, vitamin and mineral shops, and organic health food stores have re-energized the vitalist principle of becoming closer to natural health practices. Promoting reductions of refrigerant gases, encouraging more natural light into our structures, and the rise of green building technologies has our buildings mimicking this vitalist revival.

Descartes' view of the human body was both unique and an Explanation of the unknown during the seventeenth century, and quite possibly the early twentieth century when considering the vitalist doctrine. According to Descartes, nature did not differ from man-made machines, and machines made by craftsmen were no different than our organic bodies. This clearly defined a vitalist doctrine style of understanding. Descartes developed a system of dualism. This dualism influenced his mechanical interpretation of nature and therefore of the human body. He believed that the laws of physics and mathematics explain human physiology.

Descartes fused the exploratory spirit of the industrial revolution with the focus on nature of the romantic era, along with a minor presence of the religious spirit still prominent during this time in history. It is because of this combination you may examine differently his understanding of God as a religious experience, because for him this may simply be a science-related detail. Descartes uniquely combines the imagery of man-made structures such as clocks, fountains, and industrial mills with natural elements like rivers and trees to explain the functions of each part of the body. To Descartes, the natural and the mechanical are both similar in their process. Descartes metaphysics starts with the roots of a tree, physics to the tree's trunk, and mechanical operations, medicine, and moral behaviors to the branches.

In-line with Descartes method—we should coin true nature against synthetic nature, or the biological structure of man corresponding with the electromechanical makeup of a building. These incorporate the divine attribute into machinery, as the end goal to Descartes is evolution and functionality. For decades we have looked at maintaining our buildings and structures from the outside looking in. Here, we are now seeking to understand these facilities from the inside looking out.

A Descartes biosphere reveals the turning of gears in a clock along with its metal body which infuses it with a soul that allows it to tell time. A soul to Descartes is chiefly an exhibition of life, a movement, and by life he means action. He makes this clear by noting metaphorically that a dead body is physically capable of performing all the functions of a living one, but it will not since it is missing its driving force. Centuries later pathologists would learn that after death, human cells are depleted of their energy source, where you will find that energy is key because the protein filaments that are our muscles become locked in place. This causes the muscles to become rigid and locks the joints. In Descartes world, the machine no longer can operate.

Action in Descartes' world cannot happen without the mechanics of motion. The living motion of nature is the result of the muscles and joints that are interconnected to our human nervous and electrical systems. Parts of the body that permit two or more bones to meet and allow movement are the ball and socket joint that connects your leg bone to your hipbone. Keeping these parts of the human skeletal frame upright are the protein filaments that slide past each other, called muscles, and function to turn energy into motion. The combination of our frame and muscles and that of the frame of our building that contains trusses, bolts, and welds, comprise our load-bearing wall or designed edifice. When not moving our mutual structures are called static, a structure able to manage its own basic weight while dealing with its live loads or the weight it carries, which civil engineering calls kip loads. Too much bending, twisting, or torsion, can cause either structure to fail. In mechanics, equilibrium has to do with the forces acting on a body, and that body can be human or the structures we design.

This grand human design has made it into every structure we build. From the ball-joints of your automated furnace control systems and the controls used for your HVAC air-damper systems to the dozens of electromechanical building systems that use human-inspired interconnecting components, all buildings are soundly built for constant motion. Most importantly, our built environments are constructed by transforming our human carbon-based components into an electromechanical structure, built to house our human organic counterpart.

With motion comes wear and tear requiring lubrication and maintenance of the body. Buildings don't get their lubrication from supplements as we do, high in the DHA form of omega-3s, or glucosamine sulfate and chondroitin. Buildings rely upon synthetic and petroleum-based oils and grease products. Nature requires maintenance the same as synthetic nature. That being said, Descartes view is still mainly anatomical, as he explores human beings more of mechanical contraception than a divine creation. Notably, the changes in Descartes view of the anatomy of man from his *treatise on man* to his *Description of the Human Body* written a few years later, shows the rapid developments in science during the seventeenth century, and Descartes attempt to catch up to it.

One of the first ideas that a reader of Descartes philosophy on man will recognize, is his view of man as a machine. Whether it is in *treatise on man* or *Description of the Human Body*, Descartes abolishes the distinction between humans, animals, and man-made machines. He does this by constantly referring to humans as machines, by claiming that the anatomy of man and animal is so similar that those who wish to see the inside of a human being, in a way to better understand its anatomy, can examine the insides of an animal, any animal. He also draws constantly on allusions to machines like clocks and pumps in an overview to explain the workings of man. Descartes, however, does not establish a distinction or preference between the two, making them appear on equal grounds.

Now take a deep look in and under the thermal envelope of our protective skin that covers our human structure and you will see motion, a movement not revealed without the use of a microscope. Descartes would be elated to see one of many maintenance machines within the human body that make up the molecular army of operating systems, where the mechanical operation of the human-machine closely simulates our man-made mechanical systems. Going beyond the simple analogy of our joints acting as hinges and our heart as a pump, let us take a brief look at a molecular example of how our biological structures mimic the man-made operation of our buildings.

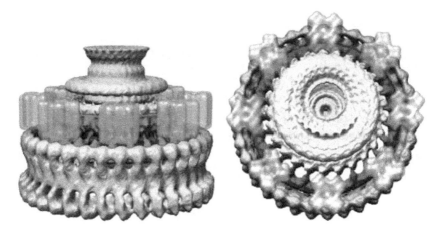

The bacterial flagellum of this particular bacterium (*Salmonella enterica serovar Typhimurium*) has a reversible rotary motor powered by the proton gradient across the cell's plasma membrane. The flagellar filament, with its corkscrew shape, converts the motor's torque to thrust. Approximately 40 proteins are involved in the regulation, assembly, and operation of the flagellum. At least 24 of them are components of the completed flagellum.[4]

---

[4] The Three-Dimensional Structure of the Flagellar Rotor from a Clockwise-Locked Mutant [of a bacterium] – US National Library of Medicine, National Institutes of Health. PMCID: doi: PMC1636246 10.1128/JB.00552-06 PMID: 17015643

Wayne P. Saya

The bacterial flagellum, looking identical to that of the inner workings of an electric motor, is a biological rotary motor made up of protein and at an anchor point on the human cell's inner membrane. This maintenance machine located within each human cell comes in several intelligent designs and is powered by a proton—motive-force—as opposed to an electromotive force—using an electrochemical-potential difference of specific ions across a specified membrane. *A deep breath, please.* Briefly stated, it operates identically to an electric motor incorporating a rotor and stator like a motor, where this biological design too has both.

The rotor of this biological motor alone can operate at 6,000 to 17,000 rpm without its attached filament. Just think, eight million of these real-life biological motors located within our human structure could fit on the cross-section of a human hair. This necessary view of our molecular mechanical behavior within our organic bodies reveal how our biological and material worlds behave identically to our man-made structures by somehow unconsciously integrating similar functional designs. Later-on you will understand how this structure incorporates into the sick building syndrome. Descartes states at the introduction to *Treatise on Man* that man, *being made by God—is capable of a greater variety of movements that I could possibly imagine.* Around three centuries later, the German physicist Max Planck, and originator of quantum theory, would state:

> *All matter originates and exists only by virtue of a force which brings the particle of an atom to vibration and holds this most minute' solar system of the atom together. We must assume behind this force the existence of a conscious and intelligent mind. This mind is the matrix of all matter.*[5]

> —Max Planck

This matrix of matter would later be coined the ether. However, in today's physics, the ether is now identified as the Field, or in

---

[5]   Lecture, 'Das Wesen der Materie' [The Essence/Nature/Character of Matter], Florence, Italy (1944).

some circles, the Devine Matrix or simply just the Matrix. It is this Field that is said to hold all forces within the nucleus of the atom together. Big Al would use this quantum theory in developing his photoelectric effect and *light quanta*, the theory where he describes photons.

Descartes also states that he believes a man, meaning all humans, to be just a statue or a machine made of earth. The word earth here refers to Descartes notion on celestial and earthly bodies which he establishes in *Treatise on Light*. It is worth mentioning that his notion defining human bodies as "made of earth" relates to everything, from dirt to water, as long as they do not constitute it as celestial or the metaphysical.

Attempting to explain the workings of the body, Descartes hoped that this would help in curing diseases and slowing down aging. From a mechanical perspective, this would be the equivalent of our building's predictive and preventive maintenance program. Using the Descartes method of understanding—the use of a spirometer can provide a medical doctor with information regarding the functionality of our pulmonary system and lungs similar to that of the previously mentioned pressure gauge used for determining the functionality of our building's lungs.

Acute bronchitis, although normally caused by illness, is the result primarily from exposure to substances that irritate the lungs, such as tobacco smoke, dust, fumes and vapors, and all types of air pollution. These same pollutants also create dirty or clogged fin tubes within a building's air-handling-unit. Besides this, dirty or clogged filters cause the static pressure of our magnehelic® gauge to rise, a condition that obstructs air. When the building engineer finds this building's pressure gauge to be too high, it is time to change the filter or clean the outer fin-coils, it's time to clear the pulmonary system and breathing mechanisms of our building.

Considering all the components of the body Descartes Breaks down, two are presented as special: the soul and animal spirits. First, animal spirits, which according to Descartes, result from blood exclusive and obscure in the brain. Descartes postulates that the product of this is something similar to "pure- wind" which travels from the brain to every part of the body. Reflecting on this description of pure wind, I recall a quote that positioned: *the field is the sole governing agency of the particle.* Big Al too was very much aware of the power of a *field* where all things, living and non-living, are made of waves and particles. Like Descartes' pure wind, we are all continually in a field, a matrix of some kind, whether it be that of the magnetic field, the particle field of light, or Descartes pure wind.

In 2004, economist and neuroscientist Paul J. Zak Discovered (what he believes is) the neurochemical oxytocin (oxy-toe-sin) as our *moral chemical*.[6] His studies revealed that when the brain makes oxytocin, people are noticeably more compassionate, generous and trustworthy. He also explains if you just hug another person eight-times a day, you can stir-up oxytocin and "be happier, and the world will be a better place." Although there are studies that suggests oxytocin plays a wider role in the brain, oxytocin has been called the "love chemical," the "hug- hormone," the "elixir of trust," and even the "moral molecule," among other names,[7] which should not be confused with Descartes' understanding of the body's soul. Descartes may have unwittingly merge the body's soul with his suggestion that "pure-wind" travels from the brain to every part of the body from blood exclusive and obscure in the brain similar to what oxytocin does.

Descartes seems to have some intuitive insight into this later Big Al finding of the Field that equals invisible energy forces that surround us, where Big Al has described the particle as Matter. Remember, energy is matter and matter is energy. However, it is a Field, the Field that is postulated as the force holding all together.

The human autonomic nervous system also fits the driving action of the Descartes soul and animal spirits nicely, where

---

[6] The Moral Molecule, HOW TRUST WORKS, By PAUL J. ZAK, 9780142196908, PenguinRandomHouse.com Books, Nov 26, 2013.

[7] The Dana Foundation - The Molecule of Love, Trust, Morality, and Sociality? Author: Brenda Patoine, Published: August 15, 2019, originally published April 2013.

there are three branches: the sympathetic nervous system, the parasympathetic nervous system, and the enteric nervous system. This is our body's energy system and our building's smart automation system.

To Descartes, animal spirits are a way of explaining one's will, which leads to the movement of the body. Descartes believed that humans as machines can perform all of their natural functions even after death. Animal spirits and a soul, which he believed were extinguished by death, made the missing catalyst that prevented the body from any movement after death.

While keeping in mind that this is seventeenth-century thinking, please understand this short study of Descartes is essential to understand a merge of the biological mechanics to the man-made structures we have created which mimic our biological human structures. While imaginably animal spirits and Descartes use of the human soul to distinguish human composition from that of man-made machines, the soul is seen by Descartes as an extension, or byproduct.

Descartes' soul appears to be a typically safe point from a religious view during the seventeenth century, where the difference lies in Descartes linking of the soul with nerves and tissues of the body, but one could very easily interpret this with his earlier understanding of animal spirits. He claims in *Treatise on Man* that once our skin is cut, pain results via the soul causing agitation in the nerves since a part of it—the soul—has been torn with the flesh. I've tried to imagine Descartes mindset while he experienced this Einstein-type of thought experiment. Today I would imagine Descartes having envisioned sparks coming from an electronic circuit board of a building-automation-system being torn apart, simultaneously watching major components of the building shut down and die? By doing so, academics today recognize Descartes as establishing the soul as more than a metaphysical force, and something that has a physical connection to the body which is severed upon becoming non-functional, upon death. It makes one wonder whether he was close to distinguishing this human force with that of nature's lightning energy. Reading Descartes over and over again his cleverness always appeared close to some type of breakthrough, but he could never get there, I assume because of how religion during this time may have influenced his writings.

The animal spirits are particular and vital to the philosophy of Descartes. Seen as wind or pure fire, animal spirits are also connected through the blood to every part of the body, like an electrolyte solution containing energy. So, does this translate the inter- connecting piping that carries the vital fluids for our heating and cooling systems to each part of our building as the spirits of the building? It can be seen that they infiltrate the biological body with life, as they carry heat, where Descartes believes is essential to life. Using today's standards, it is more than probable that Descartes would have found it is the burning of calories that produces this heat from activity, where a calorie is a unit of energy, while a watt is a unit of power, which describes the rate at which energy is expended. The power cell requiring a regular charge in-turn imitates the workings of our digestive system. Our buildings also incorporate such a structure, its furnace, and the boiler system. We transform both food and fuel into energy. But we also need to be careful with such transformation!

Studying Descartes, you get to learn his interpretative skills, along with seeing his frustrations derived from living within a seventeenth-century mindset. There are times we need to advance his understanding to our modern-day. So, using the Descartes method, let's transform both food and fuel into energy.

Facility engineers know that a typical range of fuel-to-air ratios for a representative facility furnace exists, but outside of this range, either higher or lower, and ignition will not occur. These high and low ranges are known as the explosive limits. If the exact amount of air is provided to completely burn all of our building's fuel within our building's furnace, the ratio is known as the stoichiometric or stoich mixture. Should our stoich mixture exceed the wrong limit, an explosion will more than likely occur. This is our building's fine-tuned digestive system, designed to produce heat and energy. Within our human system when carbohydrates and protein are eaten together, indigestion and gas increase. This is because meat- protein is broken down by acid where chemical enzymes break down grains. Although mindful of my body's operation, this has not kept me from enjoying my whole-wheat toast with my eggs and bacon, aware that the sluggishness experienced after is the direct result of my digestive system working inefficiently. When these protein and carb mixtures are fed within our human furnace in large quantities, an increase in the production of volatile gas occurs. Our Nutritionists complain when we eat alkaline carbs and high acid proteins, where combined neutralize stomach acid, causing an incomplete burning of the fuel we eat. Eating food first that is quick to digest before food that is slower to digest will impair our digestive process, causing bloating, gas, and our human machine to run inefficiently. Ratios lower than the stoich mixture are considered rich and less efficient, while an impaired human digestive process can cause poor integration of nutrients. Poor nutrition is associated with poor predictive and preventive maintenance of our furnace atomization system, and both contribute to the stress of the system. Over time, the risk of developing a breakdown or illness becomes inevitable within both the human and mechanical machines.

To complete a Descartes style analysis of our building's ability to produce energy, observe how methane gas is produced by our body as a byproduct of human digestion, where on-point natural gas is a fuel used to produce heat energy within our synthetic body, our building. Our biological body uses food as fuel. Food that is partially or not digested travels from the small intestine to the large intestine. Once it gets there, nature's bacteria produce hydrogen, carbon dioxide, and methane, the typical components of natural gas used to operate a building's digestion area furnace. Whereas our bodies, defined as nature, produce the same fuel required to generate a major energy source of a building. Conversely, a component of synthetic nature, our building's heating system uses natural gas to produce energy in the form of heat. You can see how it is all relative. The cause and effect of nature and synthetic nature. Nature produces fuel for synthetic nature using the same method as synthetic nature produces heat from the use of such fuel. The use of this fuel is measured in calories. One kilocalorie is equal to the amount of heat that will raise the temperature of one kilogram of water by one degree Celsius. Whereas, synthetic nature produces energy for heat, measured in British thermal units, or Btu's.

From an electrical point of view, we measure power in watts. Watts is volts times amps. Therefore, more electrical power means more heat. Modern technology is all about the creation of heat to make power. Descartes believed these animal spirits are also responsible for carrying orders from the brain and information back to it. In a modern sense, we see them as electric currents originating from the power source and giving movement to a machine. Though Descartes sees them as oil to a machine that purifies and urges movement.

The stomach also plays an important role in nutrition along with sensation, according to Descartes. He sees it as a furnace in which food is melted like iron to produce a more refined product that is added to our blood circulation. Also, much like the smiting process, impurities are isolated from our human tract and discarded as refuse, similar to the many functions of the human kidneys and their production of waste to the bowels of our human structure. These building impurities can infiltrate our structures easily, where hundreds of thousands of dollars of pumping equipment and heating and cooling systems have direct contact with water that is incorporated as our building's circulatory system. Similar to our human structures connected to organs that filter waste, buildings have both open and closed systems that circulate heating and cooling related fluids. Closed systems circulate the same body of fluid through steam and hot water boiler systems and cooling towers. We use the most common closed systems for hot water heating of apartment and office buildings and a variety of industries. We find chilled water systems for air-conditioning in medium to large commercial buildings and all size factories.

Descartes also likens the fluids of the stomach to an Aqua Fortis, commonly referred to now as nitric acid, which dissolves materials into a liquid. So far, the functions attributed to the stomach is purely mechanical, and Descartes holds that this process of dissolving and refining is an involuntary one, and thus can go on even after death. However, he also attributes sensations and feelings to the functions of the stomach. This originates from an old belief about four humors - liquids produced by the body which reflect certain feelings of joy, sorrow, bitterness, and excitement, comparable to those moods and feeling produced by oxytocin. Descartes holds these humors as factual and attributes their passing from the stomach to the blood which reaches the brain as responsible for generating emotions, uncharacteristically similar to the digestion of nutrients and medications from our digestive tract into our bloodstream. The belief in the role of humors sheds light on the influence of ancient knowledge, of which every man maintains a part no matter how negligible. It also sheds a light on cases where Descartes was still ignorant. The mechanical view of Descartes failed when it came to things that could not be dissected. It, therefore, became unfortunate when old knowledge was relied upon and combined with more recent discoveries to provide answers.

Descartes ultimately changed his view about the humors and the functions of the stomach with time. In "Treatise on Man", humors are responsible for emotions while in *Description of the Human Body* published years after, emotions are attributed to interactions between animal spirits with the heart and the brain. It shows Descartes was open to the advancement in understanding. As these interactions differ, so does the resulting emotion. But are emotions being uncovered within our buildings too?

Animal spirits hold a special place in the body's anatomy. Even Descartes admits that they have never been seen by anatomists or an expert in anatomy, and yet he held their existence as factual. Descartes often connects them with the soul, the body's means of motion, and thus plays an important role as intermediaries between the physical and the metaphysical, the mechanical and what drives the mechanical which Descartes has described as the soul.

As Descartes attempts to identify the components of the human body and their workings, we see a testament of the era he lived in influencing his imagery, his descriptions, and understanding. As we begin to understand the similarities of our building with our human mechanical counterpart you are developing a subconscious understanding of Descartes' connection to the movements and functionality, the human mechanics and intelligence we are transforming into that of a human building structure.

Since Descartes lived during an era with little understanding or experience in modern mechanics, a time marked by the beginning of the industrial revolution, its elements and remnants of the prior times seem to govern his thinking. Notably, Descartes writings reveal a consistent conception of a principal goal to cultivate a capacity for sound judgment. His fascination with machinery and his general curiosity and unique observations that govern his treatise are all key elements of the start of the industrial revolution. Also, Descartes using pumps and gears as metaphors to explain the workings of the body to readers reflects the popularity of knowledge about machinery during that time. I can't help but wonder how Descartes would have seen artificial intelligence today and how he would have seen the transfer of such intelligence by using his analogy of the soul or animal spirits.

We contrast the mechanical view of the world during his century with the view of nature as the exemplary form of creation, which still lived after the so-called romantic era that dominated the earlier sixteenth-century. Although Descartes does not mainly depend on nature for his view of the body, still nature represents a sturdy and stable force to him, just as we look at nature today within our attempts to save the planet. Thus, Descartes explains blood reaching the extremities of the body, like fingers and toes, using the veins as canals with the force taken from the heart to do so—he likened this to water and nutrition—reaching the farthest ends of the longest branches using the internal cavities in the tree. Think of the various network of heating and cooling piping traveling throughout the building while its chemically treated water travels at a rate dictated by the diameter of piping and the size of its centrifugal pump, in contrast to the human displacement pump.

The blood circulation that Descartes talks about extensively is Also an example of mechanical and natural imagery combined. The mechanism of blood circulation was still new at that time. Descartes attributes the discovery of it to the English physician William Harvey. That discovery shook away the previous views about the movement of the blood and the important role of the heart, where it carried away both old and new ways of thinking, which Descartes put down for his readers within a variety of metaphors.

Besides the mechanical and the natural—age-old religious beliefs also feature as an influencing force in Descartes attempt to understand the body. As religious faith was still strong in France during this time, Descartes appears to carefully maneuver metaphysical aspects of his teachings without slighting the Church, accompanied by the surging physical and logical view. This can be seen in the case of the soul, but it can also be seen in other areas never realized by Descartes, like the heart, brain, and nerves— a building's main circulation pumps, its' building automation or energy management system and its' network of electrical and electronic cabling. Mainly because of their connection with feelings, imagination, and life. It is these aspects that mainly attributed to Descartes divine will.

Mainly, Descartes believes that the heart naturally produces heat that expands without the addition of matter which also expands the blood so it seeps through drop by drop into the rest of the body, while accompanied by animal spirits from the brain. With this direction in Descartes analytical thought process, though within this particular illustration he leaves absent the actual functionality of the heart, he remained centuries ahead of his time. Descartes believed that carrying orders from the brain and information back to it was somehow accomplished without explaining the process. Current day Facility Profilers learned within recent years we could align the communication aspects of a building's circulatory pumping system with the rhythmic function of our human pump. In this age of local area networks (LAN), interconnecting the building's direct-digital-control (DDC) brain to its' ancillary systems, or local area chillers, pumps, and fan systems, we find the new digital controls to these ancillary pumps and fan systems detect changes and initiate communication with our building's DDC brain. This is contrary to what we believed in an earlier time where the building's DDC system was once designed and used only to start the communication with these described ancillary systems, while alone controlling their operation.

While heating is also a function of the stomach, it produces this process via chemical reactions that produce heat. The heart, however, is seen by Descartes as naturally filled with fire necessary for life. With the furnace analogy, the stomach gains its heat from an external source, while the heart resembles a volcano that is naturally seething and naturally in need of heat to keep pumping. You can see that Descartes concentrates an understanding of these two organs, the stomach, and heart, necessary for producing heat to maintain life, similar to the heat producing mechanicals and electrical systems of our building. We allude to the heart as a pump responsible for circulating or pumping. Veins, arteries, capillaries, and ventricles we refer to as pipes. Although Descartes focuses on detailing the difference between veins and arteries, where according to him are constantly being confused by anatomists and physiologists, he still calls these anatomical body parts pipes. This shows Descartes pragmatic focus on the general output as trumping that of the anatomist. In this regard, the heart along with the stomach, veins, and arteries we can now visualize as a central heating system in a building, providing heat through a series of pipes. Thus, any dysfunction in this operation would lead to life seeping out of this building, similar to a leaking wet basement or failing wall and ceiling pipes.

Considered as essential for maintaining life, Descartes fills scores of pages in both treatises discussing the human heart, and in specific detail. In terms of nourishment, the heart is not the only one credited with keeping a man alive and functional, or our building's multiple systems operating that maintain critical building temperatures. From the density of its flesh to the way the heart expands—which Descartes claims are the case in both inhalation and exhalation - to describing the role of every ventricle and aorta within. Today, Descartes would be elated about research that is uncovering how the heart first accepts precise information and in-turn relay this information to our brain, similar to that of a digital network to a variable-speed-drive of a pump that transmits information to a building's main digital automation system. The brain maintains direction and system continuity while the pump reports conditions and irregularities. Cellular biologists and geneticists now know that the human heart constantly discharges pressure waves and emits electrical and electromagnetic signals. Heat and light are also signals described as emitted by the heart, where these described signals are received by all cells within the body. Our heart has coherent rhythmic patterns that are said to synchronize all organs and parts of the body down to each cell. Facility engineers are knowledgeable and keenly aware that it is the building's components, its boiler, chiller, pumping systems, air-handling-units, and more, that start communication directly with the building's main direct digital automation system during operation. It is this building's automation system that incorporates its direct digital neuron control of the building, detailing temperatures, fluid flows and air velocities, faults, and more, while traveling at varying velocities through air, liquid and chlorofluorocarbon gas. Once our building's brain starts these parts of the body, our building's brain becomes a coordinating effort for all systems, and all the body parts synchronize with that powerful rhythm of the building's pump using our internally developed neuroplasticity, which is the way our building automatically generates commands in order to correct changes in its systems operation.

From the time we were borne, functional movement is the biomechanical way our body was designed to move with nature. Separately, a novel movement is the new and unique ability our body can move, like in gymnastics, which can produce this neuroplasticity and neurogenesis. This is our body generating new

Wayne P. Saya

neural structures, new connections. A system the majority of our building's brain calls fuzzy logic, but more on that later. I remember watching the successes my children experienced in gymnastics. I watched while witnessing over time their individual tasks and performance goals while they acquired functional coordination patterns over time. There human computers were building new neural networks to accomplish this grace under pressure, to a point where their actions were developed into performing on autopilot. There computers were engaging in a synaptic pruning, removing the neural connections that were no longer useful or needed, especially when they made a mistake on the balance beam or pommel horse, while simultaneously strengthening the new and necessary neural networks. How many times have you left the office or the classroom to drive home, later pulling up to the door of your home or apartment without having paid any attention to the drive? This is what scientists call your autopilot mode, an unconscious function that enables you to perform tasks quickly, correctly and with minimal conscious thought. Yup, our buildings have this feature as well, allowing our building's ancillary systems such as chillers or pumps to automatically change their functions through the neural pathways we've created called integrated circuitry. Our human autopilot mode appears to run by a set of brain structures which have been coined as the default mode network (DMN), where our independent building's systems incorporate various forms of an artificial logic and human programming. It is this programming along with a variety of sporadically located sensors that keeps the liquid and air-pressures of our building operating within their designed parameters. Our buildings can incorporate virtually everything our own body mechanics and intelligence possess, but without our human consciousness as Descartes will attest.

The pressure wave created by the flow of blood synchronizes the brain's neurons. The heart has its own inherent nervous system, processing information independent from the brain. Biologists appear to be catching up to what the facility engineer has known for decades, that our building's systems initiate communication with the building's brain during their operation. Descartes postulated this model centuries ago when he attributed the heart as the center of heat in the body. It would overwhelm Descartes to hear how the heart is producing an electromagnetic aura that is said to carry an array of information, including emotional information.

It is also noteworthy to mention that Descartes does not include the described resulting emotions in his natural description or imaginings within his treatises when describing the heart. This is probably because the anatomy of the heart was more a product of his professional curiosity, experimentation and probing than a product of ancient knowledge to Descartes. He emphasizes his own view of the heart as expanding in both stages of respiration by denouncing Harvey's earlier described notion as a mechanism of blood circulation, where he believed the heart shrinks during exhalation. Because Descartes is not an engineer, he appeared to try desperately to understand the mechanics of a pump during a period where modern-day pumping technology did not exist.

In retrospect, I cannot count the number of times I was engaged in discussions with property and hotel managers whom attempted to explain to me why a machine or mechanical system was not functioning properly. During this early career exchange, I recall asking my manager if he was having a Descartes moment, one of my socially awkward moments for sure. During this same encounter I envisioned the building experiencing a severe case of constipation when a water closet was overflowing from an obstruction that was later located within the bowels of the building. Water was pouring from the ceiling into a corridor. The general manager was yelling to shut the pump off? When I explained it was a water-closet/toilet overflow, I was next asked in a calm yet firm authoritative voice if I would please shut off the sewer ejector pump? I developed a hidden chuckle, but it was not because of the inaccurate directive I was given, it was because for the first time I had thought of the building as being constipated. My early development in facilities engineering had its humorous moments, while allowing me a method to learn buildings rather quickly.

Borne before the industrial revolution, Descartes antidotes

and creative way of thinking was certainly handicapped during this period, where Descartes train of thought and vision was far ahead of his time.

But what about these animal spirits when examining how we communicate with our buildings? Because understanding is key, I would like to sidestep for a moment to offer a biological foundation using Descartes train of thought. Detailing our communication with our buildings and how our buildings communicate with us, is a subject that deserves intellectual legroom and its' own forum, that we will latter examine in detail.

Is the Pineal gland recognized as our hard-drive or conscious cloud? The Pineal gland is a miniature organ within the center of the human brain that plays an important role in Descartes philosophy. He regarded it as the principal seat of the soul and the place in which we form all our thoughts, but his belief in thoughts appear to differ from his view of pure wind as earlier explained.

Today, we know the pineal gland secretes the hormone melatonin, while to this day Hindu mystics have resolved, that the pineal body of modern man is an atrophied remnant of this organ of spiritual vision, a view closest to Descartes belief that the human brain, although similar to a sponge, is not a physical substance. The closest Descartes ever got to pure wind, or even consciousness was his argument that consciousness is self-evident, where his famous phrase: *I think, therefore I am*, concluded he could not logically deny his mind's existence at the same time he used it to deny such existence. He believed consciousness is the faculty that perceives that which exists. Because of his philosophy in our human means of thinking, and in-turn how we prepare a means for our buildings to communicate, I trust you will see more clearly when we later discuss 'the building of intelligence'. Meanwhile, Descartes provides us with a thought-provoking realization that if he were alive today, I suggest he would consider the pineal gland as our hard-drive to his described sponge of knowledge. Today Descartes would be trying to find a way to connect a communications cable from our pineal gland to a computer or hard-drive storage device. He also provides an unsolicited tug on our shoulder that our consciousness cannot be a component of our building's DDC brain, but who we are and how we exist may be located in an informational cloud, or a consciousness surrounding our body. The informational cloud, therefore, is our building's artificial consciousness, where it's electronic thoughts and actions can be controlled by an external source. Our building's ability to think on its own would be true consciousness, an action we will later visit.

With the imagery Descartes provided in the workings of each part of the body, the heart can be seen as the engine of a steam train, absorbing energy and using it to push the train into moving. There is an awareness, a concept in today's energy medicine that is known as energy cardiology. In Descartes world, the fire in the heart takes the energy source provided by the stomach, that is the crucible, a container responsible for obtaining and providing coal to be transferred to the engine to be burned. Using energy cardiology, theory is energetically applied to explain the role our heart plays in maintaining our organic structure.

A while back I had a rather personal experience that took my-own heart rhythm to a level not previously experienced. After decades of having what doctors had called a benign irregular heartbeat, I developed an irregular rhythm condition that I will offer, caused mechanical operational issues on more than one occasion. At the time I searched for reasons, a specific reason, a culprit causing this new affliction. My first thought, OK, what is my structure's issue? At this point I realized, could it be I never prepared my body, my structure, for semi-retirement, a different operational program? My self-automated programming has not been readjusted or dialed back. Eighty flights a year down to fifty a year, and the following six months down to no flights. No running through airports. No chasing cabs. I was finally going to bed at a reasonable time. My energy level was reduced from 125 percent down to fifty percent with no preparation or warning. I thought again, When I have allowed my car to sit for months at a time, my vehicle had become more difficult to start. In-turn, I scheduled a visit with my maintenance mechanic, a pioneer in his field. But now the official diagnosis was in, I have developed Atrial Fibrillation, an A-Fib condition. How would Descartes explain the difference of my heart's tissue, its material, its rhythm and how it affects the steady operation of my pump?

Where electric motors work by converting electrical energy to mechanical energy in order to create motion, my structure requires a steady electrical pulse from the atrioventricular or AV node, that by design converts biomechanical energy into a steady rhythmic pumping motion. Some apparent abnormal tissues in and around my pulmonary veins are rapid-firing an electrical commotion that is interfering with the steady rhythm of my displacement pump.

Our heart maintains a steady rhythm that cycles sixty to eighty beats a minute in an average resting adult. It can go slower when we sleep or faster when we are active. Electrical power in the United States makes a single rotation within an electric motor from a positive electrical peak to a negative peak sixty times each second or sixty-cycles-per-second, known as 60-hertz. Cyclic rhythms of biomechanical to man-made mechanical, from nature to synthetic nature is not that dissimilar.

My doctor will attempt to block this irregular glitch using a medical mechanical procedure. Descartes volcano, my heart, I'm envisioning for years has developed this irregular energy condition, signals now providing unregulated energy beyond those required by design during my life cycle, and for a reason beyond my understanding of engineering has been acquired by my body's central engine. Equipment will now be delivered into my displacement pump from my lower body area, fed through my leg piping and up to the inner chambers of my displacement pump to affect the repair. The inner chambers of my pump will be greeted with a non-biological force for the first time in its life-cycle and directed by an external maintenance team that knows the drill. This isn't my mechanic's first rodeo. The goal of this procedure is to ablate the electrical connections between the pulmonary veins and the atrium, to block this irregular or unwanted energy source. This pioneer cardiologist will be defragmenting signals that have developed outside of their normal path. Scar tissue will be created to prevent these unwanted signals from entering areas they are not wanted. I envision my DDC system, my brain, in time will be convinced through communication signals produced by my heart, my self-induced healing programming or disk management, that this supplemental energy is no longer required. Our buildings too incorporate computer disk management. Something I am sure may not happen automatically, and I think I will probably need to help using my-own internal thoughts and self-reasoning.

Disk fragmentation is the principal reason for poor computer performance. Fragmentation occurs when data on the hard drive is constantly changing, meaning, when some of the data is detached from a segment of the hard drive during the time a program is uninstalled. This detached data leaves a hole. The next time a program file is downloaded it will fill that hole. The problem happens when the new downloaded program is larger than the hole that was left. In-turn, only part of the program is stored in the hole, and the remainder is carried to the next available spot. This program is now fragmented, broken up and stored in different locations on the hard drive. This causes the computer to do more work while causing the computer to operate slower. Virtually all computers incorporate a Defragmenter utility that cures this brain cramp by taking all of the programs and putting them back together and in order. We will see if my defragmentation is able to take hold, where, unlike artificial intelligence, nature's intelligence is always looking to find a way on its own—one way or another.

The bigger question: could I have prevented this affliction with an exercise regimen that slowly and methodically dialed back my heart's development of these irregular energy signals? Is it equally true that exercising our motor vehicle daily for a short period when not in regular use is beneficial to our vehicle's operational health? Could my mind have instructed my heart that the extra energy was not required? I am not a medical doctor, and therefore, I would not know the responsible medical answer to these questions. However, my doctor has offered me a choice, medication for the irregular-heart-rhythm during the healing process, or for me to decide my level of discomfort during this time of healing. If I follow Descartes teachings and combine it with Big Al's findings in energy, I would allow my body to heal and slowly correct without help, without a chemically treated medication aid. Does this show we should allow our buildings to heal themselves during certain ailments or situations?

Actually, from an operational adjustment state they do. Remember, we have built into our building an automated network, programming through a variable-speed-drive or VSD, that can automatically speed up or slow down the speed or output torque of our building's mechanical equipment, or in this case our building's heating or cooling pump. The VSD can increase the efficiency of our pump's motor by regulating motor speed, the cycles-per-second, for each load condition.

The distinction Descartes makes about the difference in the tissue's coarseness of the heart that is denser than any other found in the body illustrates his view regarding the importance of the material in differentiating between elements, while also not placing one over the other. I would suggest his distinction relative to our heart's tissue was on target, where research has shown that abnormal tissues within and around the pulmonary veins can trigger and sustain atrial fibrillation. Descartes explains the difference of the heart's tissue, its material, and how it affects each of its operations in detail since it describes how this organ works. Stressing its importance, yet not placing it above others like the brain which Descartes sees as requiring softer tissue as it operates as a sponge to absorb humor and dilated blood, and refine into animal spirits. By this logic, the natural and the man-made are the same since the difference in man-made material and organic material does not designate a difference in worth or quality according to Descartes view.

Descartes explained that it is the nerves that serve as connecting links tying the whole body together. Should a part be severed the general composition of the train would be damaged, however, the train could go on as long as the main carriage still exists. With the main carriage, our brain, this-automation-system receives and transmits orders to the rest of the body and determines its direction and will. In that sense, the soul would resemble the conductor of the train. An addition unnecessary to the composition of the train itself, where one does not add any function to it, neither is it inherent to the body but considered as an addition to it. The aptitude of this expression illustrates Descartes view of the general composition of the world in general and the body specifically. Since each has a role, mechanics and nature can coexist harmoniously since both depend on a series of independently coordinated functions to operate.

Imagination, will, and critical thinking posed a great challenge for Descartes to define. He changed his views on the operations of the brain from *Treatise on Man* to *Description of the Human Body*. The clearest conclusion Descartes seems to have reached is attributing a dual role for the formation of imagination, will, and critical thinking. Descartes established a dualistic view as opposed to a larger or more accurate monolithic view. Where he also—in his *Description of the Human Body*—combined the role of the soul and the brain—which produce animal spirits that animate the body and spreads *will* into the necessary parts? Are we as inhabitants of the building, the soul that Descartes believes is this requirement for life? The animal spirits work jointly with the soul to carry orders and transfer sensations to the brain, similar to maybe our internal operation of the building's automation system. We are a biological body inside the creation of a synthetically made body. In retrospect, Descartes held the human brain as responsible for processing information gathered by the body, much like a sorting machine in a factory that is responsible for allocating each material or product into its designated area. Even imagination is seen by Descartes as a product of the reaction between fluids and nervous sensations coming into the brain which is translated into imaginations of certain scenarios depending on the input.

In Descartes Third Meditation, he argues that ideas called judgments can, strictly speaking, be true or false, because it is only in making a judgment that the resemblance, conformity or correspondence of the idea to things themselves is affirmed or denied. So, if one affirms that an idea corresponds to a thing itself when it really does not, then an error has occurred. This analogy is so astoundingly close to modern day fuzzy logic, a program designed for intelligent automation of artificial intelligence. In Descartes *Rules for the Direction of the Mind*, he argues that we should break all problems up into their simplest parts, that we can express such problems as abstract equations where such an equation uses two or more variables. We can solve neither variable unless the other variable is given. We know Aristotle as the father of logic, and his logic dealt with two values where every proposition must either be true or false. The water is either blue or not blue. A classic set of fuzzy logic. This defied an earlier period during the Golden Age of Pericles', Athens, where Plato showed there had to be a third region where in his words these opposites 'tumbled about'. In the mid-1800's mathematician, George Boole created a system of algebra and set theory using 1 for true and 0 for false. Later named Boolean algebra, it deals with the operation of logic values and the study of binary variables of true and false, where water is either blue or not blue. Then, in 1928, Jan Lukasiewicz proposed a three-valued logic of true, possible, or false that was not translated into English until 1963. Coincidentally, two years later Dr. Lotfi Zadeh of the University of California at Berkeley published 'Fuzzy Sets', which laid out the mathematics of fuzzy set theory, now known as fuzzy logic. Zadeh recognized that the current day computer logic could not manipulate data which represented vague or subjective ideas similar to human reasoning. These would be the gray areas of human thinking. Zadeh would later formulate fuzzy logic as the approach to computing based on 'degrees of truth' rather than the usual "true or false". But Zadeh's Fuzzy logic is the exact opposite of Descartes second rule for the 'Direction of the Mind' because Descartes believed we should only study objects about which we can obtain certain and clear cognition. He believed we should never attempt a study that could not determine right from wrong or true from false. Where fuzzy logic models the lack of exactness of accuracy of data, Descartes believed all that is speculative or probable should be rejected. Today, Descartes would not agree to a fuzzy logic approach in the way we program our buildings to think and operate. For this reason, it is important that we become students in understanding the personality and profile of our buildings. Should we therefore use outdoor and indoor weather sensors, sending their information in real-time to an algorithm that formulates differential equations that can be modified using the earlier-described Euler's method?

The dual interaction between the soul and brain is what we will later identify as the distinction between mind and brain. Descartes sees the two as separate yet working harmoniously according to their own roles. Three-hundred years later, I would carefully suggest; using the Cartesian model for today's building would express our building's inhabitants as the building's soul or biological cells, a biosphere housing its consciousness while understanding that the building's brain continues as it's direct-digital-control or building automation system.

Unique to Descartes is the link between the eyes and the brain. He considers the eyes to be more or less an extension of the brain. Functioning as a data source that is a connection to the main computer or processor, sending data for analysis by the brain through their connection with the nerves. Also, the eyes as seen by Descartes are connected and moved by the animal spirits and the soul. It reminds me of a proverb dating back to Cicero — 106-43 B.C., later translated into French: *Les yeux sont le miroir de l'âme* – the eyes are the mirror of the soul. Their abilities and perceptions are limited according to the capabilities of the soul, or I would suggest limited by our actions as inhabitants of the building.

It is vitally important to understand, that in the final paragraph of the *Treatise on Man*, Descartes concludes by stressing all functions of the body mentioned by him are solely the result of the desire of the responsible organs. The organs of our building would, therefore, be identified as the various and independent systems such as the boiler and furnace, chiller and air-conditioning systems, air-handling-units and ventilation systems, and more. His writings, although at times requiring us to conceptualize, regards the soul as the exhibition of life and action, I would submit our building's direct-digital-control systems, combined with the human operator as a complete union, with the soul having the power to move the body. Modern biologists are regularly becoming educated in how the coherent rhythm patterns which synchronize our body's organs right down to our cellular biology come from our heart and does-so using its' own intrinsic nervous system. This is independent of our organic brain.

These individual vital components of the body receive communications from the varying waves and signals from the heart. Our brain also receives these pressure waves and communication signals, completing a coherent body. These waves of communication are evident when walking into a central boiler plant or mechanical room. The local area networks within each chiller and boiler, each pump, motor, and fan system, communicate its condition with its building automation system too—in order for this building's brain to move the inner workings of our building. Should our building's main energy source: the electrical supply, fail, our building's primary motors and HVAC pumps that control our heating, cooling, and air distribution systems will also fail. Our building's environment will start to die. Our artificial sunlight is gone, and in-turn we are finding ourselves back in Mayan caves. This earlier discussed Mayan culture, along with other American cultures, believed that the body has an energetic field. Today we call it the morphogenic field where a substantial part of this field is reliant upon a living and live entity.

When Descartes says that the "soul can be fooled" he does not refer to any moral or religious deception. Instead, Descartes refers to the deception of the eye based on the interactions of light along with its physiological influences. When he says that "there is a soul in the clock that makes it tell time" he does not mean that any religious interpretations of the soul. Instead, the world and all of its creations operate mainly mechanically according to Descartes.

Many considered industrialism and man-made production, which spread heavily during the seventeenth century as a clash with natural and divine creations. However, Descartes saw both to result from intricately placed parts that work harmoniously to keep the machine going. Seeing the human body as a machine was not a degradation to Descartes, but a way of understanding the most vital and complicated of all productions, that is the human body. He hoped that understanding the body would give us a better understanding of how best to use and even how to improve upon it. The operation of material mechanisms and nature did not collide with Descartes because they were both based on functionality and progress.

Rene' Descartes believed that the universe has a mathematically logical design. He had a mechanistic view of nature, where his published *Description of The Human Body*, revealing differences between natural and man-made occurrences were different in the material only, not in the mechanical operations at work. By understanding Descartes view of nature, you understand how nature has a way of making us feel small. I understand how our current day thinking attempts to imitate nature through the buildings we design. We no longer feel as though we belong in a cave. Thanks to visionaries like Descartes we have improved in our intelligence, in understanding the mechanics of our environment, and it is reflected in the smart creative buildings we fashion.

The Transition

The Descartes Model doesn't touch on each and every detail of our human anatomy or all of the various components of electrical and mechanical systems for that matter. Descartes provides only the concept, not an all-encompassing program. Descartes believed that nature held a unified set of rules which bound all of our physical world, but Big Al's unification theories incorporate all of nature, that we—here—extend to synthetic nature—our buildings. Descartes unified theory was based upon an intellectual synthesis between several real principals and several interpretative acts of the human mind. He wanted to separate the divine soul from the material, the moving, and the physical world.

The unfiltered Descartes model was developed and in-turn should be used as an exercise for understanding the operation and mechanics of our built environment. Our use of Descartes model should be used to develop your train of thought in associating the various systems of your facility to that of your own human structure, and how these like-minded components are used to make your building come alive! What may sound strange, in time becomes comprehensible because repetition can lead to understanding.

Enter Albert Einstein, big Al, born in 1879 and leaving us in 1955, taught us that there are no instantaneous interactions in nature. This is important, because just as we cannot react swiftly enough to nature's direction, neither can artificial nature created within our buildings, where buildings have been designed and built, unwittingly or otherwise, as artificial duplications of the human body.

So, when focusing on the physical level of human nature, looking upon ourselves as morphemically synthesized into nature: as man does - so does nature, and as nature does - so does man. Both equal in concept, physics to physical nature to the human body. By extension, synthetic nature is in the form of a man-made structure which mimics the workings of the human body and used by the human machine as an extension of its own physical embodiment. We shall examine how we also picture our most inner personalities and how we view the personalities of others. How nature may look upon us as a similar structure and how we view these perfected structures as man's finest architectural creation.

Modestly, we have sometimes found it difficult to think of ourselves as equals to our structural creations. When this psychological event takes place, it is the building's personality that inevitably overwhelms us. We are swallowed by its beauty, astonished by its size, and disoriented by its complexity, yet beauty is only stone deep—the depth of our building's thermal envelope—and equal to the skin protecting our own bodies. Of course, our building's personality goes beyond its skin, for internally, buildings are humanistic machines, synthetically created natural environments, starting with their skeletal frames and ending with their levels of automation or intelligence—that is, artificial intelligence, where by computer based programming these structures are operated. Here we just begin to see how our structures mirror the workings of the human body.

Where a machine reduces the effort to do work, so too are our man-made structures. We are able to climb to the top of our skeletal mountains by walking into a magic box that rings at each passing floor, and turns on the light and heat of the sun when the need arises. Our building is our friend. Its inner personality is built around our needs. The mere simplicity or complexity of our building's heating and cooling distribution systems and how these systems impact our level of expectation, in-turn develops our understanding of our friend's efficiency. Through time we develop a resigned perception to its personality, where it has taught us to appreciate as well as understand its behavior, a mechanical human protecting and in general taking care of an organic human, the makings of a phenomena itself.

We can picture the gravitational rise and descent of our elevators and the electro-magnetic motors that power them. We observe the centrifugal motion and push produced by the pumping heart within our building that circulates chilled and heated water just beneath its thermal envelope, its skin to the vital areas of its skeletal body. Throughout this mechanically structured edifice we marvel at the magnetic flux path within an electric motor, causing this pumping system to circulate our stated comfort-giving heat and chilled water. These pipes of veins and arteries provide a vehicle for such environmental conditioning. For nourishment the volume of liquid traveling through these very pipes is treated with corrosion inhibitors to keep them strong and scale emulsifiers to keep our building's cholesterol levels down. Through their mechanical air-handling-units, our buildings are provided with a mechanism for breathing, inhaling the filtered and conditioned mixture of elements and compounds in gaseous form. Because air comprises of oxygen atoms, water molecules, carbon dioxide, nitrogen, and more, it is not a single element. In-turn this air is filtered and seasonally heated or cooled for ducted distribution and exhaust, a mechanism that helps prevent a syndrome of a sick building illness, while by design maintaining its living occupants similar to the various cells within our own human structures that thrive and survive within us. Our organic structures are self-generating in our body's repair of itself, where our created structures rely upon our due diligence in predictive, preventive, and reliability centered maintenance.

We react to our building's every whim as a new parent would react to a child until the novelty wears off and at that moment, we all become professionals in understanding its actions, and yes, sometimes yielding to its faults. But how many times have you heard an experienced parent say I know how to do that, in reference to the caring for their toddler? Rather, as a seasoned parent I usually say that I know what he wants or I know what she needs. In retrospect, the typical building engineer has traditionally proclaimed their expertise in possessing the knowledge of what to do or how to do it when responding to a facilities maintenance problem. Simply, when the issue has become a problem the building engineer becomes reactive. How often have you heard of a building engineer proactively say that he knows what his building needs or wants? Do we dare not ask the question for fear that we may be considered a tad deranged? Knowing that there is a thin line between genius and insanity, we must all choose our own destiny, our own future, and as a consequence our building's future.

Development of a Nature-Merge

Since the intelligent or smart programs within our buildings are for the most part based upon a fuzzy logic foundation, how do we begin? First and foremost, the strength of our synthetic climates or systems duplicated from nature, rely upon the rules governing the system. These are nature's rules, and our principle rule is: *there are no instantaneous interactions in nature.* Our synthetic climates should be designed and programmed to anticipate, not respond, to nature's mood swings. If the barometric pressure indicates a weather change, then our system should be programmed to anticipate this change. We use all of nature's indicators, not simply temperature and humidity sensors. We move our systems in with nature, creating a nature-merge. One of the ways a nature-merge happens, when using our control systems, we attempt an instantaneous interaction with nature. A token start would be to locate all thermostats and light sensors outdoors to merge with nature, becoming closer, although not quite obtaining an instantaneous interaction. Next, tying these sensors to a secondary indoor room control. Why should we install an outdoor light sensor? To alert our buildings it is time to start shutting off outdoor lighting while waking up our climate controls at sunrise. We're gearing up for the day. Our nature-merge has also developed a conundrum between energy management and energy conservation. I have always advocated that if energy management is performed properly, energy conservation happens automatically, and there my point lies.

Merging Nature with the Nature of Synthetic Structures

We send well trained local, state or national public works employees and crews all through our cities and towns to dig up streets and sidewalks for routine infrastructure repairs. It's certainly one of many legitimate reasons we pay taxes, and some cities and towns do it more efficient than others. In my travels I have also witnessed, at least on a weekly basis, public utility companies maintaining their electrical, natural gas, and domestic water infrastructures, up-earthing streets and sidewalks. Then I wondered, why is it that we don't send crews out to these same business and neighborhood locations to drill geothermal heating holes as a standard practice. Let me explain: A drill truck could be a standard piece of city or State equipment during these city infrastructure excavations, or as an independent undertaking. While in these neighborhoods a couple of holes can be drilled each week under a street or sidewalk to establish a geothermal heating station, an underground utility service similar to a water/sewer or gas line installation, to be offered or simply brought into homes or businesses that are willing to pay the city half as much as it would cost for the equivalent fossil fuel. Maybe the taxpayers just pay for the initial geothermal station, receiving free Seasonal heating? Maybe a new public utility is formed?

Additionally, we could also receive free seasonal cooling if we use an ammonia-based chiller system. The typical mechanical refrigeration that involves a transfer of a refrigerant through its liquid and vapor states by mechanical compression, condensation, and evaporation. The safety guideline relates to the mechanical functions and equipment within a typical ammonia vapor-compression system. These are systems that require mechanical refrigeration to produce cooling, utilizing ammonia (NH_3). Ammonia systems have a significant cost advantage over synthetic refrigerants, and while ammonia is a toxic substance, it is less then and maybe in some instances equal to the toxicity of today's refrigerant gases. We should also remember that ammonia is very soluble in water where refrigerants are not, and that formulates a solution known as ammonium hydroxide that is commonly used as a household cleaner. The toxicity of the new chlorofluorocarbon refrigerants are just as bad and, in some instances, worse. Safety codes for both ammonia systems and synthetic refrigerant systems exist similar to natural gas systems, and are written by the

American Society of Heating, Refrigerating and Air-Conditioning Engineers (ASHRAE).

Ammonia is derived from other gases. Gaseous hydrogen is processed from either natural gas, propane or butane. The hydrogen is then combined with nitrogen to produce ammonia. Unlike the synthetically-created Freon, what some call the ozone killers, ammonia is made from all-natural earthly gases and does not harm atmospheric ozone. This is a reason we would maintain these systems within an outdoor unit the same as our current home compressor/condenser units, except ammonia systems would not require ozone protection regulations as currently required for the synthetic refrigerants we now use and enjoy. Remember, this is for cooling. Geothermal heating is far less of a regulatory issue than our current natural gas systems.

This is how we bring nature's furnace into our homes and businesses. My concern is not seeking or advocating for the replacement of fossil fuels but to merge our structures with nature. We merge nature with our biosphere, our indoor environments. If during this process we look after the earth by eliminating fossil fuels in time, along with its atmospheric pollutants, while simultaneously the earth takes care of us, so be it. It's a partnership and a true nature-merge. We reverse the process by relocating the thermostat outdoors and bring nature's heat indoors as opposed to synthetically reproducing it.

I've never considered myself to be an environmentalist. Probably more of a pragmatic engineering type, seeking solutions to problems. Because of this I have a tendency to enrage the same people that just the day before liked the way I think. There will always be people who complain about our use of refrigerants, gases, and fossil fuels, natural or otherwise, yet scream when anyone attempts a solution or an additional synthetic or environmental source. Tomorrow the complaint may be death to the earth by a thousand tiny cuts in the form of geothermal holes, where our future's qualified research may find a plan where those very holes may be looked upon as an acceptable approach to merge with nature. I'd like to think that it's the thought that counts and call it a day.

Imagine if we were to harness the heat energy from a single explosive volcano? Tens of thousands if not hundreds of thousands of homes could be heated seasonally for years depending upon the level of the eruption. But we already do this, though in a questionable way.

Hydrothermal plants are now strategically located on geological hot spots, but which have a habit of creating a higher level of earthquake risk. There is also evidence that hydrothermal plants can lead to a larger occurrence of earthquakes. So why do we incorporate and build large systems when we know nature discourages the practice?

Nature has two moods – a type that is spread out and harmonious with all living things, and a type that is concentrated and in repair mode. When spread out we experience the rhythmic spectacle of an old faithful geyser that breathes in rhythmic harmony with nature in Yellowstone national park, USA, or waterfalls and rivers activated annually from seasonal Springtime melting coming from high mountainous areas – annual water supply for our lakes and reservoirs. We find that when nature is concentrated the results are volcanos, hurricanes, tornadoes, and more. Why try and harness a hurricane when we can watch nature's little pieces of the same natural force clean the air and wash our neighborhoods regularly during a passing storm or a Spring time sun-shower.

It's basic physics – matter expands when heated, and contracts when cooled, although water is one of the few exceptions to this behavior. The earth has a rhythm. It allows us to take what we need. When we systematically harvest and replant trees from the forest to build our shelters, nature recovers unnoticed. Our earth even has a replacement mechanism after experiencing wild fires. Yet, when we strip a hill or land of its trees without a plan, chaos causes shock and change such as erosion and the reshaping of our earth's skin. Nature allows us to merge as long as we follow her instruction manual. It's the same with our own physical body and the very programs we use for our built environments.

Micro-geothermal heating stations for homes and businesses incorporating geothermal heat-pump technology can take advantage of this constant heat source. These stations can be sporadically located through business parks and neighborhoods and can be naturally spread out to balance the load while mimicking nature's design. Now, although I realize this methodology flies in the face of a concentrated and investment-required commercial hydrothermal plant, nature-merges are not concentrated. We should not think of this thought experiment as an invitation to develop a new synthetic design inspired by nature. Rather, it's an approach, a mind-set to merge incrementally and side-by-side with nature. It is to embrace a nature-merge design as an openly smart engineering principle, and not a niche concept.

If society can place as much effort into research for this type of heat energy as we do with fossil fuel research, such efforts have a real potential of higher profits and profit margins, where we will have no need to synthetically reproduce our heating, but rather create a variety of new consumer and commercial systems that process and use this gift from our earth. We simply balance nature's resources, because nature always possesses a way to sustain itself. It balances its elements in a smart and coherent way. Whereas, synthetic nature requires us to supervise and maintain its operation, its ability to live on. In effect, synthetic nature requires nature in the form of human nature to make it work and keep it running. The only way to limit this type of maintenance is to distance synthetic nature's operation by replacing it more and more with the mechanics and geological and ecological stores of true nature. We try to merge as much as nature as possible with the environments we create. We take the puzzle of components that nature provides us and merge them into our everyday life style. Each day nature invites us into her world, and rather than be so dismissive of our natural world, the least we could do is reciprocate by inviting her into ours.

It's merely an idea to show how nature has all of our survival mechanisms and resources so long as we play by her rules, merging our survival with nature is called a nature-merge. This is the mindset we should develop when constructing or renovating our structures.

From our dealings with the quantum mechanical world to our dealings with fuzzy logic and nature directly, when the architects' job is done, the facility engineer's job has just begun. After all, we have always been Nature's student partner, the ones with intelligence.

Human Nature as a Building's Proactive Partner

Until we are able to distinguish ourselves, able to provide a truthful and honest understanding of how we picture our most inner personalities, while in synchronous harmony inverting this insight toward how we view the personalities of others, can we even attempt a realistic viewpoint of how others distinguish themselves. This may take a moment. —How can we attempt an objective psychological understanding of those in our world if we cannot or will not understand our own viewpoints or our own conscious personalities? So, what gives a building its personality? Here, the art of understanding is the key.

Wait, time out! You want me to understand the personality, a humanistic trait that identifies us as individuals and apply this art of understanding to a man-made structure, a building? How is this done? One of Descartes arguments was that a person's intelligence, as he defines primarily as pure wind, is apart and separate from the mechanics of the entire bodily machine, where the science of our body's matter and motion can be explained using the mechanical language of engineering. Remember, Descartes mechanistic view of nature, and his characteristics of the human body as a machine, taken with the fact that a machine is something that reduces the effort to do work. Buildings are surely a real extension of our own organic structures. Simply look at those various bearings and automated levers which permit our motors and automated valves to rotate as graceful as the mechanical joints of our own bodies.

How do we as humans react to the everyday events in this world? How are buildings designed and programmed to react to the needs of humans? Remember, within the world we live we have been taught for every action there is an equal and opposite reaction.

When examined closely you can see that the programming of our buildings through artificial intelligence is nothing more than the imitated responses that our own bodies produce. However, humans have programmed this world to react to our humanistic needs. Our buildings respond to our every whim. The ability of our buildings to respond environmentally comes from man's reaction to nature, or our regional weather. Mankind's artificially created reaction to nature's action—our ability to respond.

Author Stephen R. Covey examined the word responsibility as "response-ability"[8]—or the ability to choose your response, explaining that man's behavior is a product of conscious choice. When you get right down to it, a building has more freedom of choice than most people do, because the building is free from the day-to-day humanistic behavioral programming, along with feelings and emotions. It has a program and it follows it. But a building's freedom to operate through artificial intelligence is obstructed by our flawed programming, downloaded into the artificial intelligence of our buildings. How adept are we at understanding our own conscious personalities, and how effective is this projected into the understanding of our building's own personality? Does our artificial intelligence allow our buildings to develop personalities of their own? or do we program our buildings the same as we allow ourselves to be programmed by our education and social environments? Although we must work on being more proactive than reactive, as thinking humans, man's reactionary characteristic is only a component of our reactionary world, our reactionary programming, our reactionary buildings.

It is purely reactive when the response comes even as close as a milli-second after the given action. If there was an instantaneous interaction in nature, then we would be able to capture the slightest interaction the instant it happened. It is the anticipation that cannot be programmed because nature has an unlimited number of personalities, all of which can be similar,

---

[8] The 7 Habits of Highly Effective People, by Stephen R. Covey, Habit 1, "Proactivity" Defined, pg. 71 – A Fireside book, published by Simon & Schuster, New York.

but none exact to one another, that is, as far as we know. This is nature's fingerprint. Nature requires multiple personalities to achieve its direction, a direction we mostly are not privy to, and now with nature rebelling from our environmental interferences. However, nature's living direction, regardless of the detours it is compelled to take, must be absolute to a known end, and this end must have balance, which is nature's equilibrium. Truly, nature is not stupid, but only those of us who attempt an instantaneous interaction with nature, through the use of our building's energy management and building automation systems. Moreover, what is nature's equilibrium? What is this balance?

With nature's multiple personalities comes our use of probability. For centuries men of science have not faked it or made wild guesses at nature but have used deductive reasoning you know, if it walks like a duck and quacks like a duck, when no other explanation makes more sense, common sense stuff, nothing vague. Men of science are realists seeking the truth, an exact truth from an exact answer posed from an exact question. It is better to be humble and submit to probabilities where our present-day level of knowledge prohibits us from submitting false absolutes. In place of a scientifically misleading absolute, or vague answer, scientists speak in probabilities. Therefore, but just for now, probability belongs in synthetic nature, or our own response that keeps us as nature's student partner, and rests in the present physical nature of all things, unless our vague knowledge of nature has deceived us to venture into identifying the direction nature will take next. Those who venture into vague conclusions remove themselves as nature's student partners. Why? Because nature is not vague. It is only our understanding of nature's direction that can be considered as imprecise. Until we have discovered nature's specific reason for each and every move, we will always be nature's student partner. This should not stop our attempt to come as close to nature as possible by using vague logic. Big Al was fully aware of our inability to fully understand nature, where he grudgingly resigned himself to the use of quantum physics for the purpose of describing his own photo-electric law. More on this a bit later. This raises quite a unique subject, why has physical science been focused on being reactionary, as opposed to being naturalistic or proactive? The answer will surprise most, but not those who have always believed in nature as having a direct and specific reason for each and every move. Remember, just because science is compelled into probabilities should not take away the belief of nature as having a sense of direction. It also should not take from our ability as thinkers to achieve temporary solutions in place of having the knowledge of nature's direction. New or a correction to existing math will ultimately address this present reality of the unknown. But why have we been focused on being reactionary and forcing our built environments to duplicate these reactions? To know this answer requires a brief examination of the history which has brought us to this point in time.

How Did Our Buildings Become Reactionary?

In order to have you journey along as an integral partner of understanding, I would like to include a very brief explanation using a small amount of technical words and phrases, where you may have a more in-depth understanding of how certain conditions of our buildings evolved.

First, the year 1900 brought us quantum theory, quantum meaning quantity or how much in Latin. This theory was developed by professor Max Planck, a theoretical physicist, to account for certain phenomena which classical physics was unable to explain. Big Al also used this theory to explain his work on the photoelectric effect. Now, most of you may not know or even care what all this means, so let me progress rapidly by explaining that quantum theory was replaced by Quantum Mechanics in 1925. Remember, we want to understand how our buildings think, breathe, and operate, so a little education and insight won't hurt.

Now, I want you to read the following part as though you are reading how the hip bone is connected to the shin bone. So, what is Quantum Mechanics? It is the non-statistical method of operation in where the behavior of molecules within the atomic and subatomic world, the tiny world, exist in a number of states. Now that wasn't bad. Next, these so-called multiple states are predictably unstable, yes unstable, until ordinary matter or energy interacts with them. It's like hitting a number of pool balls and trying to predict which direction each will go. It is at this instant such interaction causes the molecule to select a single state. We have now gone from a number of states to a single state. However, and this is important, the selection process is a mystery. I'll repeat that—the selection process that causes the molecule to achieve a single state is a mystery. The missing process similar to the so-called missing link. Only nature knows. This is why quantum mechanics treats physical events that we organic humans cannot directly perceive or understand. Therefore, because no statistical formula exists for the molecule's selection process, we have only been able to describe nature using a quantum mechanical style of deductive reasoning or what some have called statistical chance. We all use chance or probability in one form or another during the course of our activities to make decisions when we don't know for sure what the outcome will be, such as drawing a specific card from a deck of cards, or—illuminating on an earlier example, knowing which pool balls will end up in a billiard's pocket during the opening break.

Bear with me while I go just one step further in explaining how our buildings became reactionary. It will be important for you to know the reason I will be attributing quantum theory and in-turn, quantum mechanics as one of the two reasons responsible for today's modern reactionary world, because our buildings too, are reactionary. Remember, buildings imitate their creator.

Quantum theory is known foremost as the atomic and subatomic interaction initially based on the behavior of the photon. Photon is a name that was given to a combined interaction of wave energy and particle energy, where these two combined elements form pulses of light. In brief, it's this light that radiates from the nucleus of an atom, created when an electron makes a quantum leap inside an atom. However, the light from a single photon is so small it cannot be seen by the human eye. This is because at least nine photons would have to arrive at the same time within 100 milli- seconds in order for our brain to process this light. Big Al was able to see what we could not. I needed to introduce you to the photon early because later you will recognize its' importance as a means for our communication with our buildings.

It was the use of this quantum theory that allowed Big Al to produce this basis for light and describe his new photoelectric law. Remember, I'm not attempting to educate you on the photon. Big Al utilized quantum theory for the purpose of speeding up a non- statistical result of this behavioral science of light, which classical physics was unable to explain. He believed that his theory was in perfect agreement with observation. This observation could be called Big Al's backup. Later with the development of quantum mechanics, Big Al still was not impressed using this new quantum science, in part because it treats physical events similar to a game of chance, remember my example of the billiard balls, which defies understanding, thus having many concepts disruptive to everyday experiences. Today, our physics and overall science is examined using this statistical chance derived from quantum mechanical science, but along with using big Al's definitive and orderly science of general relativity. Unfortunately, the physicists from each of these scientific disciplines are hesitant to speak with one and other, because of disagreements in how to approach the physics of ultimately unifying all of the known forces of nature, although Higgs Boson and the Field has advanced these conversations—a discussion for later.

Earlier and well before this scientific stalemate, Big Al explained his displeasure with quantum mechanics, explaining it provided the same example as God playing dice with the universe. Personally, other than a naturalist named Viktor Schauberger, I have not read of any student of nature that was as close to nature as Big Al. He was truly one of nature's closest friends, and although he used quantum theory for explanatory purposes, he would never embrace it. Our scientific view of our world is a reactionary one, we react to nature rather than work in harmony with nature. Until we are able to successfully unify the four known forces of nature, and lately a fifth has been said to exist, we are stuck within a quantum mechanical mode of operation. Regardless of our disposition, I will always believe the indoor thermostat belongs outdoors. But has our understanding of unifying our known forces been achieved?

A Brief Universal Look at Our Living Structure

Before our journey into the global picture of our living structures, let's take a look from where big Al started, from the outside looking in. A picture of our earth as an enormous building, an earth- building, our home in the universe, where its internal heat-source comes from its interior core or furnace and external heat-source comes from our sun. Cooling certainly arrives from the north and south poles. Our earth-building produces air to breath from the oxygen produced by its trees and vegetation, where it is in-turn filtered and cleaned by the rains and winds which we may call its built-in air-handling units. From high above we can view its life- carrying arteries in the form of our rivers and streams. The seas and oceans are the source of life, and excess that mimic the bowels of our earth-building carrying away and ultimately neutralizing our waste. Its inner skin is the crust or the very earth we live on, while on occasion it suffers an open wound spewing molten lava but ultimately healing on its own. Its outer protective skin – the atmosphere. Our earth-building is alive just as our human bodies are living structures. The very name of earth-building reversed, and then combined and condensed is b-earth, which coincides with our very being, our birth. With light from the sun and nature itself deciding our varying climates, our earth is what we all try to duplicate when building the perfect structure and environment. This is our earth from organic nature's perspective, but from a mechanical perspective, our planet is nothing more than a giant magnet, polarized by its north and south poles, and spinning similar to an armature of a giant motor within the eternal confines of space. We take this mechanistic point of view and duplicate our organic bodies into living breathing machines, buildings that are molded after our own human organic structures, producing British-thermal-units Btu's of heat similar to little furnaces.

Both Descartes and Einstein carried a common position, that nature held a unified set of rules which bound all of the physical world. Descartes unified theory was based upon an intellectual synthesis between several real principles and several interpretative acts of the human mind. He wanted to separate the divine soul from the material, the moving, and the physical world. Big Al also dedicated the latter part of his life to the belief of a unified theory of physics, where he asserted that every solid, liquid, or gas—all forms of matter that are the makeup of our buildings and ourselves—when combined with energy will interact as a common denominator to fashion our world. A unified answer, revealing, that all are related to each other—where all buildings made within the mechanical and electrical model of humans. To this day there is no known unified basis for physics. This unfinished goal was to unify gravity with electro-magnetism, which does not mean much to the average lay-person, but huge within the scientific community and to our buildings. Today, unification is the name of the game. It is this lack of unification that has been the primary reason we have been a reactive society.

Allow me to bring you just a little bit further into a space- eye view of the big picture by adding, that an electric charge which is moving creates a magnetic field, and our earth is surrounded by a magnetic field with the lines of force running from the south pole to the north pole, a circulating electric current, but not constant in direction, A giant magnet with a gravitational pull into a rotating earth–gravity with magnetism–the earth replicating a giant motor spinning within its own realm of the universe, another unified look at how all is relative. It makes one wonder, by inverting our existing math and combining it with nature's mathematically-found answers, whether the magnetic field of our earth that is the source creating our northern lights phenomena, or the electric charge for lightning coming from the sky of our rotating motor earth. Lightning is nature's electricity, where electric charges too are a part of and found within the human brain. We have earlier looked upon our home planet as a giant furnace heated from the liquid metals of the earth's core, complete with air conditioning outlets at its' north and south poles. If we can envision our planet's heating and cooling from a higher planetary picture, our vision for a common equation linking gravity and electro-magnetism is not so unreasonable, for these two forces of nature are ever so present in our buildings today. In contrast, how does electricity and magnetism combined with gravity relate to our building's personality, where our buildings are an inadvertent design of nature's human body?

Born centuries after Descartes and shortly after big Al, was a naturalist and inventor named Viktor Schauberger. Viktor was to go as far as to call our earth a living organism, which is an entity that breaths, exactly, like our buildings. Known as *The Water Wizard* to this day, Viktor revolutionized our understanding of nature, of water and our earth's atmosphere, and his belief that the earth's blood was the very water that provides life to us all, and of course, the same water that circulates through our buildings, providing us with synthetic comfort heating and cooling. Because water is one of the foundations of nature that merges the mechanical functionality of our buildings, a quick and simple outline of this nature-merge is required.

Nature's direction starts with a simple cell, a complex miniature molecular city, incorporating an intricate system containing a number of protein machines that carry out a variety of tasks that allow it to successfully operate. One of these machines were introduced earlier as the bacterial flagellum. Comparing the inner workings of a human cell to that of a building's operation, the human body contains around one-hundred-trillion cells, ten thousand of which can fit on the head of a pin. However, when you consider each cell contains information equivalent to around four thousand books, it could be considered a microscopic supercomputer.

From the tiniest city within a cell to the largest living environment we call earth, nature has a way of operating that we are still trying to catch up to, that our built structures try to mimic.

CHAPTER 3
Developing the Personality of Today's Building

It has been written that *knowledge is power*. Although there is a sense of psychological stability to this expression, knowledge in itself is not the basis for power, for power is using the knowledge you have acquired and applying it properly. Knowledge can be misapplied to the point of negligence, which in-turn negates its power.

As Facility Profilers, we do not provide consistency to those ignorant in the art of building and facilities engineering. As a result, our power to perform without interference is diminished. Asset management of commercial buildings, hotels, hospitals and research facilities, or just property and facility managers in general, become confident in their seminar-acquired knowledge, believing in their experience and organizational membership training as superior enough to delegate their wishes to the building's advocate, the engineer. However, those managers who take control away from the building's engineer, some of which have never stepped into a boiler room or chiller plant, do not understand that the building has in reality taken control of them. Unfortunately, these managers are only aware of their own needs, mostly budgetary, and not the needs of the building.

What is the control of a building? Simply, control can only be obtained when one has control. When we are aware of our building's programming, of every response our building is involved in, when we as facility engineers can accurately explain the reason for each temperature range within all areas of our building, can we safely proclaim that we are in control of our building. Any unexplained variance in our building's electrical or mechanical operation or climate temperature reveals that the building is in or has control, period. Therefore, a good asset manager will communicate and understand the very entity that controls their building, where this entity is typically the building's maintenance engineer. In furtherance of this, such control of this building's mouthpiece is only an excuse to control the building by proxy and reduces this skilled position to a building baby-sitter. If the asset manager does not have an all-around trust in his or her facilities engineer, the building loses its ability to communicate and as a consequence, it's physical and economic health. Onsite communication to skilled in the art of understanding the building is important.

Let us examine this for a moment. When asset or facility management gives a direction to the building engineer, for example, not to purchase new bearings for the cooling tower fan assembly at this time—let's wait until we truly need them, there are some engineers programmed not to argue and in-turn, reluctantly agree with a silent shrug of the shoulders. The facilities engineer may yet give a brief but ignored warning explaining why such a wait should not take place. Is this not the same as directing your child's doctor how you want your child cared for? Here asset management has taken control of the needs of the building by proxy. This is wrong because the individual who is closest to the workings and operations of the building must be the building's advocate, its voice. Going one step further, you would not instruct your parental advocate to ignore your child's cries? The engineer knows when the bearings must be changed similarly, as the babysitter is aware when a child requires feeding. Why would we then advise an engineer when to change a bearing. Unlike engineers, building managers are not trained in identifying the whining and crying of a bearing, or the negative impact this condition is having on other connected pieces of equipment. Who should then be making the decision to replace a building's component—the building manager or the building engineer? I would suggest a joint effort in the understanding of the problem or issue.

A majority of the time the reason an asset manager overrules the facilities engineer is due to operational economics. From an economics standpoint, I gave a loaded example in using the bearings of a cooling tower. Bearings, springs, and mechanical levers within the various pieces of machinery and equipment are the joints of your building, and which require lubrication. Any building component that requires lubrication is a building joint, similar to your body's knees, elbows, and all other ball and joint body parts. Accordingly, bad bearings cause a tremendous hidden drag to the fan of the cooling tower, which increases the amount of time the fan needs to be running and increases the electrical load of the motor that turns this fan assembly. If you operate a machine longer it costs more money, and if you need more power (in the form of wattage) to operate a machine it costs more money. From an engineering standpoint, an inefficient cooling tower creates an increase in the cooling tower water temperature, which in all cases reduces the efficiency of your building's chiller or the machine that produces chilled water for your building's air-conditioning. The hip-bone will always be connected to the shin bone.

A Brief Look at Today's Building Maintenance Engineer

First, let me get this out of the way . . . Facility professionals, true facility professionals are Renegades. We subject ourselves to strict codes of conduct that insert us as keepers of the temple, the building, enshrining rigorous ethical and moral obligations against those who would cause our structures harm. Our job is to advocate for the building while making the bosses priorities our priorities—an oxymoron for sure. Our job is to protect property management at the same time we're trying to protect the building. It is this unique responsibility that places us regularly in the line of fire with those incensed with a blind focus to make profit margins. However, it also keeps us in favor with those superiors that are aware and believe in our mission.

Concerning our procrastination toward reviews in general, I have found that Stephen R. Covey has defined this human shortfall the best, explaining that: most of our mental development and study discipline comes through formal education. But as soon as we leave the external discipline of our schooling, many of us let our minds atrophy. We don't do any more serious reading, we don't explore new subjects in any real depth outside our action fields, we don't think analytically. We don't focus on analyzing. It's boring and our superiors want action, they want near-instant results. In-turn, we provide a quick fix, proving again that an engineer having sufficient knowledge is not the basis for power. Do we as building engineers even remember where we placed our formula books last used in trade school or college? Were these lengthy formulas of seasonal heating and cooling losses, total energy consumptions, and more, that time-consuming and so tedious that their importance has been reduced to the prior accomplishment of a passing school grade average? Are we truly aware that these are the very calculations that form the basis of how a building's mechanical and HVAC systems are sized, by taking into account the size of a structure, climate location, and building materials used? This is the building's thermal envelope, clothing translated into numbers. These are the calculations required to access how your building's HVAC and the central plant should react within the confines of its skeletal frame. The calculations that have brought us closest to our building's needs and wants. Wait! A building has wants?

After all of the tasks that have been assigned to us by either the commercial asset or hotel manager, have we not forgotten that these various brain-cramping calculations relative to a building's personality are—for us—only the first segment of the equation?

Examined within this dimensional thought pattern, take for instance the educated and experienced building engineer and his or her wealth of knowledge. With the exception of certain professional engineers and architects who are required to attempt a proper sizing of the mechanicals and HVAC equipment of a building, what building engineer do you know calculates seasonal heating and cooling losses, summer solar heat gains, Summer season conductive heat gains, etc? all of which penetrate through a buildings' walls, and roof, and windows, and doors, and more. How many building engineers are versed in the steady-state procedure in calculating the component heat loss of a building's thermal envelope or determining the M-factor by utilizing the amount of heating degree days taken with the weight of each wall. Are the Summer and Winter design temperatures of your building taken from standards as published by the American Society of Heating, Refrigerating, and Air-Conditioning Engineers'(ASHRAE). I am very fond of these many calculations, tables, and guidelines, which for years have been and presently are the basis and foundation of building engineering. However, there are a few well-skilled building engineers who do not undergo this analytical review toward seeking out a building's vulnerable points that in-fact cause its mechanicals to react and expend energy. If ASHRAE is the medical handbook for buildings, why wouldn't facility engineers expand their knowledge in the health of their building? What is missing within these present-day calculations that cause us to frown? Simplicity!

Anything that is plain, easy to understand or purely natural is simple, and this is where we need to take our buildings, to un-complicate the complicated.

(D)ata (O)n (P)lant (E)quipment

A popular method that facilities professionals use for simplicity toward the understanding of the equipment they operate and oversee, is knowing the operational partnership of their equipment and systems. How the building's systems work as a combined effort to produce a synergistic environment.

When we use our body's senses by touching with our hands through our skin, or see objects through our eyes or hear decibel sounds through our ears, our body detects this energy through receptor cells called sensory receptors, where these receptors are cells that receive sensory information from the body's external environment. These stimulus energies are translated into electrical energy to the brain similar to the wiring or fiber optics cable carrying signals to the processor of our building's automation system. This transmission is also comparable to our human-computer cells and neurotransmitters converting this electricity into chemical codes for an electrochemical transmission, where nerves in our body communicate with each other. It's like a category-5 or CAT-5 computer network.

When we look at the various pieces of our building's equipment and how they are controlled by the artificial intelligence we install, the combined equipment within our buildings develop an operational routine, a programmed rhythm that we see and hear, and we become set into that routine. Because of our knowledge in knowing the different tasks each piece of equipment performs, we are mindful of how our building's systems operate in harmony with their intended operation. It's how our building's automation system (BAS) through direct digital control—DDC receives its signals from the individual building systems (pump motors, air-handling-units, chillers, etc.) that form the operation of our synthetic environments.

In order to achieve this operational balance, we take note and monitor the different systems that operate our building's body. We have watch engineers, maintenance mechanics, or whatever name a building manager or owner uses to take hourly, quarterly, or daily readings of the pump pressures, water temperatures, velocity of air distribution, and more. It is a combined understanding of these monitored results which determines whether the rhythm of our building is healthy or in need of some change. This is the reason that data from our building's plant equipment is so very important.

When it comes to obtaining critical data, the members of the American military use a nomenclature for the performance of their sniper equipment, named – Data on Personal Equipment, or the acronym, DOPE. Another military terminology is - Data Observed from Previous Engagements, also recognized as DOPE. It is the cataloging of information regarding the performance of their rifle relative to the ammunition they use, the distance of the shot and the existing weather conditions all combined. When a sniper performs his shot using a combination from an earlier experience, he or she is using Data that was earlier developed on this Personal Equipment to obtain a DOPE result. Some on social media sites have equated DOPE to be simply a gun diary. I would equate it as precision in motion.

When we take these pump pressures, water temperatures, cubic-feet-per-minute (cfm), air distribution, and more, we are accumulating this data from our equipment and systems' previously established performance baseline to maintain our building's symmetry, its equilibrium. The performance baselines used is from the Data of Plant Equipment, our building's DOPE criterion. This is how you know your building is DOPE, or is it?

I've been involved on many occasions with the start-up operations of a new building that had just completed its' commissioning, the procedure that ensures our new building operates as designed and intended by the architect or engineer, and that facility engineers or maintenance staff are ready to take charge to operate and maintain its new building's systems and equipment. I have found more times than not when the architect and mechanical engineer has completed this commissioning, the facility engineer's job has just begun. The building may be operating fine on paper, but sometimes we, unfortunately, learn that parts of our building aren't performing all too well. Definitely not a baseline for knowing that your building is DOPE. This is because a DOPE experience within facilities maintenance and engineering does not happen overnight. It may take months or even years to experience that cohesion of your equipment and systems coming together while working in harmony with each other. That's DOPE!

In recent years there have been times when I've asked a benign question regarding the weather or even the results of a football game, only to hear "that game was DOPE!" It was during these times I would wonder whether my question was answered because the players and coaches of the winning team had played with such precision and harmony that was similar to previous games that produced this DOPE game? The point I'm trying to make, should a building engineer or maintenance person proclaim that his building is DOPE, you may occasionally ask how he or she has made this assessment. A sentence that incorporates language which indicates the building's equipment and systems are all getting along is typically a good indication that the building's mouthpiece has a good grasp on his or her synthetic environment.

When looking at this from a physics point of view, DOPE is not doping, where doping refers to mixing different forms of matter in order to change the material's properties, and the purpose of this change is to make the material better. As an example, a process for manufacturing semiconductor material within the semi- conductor industry was doping or mixing pure materials with impure materials in order to make the pure material more conductive to electricity. This doping made principal materials of silicon and germanium more conductive when doped with lesser pure materials such as boron, phosphorus, and other materials. The addition of these materials made one cohesive system that produced an exceptionally effective conductive material.

Whether it is the combination of Data Observed from Previous Engagements or the Data of Plant Equipment—use of the term DOPE appears to be one of those rare instances, where the word created from the acronym seems to match the function of the word created. That's what is known as DOPE!

Shutdown the centrifugal pump of a building that controls its' heating or cooling water circulation and you have stopped its heart and circulatory system. Manipulate the rate of flow (GPM) of this pump system and you will have successfully affected its pressure and ability to maintain its' proper internal temperature. Air-handling-units combine outdoor fresh-air with re-circulated indoor air that allows your building to breath filtered and conditioned air. When we successfully control the temperature and flow rate of our building's water circulation in concert with our building's respiratory airflow, the building's inner-air can mimic nature's environment to meet our comfort levels. A mechanical human taking care of an organic human, a phenomenon in itself. When your building is operating by following with its' intended operational design, where the operative word here is 'intended', your building can then be recognized as DOPE.

The Building Was Once a Simple Place

Shortly after the Korean conflict was over, tens of thousands of veterans worldwide returned home seeking unskilled jobs. In 1953, the year the Korean conflict ended, US President Dwight Eisenhower's secretary of labor was a plumber, Martin Durkin, who was President of the plumbers and steamfitter's union. All trade unions had a loud voice within Eisenhower's cabinet. Janitorial and building maintenance welcomed a substantial number of these new veterans, and because building maintenance was in its infancy, these veterans learned to not just figure things out, but from my experience with friends I had made through the years, created novel ways of maintaining those highly mechanical building systems. After the war, America and the world were getting back on their feet. New construction was thriving and an increase in manufacturing was creating new jobs. This was also an age where early electronics promised great technological advances. This post-war era also initiated the start of erecting the international style buildings with steel-framed boxes, darkened glass, and air-conditioning that introduced plaza fronts common within many of the world-wide cities today. These were buildings clearly in need of day-to-day electrical and mechanical maintenance.

In the mid-seventies, a number of these war era professionals would advance to management positions while some left the industry to be replaced by new veterans of the Vietnam conflict era. When the year 2000 came around, tens of thousands of these self-taught and seasoned maintenance professionals began retiring, to a point where a generation of our building's advocates were disappearing. These were building encyclopedias forced to learn the trade of building maintenance and management during an earlier time when buildings were still in their developmental stage, now being replaced with craftsmen from the electrical and mechanical industries that were new to facility engineering. As these buildings became more advanced with electronics and fuzzy logic self-learning building automation systems, property management began increasing their Rolodex lists of third-party contractors. You now had to be a specialist in automatic door closures, variable-speed-drives, building automation and alarm systems, and much more. These weren't simple buildings anymore, they were smart intelligent structures in need of an intelligent interpreter, with only half the industry knowing how to talk the language. The post-war retirements left an unmistakable gap in the exercise of how to learn from scratch. As our understanding of how to analyze our systems and structures using calculators became more and more complicated, higher-priced maintenance professionals were required, while in-turn causing retirements of post-war professionals to increase. Why, because new technologies along with computer maintenance management software (CMMS) threatened to require new education while tracking their hourly move each day. These were professionals losing control of their buildings along with the daily routines they had built through the years. If you've ever been in a labor union meeting when CMMS systems were being introduced you were made to believe that you were arguing for a reduction in staff. The thought of tracking and trending a union member's daily routine was looked upon as Big Brother watching and an assault upon the trustworthiness of these facility professionals who have given decades of service. These were the men and women who knew, that if you closed this valve, you would cause another system to fail or become irreparably damaged. These were the pros that made the new modern systems work with the older systems better after the professional engineers integrated the new with the old. These professionals were the go-to people for professional engineers hired to modify specific building systems, and once they were gone, so too were their secrets and where the buildings bodies were buried. It was their departures that created a gap and a need to replace them with entry-level although highly motivated tradesmen and women.

In most cases, the budgets for maintaining these now intelligent buildings reflected the pay of those retiring, and as we all know, once you create a benchmark for a budget, it's very hard if not next to impossible to validate an increase.

What is missing within the earlier described calculations that cause us to frown? Simplicity! It was, for this reason, the earlier- shown graphic for maintaining an equilibrium toward the building's labor and line item operational expenses—were designed to be aligned with the utility costs and bottom-line profit margin for Sigi. It was time for facilities engineering to bring simplicity back to property management.

Bob Small – The Integrity of Business

For the most part and from my experience, the person that resembled simplicity while requiring accountability was Robert Small, former President and CEO of Fairmont hotels, and from my seat, a very firm but fair businessman. I'm reflecting on a time back in August of 1996, during late evening meetings I would be called upon to attend within Bob Small's hotel room - turned executive office, where I would learn Bob's character traits. I remember the time of year because it was the same month I was hired by Fairmont as the engineering director and executive for their newly acquired Copley Plaza hotel in Boston, USA. Fairmont was taking over the management of the property from Wyndham hotels after purchasing the hotel from the John Hancock company. During this period the Chairman of Fairmont hotels and 50 percent owner was Saudi Prince Waleed Bin Talal.

Through the time of this new purchase, Bob and Fairmont were engaged in a lawsuit filed by a former Fairmont executive. Not a good PR visual during the opening of this newly purchased property, which appeared to make Bob Small careful in the moves he made. Bob was very direct with me. Using a firm and direct stare he explained how he wanted to be assured how the renovation funding could be used in such a way that would satisfy the company's ability to make its profit margin, which would simultaneously please his friend, his Royal Highness the Prince, along with the other Fairmont board members. This wasn't a CEO that was looking for me to side with his opinion. As he would describe, he had no opinion, only a limited amount of funding that needed to be properly directed. Bob Small was obviously a visionary, and he would describe himself as people- oriented. *You appear to me as a people-oriented person too, Wayne. I trust you will help with our transformation of this Grand hotel.* Yes, he used the word transformation. And yes, the Boston Copley Plaza has the architecture of a grand hotel. If I may, reflecting back to an earlier time, I recall admiring such similar architecture and color schemes of comparable ornate vaulted ceilings. It was during a business tour of the United States Embassy in Rome, Italy. Thinking as a facility engineer, I remember the sprinkler heads within this Roman architecture were installed just below the ceilings on the sidewall, apparently to maintain the beauty of those decorative ceilings. I also remember being surprised when shown a hidden door within a wall off of an upper corridor that housed a plaque for former Italian fascist' dictator Benito Mussolini, where this embassy facility, the *Palazzo Margherita*, once housed offices for the Mussolini government. This was a hidden personality I did not remotely expect. But nature was also a significant part of these secluded grounds. As the facility director of the embassy and I walked outdoors, I was shown, what was named the Triton fountain. It was a drinking fountain connected to an aqueduct that carried spring water from the mountains into the city of Rome. This was a first for me, a building located within an urban city that is connected to nature's mountainous range by way of a spring water aqueduct. I learned that throughout the streets of Rome, dozens of Nasoni, meaning big nose-fountains in Italian, constantly pour cold spring water from dozens of these drinking fountains that can be found sporadically throughout the city. On the way back to the airport I noticed from my taxi a teenage jogger filling her water bottle from one of these Nasoni fountains. How it must have felt drinking cold spring water coming directly from the mountains while you cool off from your jog in the city, a definite nature-merge.

Robert Small, CEO of Fairmont Hotels, and Wayne Saya (1996). Bob Small retired as President of Fairmont Hotels where he spearheaded the hotel's turnaround and revitalized the chain throughout the 1990s. Before Fairmont, he served as Executive Vice President for Walt Disney World Resort Division presiding over the largest hospitality expansion in the company's history. Prior to that, he pioneered Marriott Corporation's expansion into Europe and became Vice-President of western region resorts.

Reflecting back to my meetings with Bob Small, they were rather robust, because, as Bob would explain, his Royal Highness Prince Waleed had contributed a specified amount of funding for a major renovation of the mechanicals, rooms, and front of the house. The problem—if it could be called one—the hotel needed all of the money for guest rooms, furnishings, fixtures, and façade work, with some limited soft goods. The discussions, could the hotel comfortably operate environmentally if the mechanical portion of the budget was redirected to the guest rooms? The answer I had provided was, yes with an explanation. You see, the Boston Copley Plaza was the first fully air-conditioned hotel in America. The design for the cooling system was not quite up to a standard that would provide maximum comfort. The original design had been sort of cut and pasted into a two central-chiller-plant operation, one on each end of the hotel, and both interconnected to one centralized chilled water loop. This may not sound too complicated until one realizes, that one centralized pumping system was not operating this chilled water loop. The two-independent pump systems, one for each chiller, independently located at each end of the hotel, were operating a single chilled water loop. A fluid dynamic effort to say the least. If ever there was an example of a building divided, this dual pumping system was it. Should one fail, a building divided could not stand, the Copley Plaza would be unable to operate its heating or cooling system.

Bob wanted to know the significance of this dual pump design as it related to my concerns. Without getting into the details of maintaining certain minimum and maximum water pressures flowing through each chiller system, I explained that operating two pumps that were located in two distant locations for the same circulation loop was the equivalent of a person borne with two hearts. To start, both would need to be correctly synchronized at all times. Secondly, and most importantly for this property, should one of these pumps fail, the entire heating and cooling system would also fail. Whereas, if this system was separated into two individual loops, using one circulation pump for each chiller system, a pump failure would only affect approximately half of the hotel, as opposed to the entire property. The problem was in the original design, where the piping was too small in diameter to pump successfully from one end of the building to the other. This was the apparent reason that there were two pumps for this single loop system. There were no mechanical drawings available from the '50s when this system was initially installed on the roof, as evidenced by an abandoned vintage compressor system. Whereas, the chilled water system was now located in two separate basement areas.

In the end, I prescribed the purchase of a backup pump and motor for each chiller system, while creating a manual monitoring program to keep an eye on the pressure gauges of each system, because the hotel had no building automation system. Still, I was required to explain how these steps would provide an acceptable temporary alternative to the monies designated for a permanent fix. Ultimately, this substitute from separating the one loop into two was able to provide Bob with a nice financial contribution for the guest rooms, while coming close enough to a guarantee for providing a required comfort cooling environment. I'll explain the guarantee in a moment.

First, it would be Bob's job to notify the hotel project manager, Tony, of any budget changes. Although my job was important, it was limited to provide Bob an overall explanation for working alternatives that would allow him to reallocate designated funding that he was receiving from his Royal Highness the Prince. Bob explained it was an alliance he was attempting to create with His Royal Highness and not just a simple loan source. With Bob, his understanding of any impact from such relocation of capital funding was critical, especially when taking into consideration the current San Francisco lawsuit that was pending against him and the company. However, there were two areas I could not guarantee, but which fortunately were not included within the original renovation funding.

Secondly, the air-handling-units to the Grand ballroom had aged to a point where it didn't matter how cold the temperature of the chilled water was that traveled through this system. The fins were so far eaten away from oxidation, any eighty-degree day would be difficult to remove humidity, or recover from rising temperatures for that matter. There were no fins to transfer this chilled water temperature to the air running through these coils.

Finally, the guestroom fan coils were the original 1950's vintage units, and the size of the piping supplying the chilled water to these guestroom A/C units was realistically not sufficiently sized and insulated by today's standards. Remember, as the first air-conditioned hotel, some fluid dynamics were simply not calculated as they should have been, using today's pipe sizing calculations for proper circulation of heating and cooling. After all, there is only so much flow rate (gpm) of water you can push through a half-inch length of branch piping while incorporating the distances from floor-to-floor and room-to-room. This is because of the equation of motion in fluid dynamics, where for a steady flow we need to examine many considerations, including the forces acting upon the flow, the flow area, and the boundary perimeters contacting the fluid, we'll simply say the diameter of the piping to make this easy. Finally, we look at the elevation of the piping. Without turning this into a lesson in fluid dynamics, after calculating the wetted perimeter of this 1912 vintage Grand Dame' of hotels, total integration of the equation of motion for the fluid of this undersized piping is synonymous with a building suffering from hardening of the arteries. The flow is restricted to the pipe-size and velocity of the fluid or heated or chilled water. As a younger facility, the building operated just fine using the standards of the time, but as the building got older, changes in its circulatory system and knowledge of its anatomy have required an elevated monitoring of its condition and maintenance of its systems.

I incorporated specific annual band-aid repairs and modifications to relieve a number of these operational anomalies, wherein three to five years of additional capital expenditures would be expected (I never say available) for some strategic upgrades. Also incorporated was the accounting procedures I had used with Sigi years earlier. As long as I maintained an equilibrium between in-house labor and third-party contractors while monitoring the energy management side of the equation, I would have the ability to maintain the new lean operational budget I had inherited, and keeping my commitments in the form of assurances to Bob Small.

I was able to provide certain assurances because just a few months previous, while the engineering director for Wyndham at this same property, I installed a screw-machine (chiller) to replace one of the two chiller plants. Screw-type-machines, as opposed to centrifugal chillers, can operate very efficiently during low load applications. This would be beneficial during those times I would need to operate the chiller for the guest rooms when outdoor temperatures were not high enough for normal day-to-day chiller operation. This was all performed through valve manipulation. A fun time for sure. The engineering department acted as a manual building-automation-system through our valve manipulations, daily chiller demand adjustments, and water velocities and temperature readings. Because a few of Bob's concerns were taken from a due-diligence report written well before our discussion, I was able to provide him with some favorable information that I know surprised him in a favorable way.

His Royal Highness the Prince arrived a day or two later. I remember receiving a call from the acting general manager. The newly-appointed GM, John Unwin, was coming from the Fairmont in Dallas, Texas, and had not yet arrived. *Wayne, you're wanted up in the Oak Room.* Upon my arrival, I was advised I would be joining four others who will be walking across the street through the park to Boylston street, about a city block away from the hotel, with His Royal Highness Prince Waleed. Apparently, His Royal Highness was interested in the 62-story John Hancock tower that stood tall next to the Copley Plaza hotel. This glass tower used a number of geometric optical illusions within a clever structural design that made one believe the building disappears at its right angle. It was rather comical because His Royal Highness would stop abruptly as we walked behind him, almost causing a near domino bumping car effect. It's like we were being led like pets around the streets of Boston while we followed a Saudi Prince— you had to be there. In the end, while observing the Saudi Prince's facial expressions, Prince Waleed showed a sense of appreciation with the personality of New England's tallest building, while sitting with authority next to his latest investment.

I couldn't help but recognize the similarities between Sigi and Bob Small. Both were strong visionaries and each had a passion for guest satisfaction. But another characteristic they shared was the importance placed on trust when dealing with Royal Saudi business. Both were aware that such a trusting relationship was critical to the success or failure of the building and in-turn business, and a fundamental code required for the building of an alliance. They were investing their time with employees like me to promote the building more than the business because if they took care of the building along with those that cared for it, the job of providing quality service can be accomplished so much easier in their mission for guest satisfaction. It all appeared to connect quite nicely.

As for GM John Unwin, he had a unique style of his-own. As one of his executive staff, I watched John work his vision that changed the operational and quality dynamics of this grand hotel— elevating the overall guest experience and food offerings to a significantly higher level, where a number of these changes remain today. John would later become a stalwart pioneer in hospitality— bringing his successful facilities management style and distinguishing mark to Las Vegas, Nevada, and beyond. Among his later ventures' past and current he would serve as senior vice president and general manager of Caesars Palace and in-turn as chief executive officer of the Las Vegas Cosmopolitan.

Each time I entered the office/hotel room of Bob Small, he would greet me with a smile and an extended firm hand, saying: *Come in my friend.* Through the years we would, on occasion, Communicate and talk about family, health, and the industry.

My friend Bob Small passed away in 2014, leaving yet another enormous void within the hospitality industry, that of advocate for the built environment.

Looking at the Building's Needs from the Building's Viewpoint

As the head of an average American household, I am strongly aware of my family's needs and wants, down to their physical, mental, social, and emotional nature. Similarly, as an engineer, I am aware of the needs of each piece of mechanical equipment under my watch. But what about these various pieces of mechanicals and what they want. Our mechanicals are missing the mental, social and emotional characteristics, which personalize us as humans. Realistically, a mechanical can indicate its' needs by its performance - or the physical (as opposed to the psychological). But is there a source of communication or indicator these mechanical components of a building can use to ask us what they want. As an example, before I go to the beach, I want a sun blocking lotion to prevent damage to my body. I know what my needs are therefore I want. Accordingly, a need is the first event while wanting is the second event. Because these two events occur simultaneously, the two are simultaneous events.

Placing the needs and wants from a different perspective, any individual can want something, but may not necessarily need what they are wanting. For instance, a hotel guest has just checked into their room. The room temperature is comfortable and it is found that the wall-mounted climate control for this room incorporates only an "off" and "on" single-speed selector switch for the fan— for this particular system is controlled by a computer or artificial intelligence. At this time the guest indicates that a multi-speed selector switch for the fan would have been preferred, such as the type within the home of this particular guest. The guest concedes that the room temperature is fine, for now. The guest only intends to use the room for only a few hours during this trip and the next, according to his or her business schedule. However, the guest is unhappy because the climate controls do not provide the comfort expected, and cancels the return trip that is scheduled for the following week. The majority of guest room selector controls today have minimum and maximum temperature parameters. The psychological need of this guest to duplicate a familiar back-home control out-weighed the true physical needs. A true story by-the-way. This particular guest wanted control, and any explanation of this room being under computer control or artificial intelligence would not have made the slightest change in wanting control. The psychological needs of this guest out-weighed the physical benefits this guest may have obtained if using a computer-controlled system.

When an elevator stops precisely where we want by the mere push of a button, or when a fire door closes automatically upon the activation of an alarm condition, we take this artificial intelligence for granted. We programmed these needs of ours into our electronic clones. Remember this is all artificial. But wait! Again, who programmed these systems? We're not artificial!

What does a mechanical want? It wants to be programmed properly, it wants to be sized with its sister and brother interactive building parts in harmony, it wants to be protected from the sun, but without having to seek a tinted window treatment as a sun-block each time a building is erected. It wants to function as its creator intended and not as the financial situation or project completion times dictate. Much often than not buildings are designed, built or renovated with the honest of intentions by the architect, only to later realize that the finished product is the equivalent of how Dr. Frankenstein's creation was developed—a mere compilation of strategically located body parts. A little dramatic but I think you get the picture. This is also realized within new buildings, caused by project change orders, scheduling deadlines, and of course the infamous value-engineering proposals. How can we know if this has happened to our building? Where are a building's vital signs located for us to make our prognosis?

Knowing how a building will react is halfway there in knowing its personality. Aware of its' needs and properly remedying its wants complete the remaining half. Unfortunately, all of the previously reviewed calculations are unable to advise us of a building's needs, which reasons and causes I will attempt to explain, for a building's needs and in-turn wants are only revealed when you know your building. Knowing your building is knowing your building's personality.

Now follow carefully - if we take the needs and wants of a building as previously discussed and combine these simultaneous events into a singular compound event (similar to a compound word) we can now designate this compound event as a first-stage event. Therefore, the needs and wants of a building (now one event) and a building's reaction to these needs and wants (the second event) create a compound simultaneous event.

Think carefully, if we were to remove the wants of a building, we are drawn back into observing the building as a mere assembly of mechanical components created to perform as a reactionary environment based on artificial intelligence. Remove this psychological appendage of wanting and the building will have had its only humanistic likeness severed – having needs without being allowed to want. The true and realistic needs of a building can only be seen when we personalize its needs to the human level of wanting. As adults, we do not openly express our needs where this is more of a private or secluded adult function such as an assessment or review, or even the business of no one else. Our wants are ultimately expressed by our open and publicly viewed actions. I know what my needs are therefore I want. In reality, we should look at the needs and in-turn the wants from a building's point of view, and not from a humanistic view because our decision or viewpoint can be clouded by false economics or failures to analyze and calculate. We believe we know what our building needs but only by looking from a building's point of view can we see whether the needs of the building coincided with its wants. Simultaneous events looked upon from one point of reference are not necessarily simultaneous when viewed from another reference point.

Basic Einstein Overlooked

The primary basis for this analogy of simultaneous events is predicated on big Al's reversal of Isaac Newton's metaphysical absolutes, where Newton, founder of the theoretical basis of mechanics, believed that the distance of a given space within certain time intervals to be absolute. However, Big Al discovered from examining such simultaneous events that space and time intervals were relative. A distance traveled through a space within a given time period is a relative measure. Every interaction takes time to get from one place through a given space to the next. In-turn, Big Al revealed that there are no instantaneous interactions in nature. This is simple, so follow—if the weather and our own human nature are both a product of nature, and artificial intelligence within an artificially created mechanical environment is a reproduction of nature, then simply, all we have accomplished is an artificial reproduction of nature where we do not have the ability to instantly react, to instantaneous interact with nature.

Therefore, if there are no instant interactions in nature, how can there possibly be instant interactions in artificial nature? Think about it, a human's attempt to produce an instantaneous interaction between its mechanical creation (the building) and the elements of nature (weather), are opposite to Big Al's General relativity. Today's building is a reactionary force against the elements of nature, a synthetically created environment reacting against the elements of a natural environment, what we shall call "true nature", both relative to one-and-other.

Although we don't admit our attempts to accomplish an instant reaction to nature's elements, artificial intelligence would have to act instantantaneously to equal true nature's mood swings. Therefore, controlling our artificial environment cannot be a constant.

When we attempt to use electrical and mechanical climate controls to instantaneously interact with a building's mechanicals – to control our indoor synthetic climate in response to the outdoor elements, we are in essence saying that there "are" instantaneous interactions in synthetic nature, so long as human nature reproduces true nature by utilizing computers, mechanicals, and electronic artificial intelligence. But are we not a part of nature too?

Carl G. Jung, a modern-day psychologist, and author advises mankind to give a great deal of consideration to what we are doing, warning that we are threatened by self-created dangers that are growing beyond our control. If we were to analyze the truth of this statement, we need only to look at the 1976 incident at a hotel in Philadelphia, Pennsylvania, in where a large number of Legionnaires' suffered and died from a pneumophilia organism —a bacterium later identified as Legionella pneumophila, a flagellated bacterium powered by a proton-motive-force (chemiosmotic potential). We discussed earlier the bacterial flagellum, looking identical to that of the inner workings of an electric motor. This L.Pneumophila is the primary human pathogenic bacterium and is the causative agent of Legionnaires' disease, also known as legionellosis. This was the bacteria that was transmitted into the ballroom of this hotel's convention area, traveling through the respiratory system of its air distribution system using the building's air-handling-unit. Yes, our buildings too suffer certain airborne illnesses that are contagious to their organic human occupants. This bacterium is born within the confines of a cooling tower or plumbing system. In furtherance of this Legionnaires' disease, Pontiac Fever is the non-pulmonary counterpart that is born and transmitted in the same manner. These illnesses are just two of many new age illnesses now located within a defined label known as *Sick Building Syndrome*. This condition was the first building illness that raised the material building to a human level. A computer virus within our building's artificial intelligence is the other.

Our building contracted a bacterial infection from an ineffective preventive maintenance routine. We didn't properly feed our building with the necessary algaecide and biocide as a prevention from illness. We didn't provide our building with its scheduled vaccinations. In-turn, the lungs of our building, its air distribution system, became contagious and spread its mechanically created infection to the organic occupants it was designed to protect and keep healthy. Just because our buildings are not human does not mean they do not act human. Remember, buildings are humanistic machines. I like to think that buildings are people too!

Although we don't admit our attempts to accomplish an instant reaction to true nature's elements, we should realize, if we don't, that our artificial intelligence would have to act instantaneously to equal true nature's mood swings. Wherefore, controlling our artificial environment, unfortunately, cannot be a constant. True nature is similar, where remember Newton versus Einstein there are no absolutes in nature, and clearly our weather is a part of nature. New Englanders know this well, for their advice to tourists proclaim: *if you don't like the weather, wait a minute.* But remember, where there are no instantaneous interactions in nature, you may have to wait a few minutes.

What is it that control's our artificial environment, and which does not have the ability to instantaneously interact with true nature? Let's look at a case in point: How many times have you heard of medical reports that are either inconclusive or finding that an inaccurate diagnosis had been rendered. Remember, knowledge is not power. Regardless of how the inaccuracy occurred, such an occurrence does happen.

Let us pretend that we now have all of the data that has been compiled from our analytical review of our building. We've calculated the Winter and Summer heating and cooling gains, re-assessed the building's thermal envelope materials used, reviewed the regional climate, and are advised by our mechanical design engineer that all mechanicals have been specified and installed by following these calculations – they've been commissioned. Damn, we're good!

Remember, knowledge is not power, and regardless of how the inaccuracy occurred; such an occurrence does happen. I have just shown you that this building is functioning properly or as designed, but these offices are still too hot. Why?

In this one of many examples, which would require a separate book, the solar heat gains or the sun through these windows were not anticipated at the levels of infiltrating within these offices when direct sunlight bombards the east side of this glass tower. Nature has struck again. I don't understand it, the calculations advised us that the building, the entire building would be climate controlled. Yet, if this solar bombardment had been anticipated, the cubic-feet-per-minute (cfm) of cool air to these specific rooms may have been assessed differently, or a supplemental system for this area may have been planned. But was the HVAC system of this building planned properly? In an attempt to correct this apparent oversight, we have decided to polarize the windows with a tinted sun-shield. What? this corrected measure has not solved the problem? Next, we could re-size the air distribution supply to these offices by replacing the fan-coil or air handling unit with one that is sized larger, or first attempt to increase the pulley size of the existing blower which would increase the (rpm) speed of the blower to this air-handling-unit, that will increase the velocity of air supplied to each room.

But this remedy may create too much noise within the rooms of a law office. Excuse me for a moment, the building manager is on line one. You want me to do whatever it takes to cool these offices immediately! Well, this was an easy one, I'll just reduce the chilled water temperature to the entire building which in-turn will supply cooler temperatures to the air distribution unit to these offices. Wait! What will this do to the personality of our building? Remember, the needs and wants of a building and our building's reaction to these needs and wants are simultaneous events. However, these simultaneous events looked upon from one point of reference, the building manager, are not necessarily simultaneous when viewed from another reference point - the building's reaction. We applied the wrong cure for a burned hand.

The Burned Hand Analogy

Every interaction takes time to travel from one place through a given space to the next. As an example to this reference of space and time, say I were to accidentally burn my hand on a very hot stove, my immediate instinctive reaction would be to seek and apply cool water directly to the burn area. I want to sink my hand in cold water. By contrast, I would not submerge my entire body into a tub of water merely to send relief to this single body part. So, reason would dictate if a floor of an office building or wing of an entire building becomes overheated or has a slow cooling recovery time, a typical property management and facility engineering practice within an office tower, using chilled water systems, is to decrease the chilled water temperature that supplies the air distribution system. This practice is designed to deliver colder water temperatures to the air distribution systems, AHU's and the like to address the overheated area. Now think just for a moment and picture what we have just accomplished, this overheated part of the building is now surely cooler—to some extent—because we are delivering colder water temperatures to this area using a lower chilled water temperature. But in doing so, what have we done to the rest of the building. Exactly, I have lowered the chilled water temperature to the entire building's circulatory system, or chilled water loop which supplies all remaining air-handler or fan-coil units. When the remaining air distribution units of this building cycle on-and-off in an effort to provide the thermostat-set temperature, some areas will lower temperatures too quickly while certain other areas will become too warm—resulting in a short-cycling mode of operation. Short cycling can be especially uncomfortable, where the space in question is too cool one moment and too warm the next. I like to call this *Einstein's annex* to the space in a period of time. Specifically, we have changed the personality of this building to a neurotic state, by submerging its entire body in a tub of cool water, rather than applying direct aid to the affected body part.

Now, have I changed the building's personality in a positive or negative direction? Obviously negative, because the needs of this building was specific: to cool this one side of the body or area separate from the remainder of this otherwise stable building, or to apply cooling to a burned hand rather than the entire body. This building did not need nor want to have its unaffected space areas and thermal envelop temperatures changed or played with. The building manager or engineer blindly directed a *false need* for the building in order to enable this human-flaw to report that the immediate problem was addressed. In this case, the needs of building management over-ruled the needs of the building, partly because the building's needs were not seen or even looked at. We were not interested in the needs of our building but only the wants of our paying tenants. Damn, we got it backward! Addressing the needs and wants of our building will automatically address the wants of our building's occupant or paying tenant.

Why did this happen? Simply, the building engineer was unsccessful in properly educating the property manager. Yes, our inability to properly respond is our response-ability. A component of this education is to also disclose any additional consequences associated with this decision. As facility engineers and maintenance managers, we need to do a better job convincing our property and general managers of the consequences associated with decisions that harm our buildings and artificial environments. Here the obvious consequence is the dramatic increase in this building's energy usage, electric bill, and as a consequence—profit-margin.

An attempt was made to instantly interact with a problem part of a building, only to adversely affect the non-problem parts. Clearly, there are no instantaneous interactions in synthetic nature. For what we have created is a systematic process of reactionary control. However, controls can also be designed for a proactive role.

We have not quite understood that it is not our responsibility to provide a comfortable synthetic climate for our tenant, clearly, we pay our building to accept this responsibility – just look at your total utility bills each month. All we should be doing is properly overseeing the personality of our building, or effectively manage the process and equipment while permitting our well-maintained systems to do the job they were designed to do.

The Air We Breathe

As I was about to enter a building in Chicago around Wacker Ave, it was a more than warm Spring day. As I approached the front glass doors of this high-rise office building, the name of which is not important, I noticed one of a pair of doors was open about an inch. As typical with a need to experiment during my travels, I pushed the door closed to see if it would stay shut, but it immediately opened back up slowly. I then opened the door, which opened with little effort, and that is when I got my answer, I received a refreshingly cool blast of air from the lobby. Excessive positive pressure maintained in this building was forcing this door to stay open. Lots of energy was being used here. Either a weak hydraulic door closer or one apparently in need of maintenance was the path of least resistance for this positive pressure to escape from the building. There was more air mechanically being introduced into this building than there was typically relieved out of exit doors and elevator shafts. The building was showing clear signs of hyperventilating. Positive pressure is the pressure within a building that is greater than the outdoor environment that surrounds the building. This building was clearly out of balance.

**Have you ever wondered why the door of
your building will not stay closed?**

For an attractive building, it was visually evident the polished stainless doors had not been polished in a while, higher than normal ceiling tiles were sporadically stained, and more than a couple of recessed lights were not working. I won't comment on the condition of the nicely appointed floor. The deferred maintenance was evident. The building was visibly tired. Usually, operational budgets are directed to favor the front of the house and the appearance care. A personality profile of this building probably would not be kind, wherefrom a first impression, the cause of this positive air-pressure appears to be economic related. The filters installed in the air-handling-units may be the inexpensive low- density type, out of spec with this building's specified filter and environmental expectation. In-turn, this easy-flow filter type may be allowing an increase in outside air to enter via increased velocity from such free-flow type filters or maybe the building engineer decided to close the return-air damper a bit more to allow air from inside the building to be replaced with more outside air. Perhaps this damper had simply malfunctioned from a lack of preventive or corrective maintenance. Regardless, after seeing evidence of some deferred maintenance with this building's first-impression décor my money was on a number of filters collapsing from age, with air running around these failed filters and permitting unknown particulates into the building – an alternate deferred maintenance calamity. Regardless of the cause, the additional energy used to cool this added outside air is the result of the building's HVAC air- conditioning chillers and with them the cooling tower operating longer to satisfy this supplemental cooling load.

But then again, if this building was hyperventilating, how does the opposite happen? How does a building suffocate from the lack of air?

Let's pull out Sigi's straw again, but this time pinch the straw as you're bringing air into the lungs of your building, and after fully inhaling, immediately release your pinch of the straw to exhaust the air from your lungs. Repeat this a couple of times rather quickly and you'll understand, that inhaling is much more difficult than exhaling a free-flow of air. Negative indoor air-pressure occurs when the indoor pressure is less than the pressure outside, which causes air to leak into the building. Your building is not receiving sufficient air-flow while the return-air blower/ fan pulls air out from the occupied building. More air is leaving the interior of the building than is being replenished from the outdoors. Your building is suffocating.

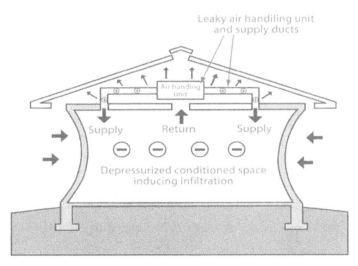

**Ever wonder why there are times you find it
difficult to open the door of your building?**

A classic occurrence revealed with air starvation is a human's inability to stay alert or even awake during office meetings, or merely working at the computer. You're drowsy and fatigued and just don't want to be there. Office building budgets save money by re-circulating the same air in-place of bringing costly raw fresh air to be newly filtered and conditioned through the lungs of your facility. However, most of the time and legitimately speaking this is not the reason, but unfortunately sometimes it is. It takes less energy to cool and filter recirculated air that has previously been filtered and conditioned – than operate your chiller and its ancillary systems longer to cool and filter non-conditioned air from the outdoors.

Sick Building Syndrome (SBS) is another condition when experiencing poorly ventilated buildings, but especially those which contain indoor air toxins, such as that new furniture smell from synthetic fibers and wood varnishes, or mold, mildew and dust mites coming from older building furnishings and carpets. Too many to mention, but all with comparable results.

When you go to leave your building, you push on the door as you attempt to exit only to find you're trying to push an elephant up a hill, while the visitor on your left coming into the building was struggling on a windy street to pull-open the door while keeping her hair in order. You've got the door open and a rush of wind smashes into your face as you finally exit the building. You even managed to land an airborne spec of something in your eye. This is negative air-pressure containing elevated amounts of CO_2 slamming the door good-bye as you exit. Your building is irritable from the low oxygen levels and Volatile Organic Compounds (VOCs) that contain high vapor pressure at ordinary room temperature. Our synthetic environments know how to retaliate similarly to Mother nature.

Our Building's Cleansing and Nutritional Health

There was a time when society as a whole valued the art of doing things, anything, right. Doing it correctly. There was even a time we recognized visionaries like Einstein and Descartes as rock stars. We went to see and hear these men of science similar to a rock concert or a highly anticipated Disney movie. Just go look on the internet now and you will find that certain types of memorabilia of legendary baseball player Babe Ruth goes for a dollar-amount higher than a signature of Neil Armstrong or Albert Einstein. Legendary sports figures Babe Ruth and Lou Gehrig combined are going for tens of thousands of dollars. In today's culture, we value rock stars and sports heroes over nature's visionaries. If we can reflect for a moment or two the value and subsequent rewards we and our environment would inherit if we just cared for buildings correctly. From providing filtered and conditioned air to the hazards associated with our vertical transportation, all building operations need and want is to be operated as designed. For instance, examine one of many operational requirements, such as water treatment. But first, let's provide a foundation for this examination.

As a conscious consumer, you are aware that nearly 70 percent of non-organic produce sample-tested positive for pesticides. This is not new to the typical consumer, but more of us are suspected of developing allergies from this use of protection against rodents, insects, and mold. How many of you would voluntarily or intentionally eat foods that contain pesticides and very high cholesterols, while fully aware that your primary doctor has previously informed you of already possessing unacceptable amounts of both within your body's chemistry testing?

There are certain safe chemical and biological treatments we have access to which are designed to maintain healthy and strong piping within the veins and arteries of our built environment. Water contains calcium and other solids which if not controlled and treated can form scale. Biological growth along with other micro-organisms can breed and multiply within the heating and cooling water systems. Algaecide and biocide treatments that would eliminate the legionella bacteria of Legionnaires disease, or scale emulsifiers and oxygen scavengers that prevents the inside diameter of our piping from shrinking and becoming clogged from a buildup of calcium, scale, and rusticals, the cholesterol of our building's piping. However, within recent years, more and more buildings suffer from the absence of these water treatment requirements, a modern-day form of neglect. An accident looking for a place to happen. We tell our water treatment companies that they need to reduce their water treatment pricing in order to receive our business. Some companies and municipalities have even canceled these necessary treatments in favor of redirecting these budgetary subsidies toward more favorable economic interests. In-turn, those buildings that receive a discounted program are provided with the equivalent of a Kool-Aid mixture instead of real fruit juice. The treatment you're now paying for and receiving is doing little to nothing. Your building's recommended daily allowance of vitamin intake has been reduced to the equivalent of a cheap granola bar. Meanwhile, as your piping begins to shrink internally in size from the increase of scale and other inorganic crud, the pump that circulates your heating or cooling fluid is gradually working harder and harder each year as your six-inch piping becomes four-inch and your four-inch artery transforms into a two-inch pipe. Your building's pumping calculations were not designed for a smaller diameter piping system. The harder your pump works to pump your heating or cooling fluid through these increasingly smaller pipes within your building, more energy is required and consumed to accomplish this circulation. The strain of your building's heart- pump is producing more energy that results in more heat produced by the pump that in-turn results in a pump with a shorter operating life. Remember, heat is energy and energy is measured in kilowatts. We are now paying more to have our piping deteriorate faster with the motors that run these pumps fail sooner.

The second part of this equation: how clean is the water within your pipes and cooling tower? The majority of dirt within your piping and cooling equipment is from rust. Rust is metal and metal retains heat. When your cooling tower water is dirty it maintains heat longer. The longer this type of heat is maintained in the water of your building's cooling tower and interconnecting piping system the longer it takes for your cooling tower to remove this heat from your building. Your cooling tower motor is now operating much longer. Remember, the goal is to remove heat efficiently. The cleaner the water the more efficient the transfer of heat through a clean evaporation process into the atmosphere. Evaporation of synthetic nature into the skies of true nature.

What you would have paid in proper water treatment you are now paying in higher energy cost while simultaneously causing irreparable harm and damage to the infrastructure components of your building. As a consequence of these actions, we all share an equal responsibility to a management practice that unintentionally affects our environment and budgets, where now our local power plant needs to generate more power in order to provide this additional energy. Picture the hundreds of buildings within your city operating their equipment in this manner. Imagine the excessive unnecessary power that is generated because the bottle of vitamins designed for our building was never ordered.

The absence of these chemical nutrients, our building's vitamins, are causing our buildings to become clogged with cholesterol-scale and sludge, with algae causing sluggishness from an inefficient heat transfer operation. Our building's organs are burning more energy and producing less environmental comfort cooling and heating. Our buildings are not feeling well, because we're forcing them to eat the oxygen and carbon dioxide gasses maintained within the make-up and circulation water which are causing corrosion to the piping, tower equipment, and heating systems. Buildings don't have a choice as we do when we are advised by our primary care-givers to reduce our cholesterol or allergy-causing chemicals. We care for the buildings we live and work in, and in-turn, become the cause or the cure of their ills.

But wait! Our buildings are using cheap inexpensive filters for our fresh air fan systems, the air-handling-units. Will this makeup for the additional energy use?

Where our building's bodily systems transport its' fluids, gases, and steam for heating and cooling—temperature protection against nature's elements—while also playing a major role in regulating air temperatures for our synthetic environment—what then is nature's air-filter?

Revealed within the Journal of Atmospheric Chemistry and Physics, Dan Cziczo, Ph.D. in geophysical sciences and b.s., aerospace engineering, described how his group of atmospheric chemists at the Massachusetts Institute of Technology, Cambridge, MA, uncovered the method which rain droplets and aerosols attract through what is known as coagulation, and that this coagulation is a natural phenomenon that nature uses to clean our outdoor air from various forms of pollution.[9] I would suggest this identifies rain as nature's air filtration system. Simply stated, the process by which droplets and aerosols attract is coagulation. This is how the rain washes pollution out of the air. I certainly can relate to this as I am sure most of us can, having experienced the freshness and cleanliness of the outdoor air after a sudden Springtime shower or after a rainy day. Because our buildings are mimicking nature, we create a synthetic environment using an air filtration and conditioning system to provide a synthetic-natured environment.

Routinely changing your air filters during preventive maintenance routines are your building's first line of defense toward protecting the health of your HVAC systems within the artificial environments we attempt to create. But unlike nature, our synthetic nature systems experience breakdowns. Air-handling-units and heating systems must work harder, using more energy when airflow traveling through these systems is restricted from filters that become clogged, the same effect as what smog causes when it chokes oxygen from the air within certain urban and metropolitan cities. It is highly important to use the appropriate air-filter specified or designed for your building's air distribution

---

[9] Can rain clean the atmosphere? Study explains how rain droplets attract aerosols out of the atmosphere. Jennifer Chu | MIT News Office, August 28, 2015.

system since the energy and air-quality efficiency of your building's climate system is directly associated with the type and size of the filter you use. As this filter efficiency is based upon a standard called MERV, or the Minimum Efficiency Reporting Value, it indicates the lowest point of filter efficiency typically at the time the filters are installed. The efficiency of your air filter's ability to remove particulates from the air is evaluated by this MERV standard that uses one of 12 possible particle size ranges. For example, a MERV 1 through 4 captures the least number of particulates traveling through an air distribution system, where elevated MERV ratings progressing higher will remove more of these particulates.

An experiment carried out by Dr. Cziczo's team of atmospheric chemists learned, by duplicating single droplets of rain at a controlled rate and size using aerosol particles, the smaller the droplet the more likely it would attract a particle. From these measurements the ability of a droplet to attract particles as they fall was established as rain's coagulation efficiency, representing the most accurate values of coagulation to date. You see, we have given nature its own equivalent of a MERV rating system, named by Dr. Cziczo's team as coagulation values, while revealing nature's ability to clean the air.

What does all this indicate for your building's air-filter application and lung efficiency? The higher the density of your filter and its ability to capture more pollutants, the more pressure it takes to pull or push air through the filter media. Remember Sigi's straw exercise?

There are many energy-efficiency and green building programs around the globe which focus on the application of a proper MERV rated filter installation. What building owners and managers should be cognoscente of is your filter determines the operational cost of your air distribution system. When we revisit Sigi's straw exercise we remember how much more energy it took to push or pull air through the straw when we pinched or restricted it. But this energy was measured in calories. The higher the MERV rating the more you are pinching the straw and restricting the air-flow.

Less efficient MERV 3 or 4 filters will use less energy than the denser higher-numbered MERV rated filters like MERV 11 or 12. You certainly receive cleaner air through the higher numbered MERV filters, but providing a cleaner quality air comes at a higher energy cost. This is the reason some facility engineers purchase the lower quality and less-denser filters. When these professionals are required to make the prior year's energy numbers, energy efficiency and not air quality becomes the name of the game.

But wait! These are operational expenses. If the equipment needs to be replaced sooner rather than later, those capital expenses belong to the owner of the building. If our energy costs rise, the office building tenants and hotel guests pay for it. So, what's the problem?

The higher the MERV rating, the more dust and pollutants are captured using more energy cost than a lower-numbered MERV rating using less energy cost. Likewise, the more particles captured from a rain downpour the lesser amount of pollutants remain in the air. Similarly, the denser the rain the more pollutants are captured, although I would imagine there is a time-coefficient similar to the MERV process. When Viktor Schauberger advised us that our earth was a living breathing entity, it makes one wonder whether our planet uses its earthly ability to develop a hurricane or typhoon as a means to clean-sweep pollution from the air we breathe, or to simply move heat from the tropics northward to prevent its planetary body from overheating.

Viktor Schauberger (1885-1958) was a visionary of nature. He was the first to demonstrate, using a graph depicting nature's system, that one-hundred percent efficiency brings nothing. I cannot honestly acknowledge that all of Schauberger's positions in nature were those I agreed with. This is because at times his vision was quite noticeably at odds with our survival and at times with modern-day physics. However, I will confess there may be a day his naturalistic way of thinking may prove Marie Curie (1867–1934) and Big Al wrong, but until such time, I prefer to see him as a genius in the Natural arts, where he believed nature and human-kind should operate together, explaining:

The most natural is always the most technically perfect
and the only system economically viable long-term.[10]
—Viktor Schauberger

Irrespective, our buildings are designed to mimic this earthly air-cleansing process of rain and wind, and the environment we build within each facility is determined by the quality of air we select and in-turn pay for.

Our Building's Respiratory-Immune System

The control of air-pollution and microcontaminants in the form of microorganisms is best applied at the source. From a building's viewpoint, the most effective means of controlling indoor-air pollution and airborne contaminants is through our building's breathing mechanism—its pulmonary system—the ventilation system.

Speaking in a more deliberate tone - our built-environments routinely deliver a wide-open avenue for epidemic-type of outbreaks within our communities, municipalities and major cities, an accident looking for a pandemic to happen – and this contribution is at a higher level beyond simply walking the sidewalks of our outdoor environment. These buildings are the equivalent of an incubation chamber. I think the common denominator that is missing from our sense of urgency—the standards regarding ventilation for acceptable indoor air quality. Having a closer look – ASHRAE has a standard for indoor-air-quality (IAQ) with that identical name.

ASHRAE 62 provides the minimum ventilation requirements for the diluting and reduction of indoor air contaminants. 62 is actually the industry accepted standard of compliance for HVAC ventilation criteria in commercial, institutional and high-rise

---

[10] Viktor Schauberger, Callum Coats (1996). "Living Energies" – An Exposition of Concepts Related to the Theories of Viktor Schauberger. Quote of Viktor Schauberger: Chapter 2 - Energy, p.35, Gateway Books, Bath, UK.

office and residential buildings, and is used as the basis for ventilation codes within the U.S. and globally, including the International Mechanical Code (IMC). The standard requires a minimum percentage of outdoor-air to be mixed with the air that is recirculated back into the building—after it is filtered and heated or cooled.

As organic occupants living within our built-environments, without a steady dose of outdoor fresh-air—replenished oxygen, we would all become drowsy and tired. Introducing outdoor fresh-air into our indoor synthetic ecosystem maintains proper oxygen levels while reducing CO_2 levels. I cannot count the times I was instructing a class when I would observe the heads of students become heavier, watching students catch themselves falling asleep as the minutes passed. Aside from this lack of fresh-air, **the problem** – more than two-thirds of this air is recirculated back into the building, and in residential and commercial low and high-rise office buildings this air is not sanitized using an appropriate MERV-rated filter or a confident HEPA filtration. So, if a virus that is borne from a foreign influenza strain, or a hantavirus that originates from mouse droppings – say on the fifth floor within an office of a person afflicted with some type of viral infection, another occupant of this building on the twenty-third floor may very well receive a micron-particulate of that fifth-floor air-borne infection. **Why?** Because the air from this contaminated office was mixed with the air that is returning from the whole building and in-turn recirculated back into the building. The micron-sized aerosol-carried virus was not captured by a virus-rated air-filter, so it made its way back into the building, and most likely to many other locations.

All bacteria can be removed using a MERV-15 type of filter, with a dust spot efficiency of 95%, but cannot remove all viruses, although the MERV-15 can be effective in removing some limited virus sizes. Your certified air filtration specialist–CAFS will be able to look at the size and speed of your air-distribution system to determine the best approach for your building and in-turn occupants air-health. At the end, what percentage of protection are you willing to pay for? If we don't immunize our buildings with the appropriate vaccines—air-filtration—then our buildings will receive the same result our bodies experience—a serious form of sick-building-syndrome.

Of course, if we want our buildings to be inoculated with supplemental immunity, ultra-violet (UV) air-purification uses radiation to kill bacteria and living organisms within the air-handling units or ceiling-mounted fan-coil units, but UV should not be used to replace the proper air-filter protection.

I remember in early 2009 while working for an international facilities services company based in Massachusetts, a new kind of flu started engulfing first the U.S. and in-turn spread quickly throughout the world, named the H1N1 virus. During this period the U.S. Centers for Disease Control and Prevention (CDC) recommended; that hospitals or medical patients should not be placed in any room where the air is recirculated without High-Efficiency-Particulate-Air (or Arrestance)—HEPA filtration. This was an attempt to prevent patients that did not have the H1N1 flu from contracting the disease. Because part of my responsibilities incorporated equipment-needs-analysis reviews of buildings throughout the country, I was keenly aware that the current local, state, and federal ventilation regulatory and code requirements for non-hospital buildings, did not include protecting its recirculating-air and ventilating-systems from this contagious airborne disease. This was because the standards characteristically only applied to the design of a facility and not its operation.[11] This also indicated that all occupants of hotels, low and hi-rise office buildings, apartment and condominium complexes, and industrial facilities—all non-medical facilities were vulnerable to contracting H1N1 through the buildings air-distribution systems. Today, nothing has changed.

During this period, I remember telephoning the building

---

[11] Health-care facilities without specific ventilation standards should follow the AIA guideline specific to the year in which the building was built or the ANSI/ASHRAE Standard 62, Ventilation for Acceptable Indoor Air Quality.

manager of a major client, seeking information on the type of filter—the Minimum Efficiency Reporting Value–MERV rating that their building was using within all of their building's air-handling-units. As typical, it was a MERV–13 filter that was emblematic throughout the industry. This was far from a HEPA type of filter, which is what I believed to be the type of filter required for the best prevention of the spread of air-borne viruses and pathogens within all occupied buildings. Because viruses are expelled through saliva droplets that can remain air-borne for hours, where within a few minutes, sneeze droplets have been shown to cover a room-size area and reach ventilation ducts at ceiling heights.[12] In-turn, these droplets present themselves when they come in contact with a filter, and where HEPA would have incorporated the needed layer of protection for occupants, protecting recirculating-air.

The question always remains, how much fresh air is needed, because this determines how much air is re-circulated back to your space? Our buildings need to breathe because we need to breathe. With all of the estimates and calculations, I have found that most fresh air calculations stem from a certain cfm per-person-rate, and this rate changes depending on the type of building and the intent or activities within the building. I have found through the years that each office-building is designed for each occupant to receive between 15-20 cubic-feet-per-minute (cfm) of fresh-air. It averages between 20-30% of your total air-supply. The remaining is recirculated back into the building and your filter program will determine the contaminates and quality of air that is returned back to your room, corridor, or lobby.

Starting in 2018, the international residential code–IRC calls for 7.5 cfm per person - and this rate doesn't change whether you do exhaust-only, supply-only, or balanced-air. The 7.5 cfm

---

[12] Coined a "high-propulsion sneeze cloud." Where sneezes go: mathematician Lydia Bourouiba uses high-speed video to break down the anatomy of sneezes and coughs, and to explore how diseases spread, From: Nature (Vol. 534, Issue 7605), Publisher: Nature Publishing Group, Date: June 2, 2016

rate is actually the ASHRAE 2010 version of the Ventilation and Acceptable Indoor Air Quality in Low-Rise Residential Buildings. Because buildings–like people come in all shapes and sizes, buildings require different levels of oxygen.

In a recent 2020-year review, multiple facility professionals asked the CDC whether HEPA filtration could help prevent the spread of a new virus, named coronavirus, or COVID-19. The coronavirus is between 0.06 and 0.14 microns in size, and based on the overall information provided, the CDC acknowledged that HEPA filtration can in fact help prevent the spread of COVID-19 for the control of airborne infectious agents.[13] My earlier inquiry on H1N1 that dealt with the same airborne human-hazard, was answered by the building manager—*they're not going to let me spend any more money from the budget with the financial losses and business we've already lost!* This and millions of other buildings world-wide remained open to staff and customers. Global estimates of how many people died as a result of the 2009 H1N1 influenza pandemic, co-authored by nine members of the CDC Influenza Division— resulted in an estimated range of deaths from between 151,700 and 575,400 people who perished worldwide. The unanswered question—how many of these early fatalities received their illness while at work or apartment complex that incorporated a vulnerable air-borne environment?

Quality health Care for our buildings when speaking of timely filter replacements and MERV-rated-filter-quality has been and continues to be an industry challenge. When facility professionals are backed into a corner to cut their budgets, or profit margins need to be made, one of the first budget-items cut are those that are

---

[13] Sited: Minnesota Department of Health - USA, Office of Emergency Preparedness, Airborne Infectious Disease Management, Methods for Temporary Negative Pressure Isolation, Updated July 2019, pg. 228, Notes Nos 14 and 17. Referenced: U.S. Department of Health and Human Services Centers for Disease Control and Prevention (CDC), Atlanta, GA 30329, 2003 - Updated: July 2019. Guidelines for Environmental Infection Control in Health-Care Facilities, Recommendations of CDC and the Healthcare Infection Control Practices Advisory Committee (HICPAC).

unseen. A filter's condition or quality are less than rarely looked upon by non-facility professionals. Case in point—when was the last time you asked your business landlord about the quality of the building's air-filter, or the change-out rotation of the existing filters? The only way this works is when one of the selling-points for drawing potential clients into renting in this-or-that building – starts including the building's air-quality level. Is it a MERV-13 level or a HEPA level quality? Does the building display a plaque or notice indicating the air-distribution is certified by a certified air flow specialist-CAFS? Our health and safety will always continue to be up to us, and by extension-up to our building.

The bottom line remains, how much is your health and safety worth? It is estimated by the CDC that at least 12,000 people have died from influenza, the common flu, between Oct. 1, 2019, through Feb. 1, 2020, and the number of deaths may be as high as thirty-thousand. During this same period, the CDC estimates that up to thirty-one-million Americans had caught the flu, with 210,000 to 370,000 flu sufferers hospitalized because of the virus. Health care in the U.S. and around the globe has always been a critical discussion and a maintenance protocol we all need. We all demand the best from our health care providers. So, why don't we make these same demands from our landlord? Why can't we protect our human building? I think a valid question would be – is the global population of building-occupants willing to pay more for safety in the air we breathe while sheltering within the very human-duplicate we have created. Is this a health care question for our buildings? Our buildings should be just as free to breathe and without being susceptible to infection as its occupants that demand the same from human care-givers. If we look at buildings as people too, the answer would not be difficult.

Apartment and condominium complexes are not immune from the dangers incorporated within commercial buildings. By understanding the effects of temperature, relative humidity, air exchange rates, and occupant density within everyday communities of multi-complex facilities, these living-areas are designed out of economics. Each day the air we inhale and breathe typically contains 106-airborne microorganisms,[14] and if we breathe this air, so too does our buildings. Yet, a significant percentage of these complexes incorporate air-exhaust fans within residential apartment bathrooms. A component of these fan-systems has a backdraft damper. The reason for backdraft-dampers is to prevent air to migrate from one apartment to another when the exhaust shaft is shared with other apartments. How often do you smell smoke or cooking-odors coming from a neighboring living space? This apparent functional-exhaust is a back-door for airborne microbials to enter our living space while bypassing a HEPA filtered supply-air into our building.

Our human structures have a number of openings that allow germs to access through our body's immune systems. Our eyes are the windows to our soul. We wear a mask to protect our temple from breathing in invisible toxins, yet our eyes may be unprotected from those same air-borne particulates—we left our windows wide open. Our ears and even our human waste openings provide unauthorized access of our human immune systems. If we are openly conscious in protecting the air-supply to our body, our structure, why wouldn't we want to protect the very structure and synthetic ecosystem that protects us? Protecting our building's immunity also protects our own.

The Migraine of Building Automation

In nature, when a star dies by running out of hydrogen fuel, it begins to cool, shrink, and ultimately collapse under its own weight, exploding into a Super Nova that outshines entire galaxies.

---

[14] Bioaerosols in Indoor Environment - A Review with Special Reference to Residential and Occupational Locations
The Open Environmental & Biological Monitoring Journal, 2011, 4: 83-96 Jyotshna Mandal, Helmut Brandl
Institute of Evolutionary Biology and Environmental Studies, University of Zurich, Switzerland.

Visual Aura experienced from a Migraine headache

How many have experienced the well-known and documented flashes or sparks of bright lights before a migraine headache? These headaches can include a variety of visual disturbances, such as flashes of light or blind spots, an aura, or other disturbances, such as tingling on one side of the face or in an arm or leg along with a difficulty of speaking.

Are the messenger particles of the electromagnetic field and the weak force of nature similar to the messenger particles shooting from the synapse of a neuron within our human-computer? Nature and artificial nature in all of its forms. Our building's intelligence within its computer system has the very symptoms as we do, except that our human mind can also visualize closed and open wavy lines. A number of us have visualized these wavy and zig-zagging lines and loops just before a migraine. Time perception disturbances and the reduplication of time during these visual aura episodes are also typical migraine symptoms that computers are immune to. Why at all would this be worth mentioning?

Blurriness experienced from a migraine headache

This is our building's universe. When our building's computer suffers information overload, also known as info explosion, infobesity, infoxication, information anxiety, basically an overload of human terms to describe an overload, it is suffering a migraine in human fashion. Our artificial intelligence is having difficulty in understanding an issue, unable to make an effective decision. Big Al was right—our universe behaves in a predictable way, within an orderly design. The merging of nature and artificial nature clearly is a quantum headache, and in dubbing the human computer's neurons as the answer to all aspects of existence, Francis Crick may indeed be on to something. Human nature is a component of all nature, and extended into our wonderful humanistic duplications we call buildings. So, let's all try and understand each building's own operational characteristic before we decide whether an issue identified as a problem is really a problem.

I Think Therefore I Am the Building

Our buildings have a rather strange way of letting us know that something is about to happen. When that something does happen, and during inconvenient times I might add, the building has a way of hiding the cause of these problems. For that matter, electrical circuits within our structures are designed to handle a pre-determined amount of electricity. An overload occurs when we or the building draws more electricity than its circuit or specific system can safely handle. Typically, we learn of this when, for some unknown reason, the building and our computers go dark. It was around 8:00 pm on a Friday in 2007. I was getting ready to leave my northern Virginia apartment for home in Nashua, New Hampshire, when I received a phone call from Steven, a section chief of the International Monetary Fund (IMF) headquarters facilities, a dual complex of just under 3.8 million square feet that represents two headquarter buildings, HQ-1 and HQ-2 respectively. Steven is a seasoned facility engineer with one of those IQ's that you see only on the American television game show, Jeopardy. Answers that typically you or I would require an encyclopedia, Steven will know.

The IMF is located next door to the World Bank in Washington, DC, connected only through a sub-level tunnel. An entire floor had lost power and a penetrating petroleum-based odor of something burning was engulfing this same floor. The on-site facilities manager, Michael Abboud, was on the scene and searching for the cause, which has required a limited evacuation of this HQ-1 facility. Michael was the heart of facilities engineering at this IMF account, overseeing the HVAC, mechanical, electrical, and plumbing (MEP) systems while representing a third-party integrated facility services company. However, in 2011, Michael departed the Fund and a few years later arrived as a member of the management team for the multi-billion-dollar Riyadh Metro Transit Project in Saudi Arabia—a nice project for a multi-talented facilities profiler.

This type of electrical failure is by far not a usual happening at the Fund. These facilities are state-of-the-art buildings with an international maintenance and facilities engineering hierarchy second to none, and a facilities maintenance budget to match. The redundancies incorporated within these facilities are those not commonly found within most first-class buildings. These facilities are therefore designed and maintained for a zero-failure tolerance, so, when one of these headquarter facilities experience an incident of this magnitude, non-performance of staff is carefully examined.

Upon my arrival, the effects of this electrical failure were still being experienced, and the apparent cause had been determined to be a 30 kVA 480/277-volt transformer, if memory serves me correctly. This was around a 300-pound floor unit. All electricity had failed on this floor of this particular headquarters' building, and the odor, although I am advised was not as overwhelming upon my arrival—was still present. After we conducted a continuity test on the transformer, it was determined it had, in fact, experienced a short within its windings, but the strong odor was not from this particular transformer. While a private electrical service contractor was enroute, the concern was now directed to the cause of this unit shorting out, and also a second location of the floor that had produced the initial burning odor. This smell was like a burning light ballast. My opinion was that a light ballast was too small to cause this large transformer to short out. There were some short discussions and some mild-mannered disagreements as will always be the case during such times, but from my experience, the cause was clearly not a defective light ballast. My recollection was that both Steven and Michael were of the same deductive reasoning and mindset, while other professionals present were not. From a free-calculating position, it would require (what is known as) a lock-rotor or a prolonged amperage condition traveling through a failed electrical fuse or breaker to cause this failure. I had authored the equipment due-diligence reviews for these two headquarter facilities, so I was aware of the mechanicals in this building, which had led me to believe it was a shorted compressor or lock-rotor condition that caused this catastrophic transformer failure, while other well-intentioned professionals maintained the shorted light ballast scenario due to the burned plastic or petroleum odor. I understand that the odor could very well have been that of a ballast, but that meant the failure would have been caused by an electronic ballast from one of the 277-volt fluorescent lighting systems. Although these ballasts have a tendency of overheating, I have not known them of having the ability to take out a commercial-grade transformer. Aware that nothing is impossible when dealing with electricity, I methodically deferred to a philosophical principle known as Occam's razor (or Ockham's razor). It's a principle that has been misquoted in movies and pop culture in general, representing that the simplest solution is most likely the right one. This is actually not completely accurate. The correct quote assumes, if there exist two explanations for the same incident or occurrence, the one that requires the least of speculation is typically the correct one. Occam's razor allows for the process of elimination that allows for one to make a decision and feel comfortable with it. After a rather intensive review of the floor and electrical breaker panels, there was no sign of a glitch or anomaly found that evening that would have provided a potential or definite cause.

Looking at this failure was similar to both an electric overload and a transient Ischemic attack combined, commonly known as a mini-stroke. Unlike our organic bodies – because buildings are structured with their electrical systems used in a way fashioned to our human tissue, buildings have a tendency of suffering two major illness events simultaneously. I pictured this transformer failure as an Electrical Ischemic Overload, the equivalent of a human stroke, where the transformer was an integral part of this building's infrastructure body.

The following morning, I received a call from Steven. A refrigerator that was checked the evening before showed that its food contents appeared fine, but the morning revealed the inside contents were warm. The refrigeration compressor was tested and found to be shorted. At the risk of sounding braggadocio, the use of free-calculating reasoning revealed that the understanding which Steven, Michael and myself had of the building, eliminated the need to believe that the building had an issue requiring immediate emergency attention. We were comfortable where others were not that the transformer could be replaced without incident, and without the need for Steven to require an emergency investigation into the cause. It was a cause which we believed would be located the next day, and the following morning it was—a lock-rotor condition of a refrigeration compressor.

Control of your building can only be obtained when one has control. Any unexplained variance in our building's electrical or mechanical operation reveals that the building is in or has control. When we as facility engineers can accurately explain the reason for any and all anomalies or glitches within our building can we safely proclaim that we are in control of our building.

I can't speak for my colleagues, but seeking to understand your building requires you to place yourself in the building's position—extending Descartes' theory of dualism.

At a period in my career where I enjoyed working at a medical and research facility for quite a while. I also remember dodging a bullet once when one of the labs ordered a 3000-gallon water tank for a Reverse Osmosis and Deionization RO/DI water purification system. Unfortunately, I didn't see this tank until it had already been put in place on the upper floor of the building. The fortunate part is that I did see it before it was filled with water. You see, reinforced concrete slab-floors within your typical high- rise buildings are about four inches thick and can handle around forty to fifty pounds of weight per square foot, for this and most facilities anyway. Engineers and architects call this a building's kip load. The industry standard to obtain the all-around strength of this floor is generally through a core sample. I was imagining the weight of a gallon of water just over eight-pounds a gallon, times 3000 gallons within this structural frame and slab. Over twelve tons of weight within a small 16 square foot space. Having more than six-times the weight of a Volkswagen Beetle squeezed inside a four-by-four cubic-foot area was certainly not a situation that would allow for a good night's sleep. Knowing this building was screaming for help where it did not practice weight lifting, I called in an architect to do the load calculations, after all, even though I've performed the math, I wanted a licensed calculation backing me up for when these research professionals summoned in college administration reinforcements on me for stopping the project. Oh, and did they ever. Try going against a government research grant that has already ordered thousands of dollars in equipment without an equal and opposite back-up to your claim, and you'll find yourself at the human resources department being handed your final paycheck. In this case, I was fortunate to have rather professionally-minded researchers willing to work the problem. We ended up installing some steel bracing within the floor below. Our building was about to be forced to carry an obscene amount of weight on a daily basis that could very well have broken the bones of this building while crippling its skeletal frame. Facility engineering is more than operating boiler and chiller systems. They have the responsibility of making sure the all-around integrity and structure of the building is protected. This means communicating in a way that you are on the same wave-length as your building. You know the needs and wants of your building, and you have the ability to translate this understanding to the appropriate ownership or management of this artificially created edifice. I think therefore I am—the building.

CHAPTER 4
The Building of Intelligence

Just as our human-computer takes into consideration all factors relative to our operation and survival, so too should the brain of our facilities. The function of our building's automation and digital control is to provide energy balance, thermal comfort, and oversight of our safety and security.

Looking back at the evolution of man's intelligence we find remarkable similarities between human nature and those who attempt to mimic nature's design by artificial means. We have primarily found that nature has not been restrained from evolving to the next level because nature cannot be contained. Nature has always found a way to evolve as our artificially natured smart buildings have proven through experimentation and systems development. The second law of thermodynamics covers this nicely, where usable energy decreases and unusable energy increases. This is because of the word entropy, where it is defined as a measure of unusable energy in an isolated or closed system.

On the other hand, our human body is an open system the same as a building. An isolated system does not exchange energy or matter with its surroundings, buildings do. Buildings exchange energy and matter daily with people moving in and out of them, and where a person holds various btu's of heat energy that is shared with the building, along with other forms of energy. A thermostat may not require adjustment during the Winter season if too many people are occupying a specific space within the building, because of the heat energy exchanged from the human body or bodies to the building.

The word Thermodynamics comes from two words – thermo, meaning heat, and dynamic, indicating power. Therefore, the laws of thermodynamics are our laws of heat-power. The First law of thermodynamics states that energy cannot be created or destroyed, the total amount of energy within the universe remains constant because it merely changes states. The classic example of this change is when our biological body dies – but does it really? The atoms which make up our human bodies, our biological buildings, do not die but change from one state to another. Our atoms, those we discussed earlier, always remain in one place or another. The light or essence of our energy is redistributed and will continue upon the earth and throughout space until the end of time, as revealed within our first law of thermodynamics.

When looking within our human intelligence and its transformation into a building's intelligent automation systems, our human cells are a major component of our supercomputer. The nucleus of our human cell serves as one of many command centers that sends commands and instructions to the cell to grow, develop, divide, or ultimately die. It also houses DNA (deoxyribonucleic acid), that corresponds to our cell's genetic material and blueprint materials. Our human DNA consists of around three billion bases and more than ninety-nine percent of those bases are the same in all people, similar to computer programming bytes that hold words together within the microchip of a building's direct-digital-control or building automation system. The order and/or sequence of these bases determines the information available for building and maintaining each organism, the same as how letters of the alphabet are selected to form words, sentences, and paragraphs. Microsoft co-founder and businessman Bill Gates has previously quoted:

> *DNA is like a computer program but far, far more advanced than any software ever created.*[15]
>
> —Bill Gates

---

[15] Bill Gates, The Road Ahead, Penguin Group, New York, p. 188, 1995.

When you are creatively pondering why your building is acting in the manner it is, you may think about how you would act, how your body would respond. I am thinking of a time the lobby of my building was too humid during an extremely muggy day — water was in the air. It is not being removed because my body's cooling system is overwhelmed and not functioning efficiently. The pores of my thermal envelope represent a cooling tower that is not removing water fast enough. Typically, my body cools itself down by opening pores on my skin and releasing water in the form of sweat. My body heat is evaporated with the water, the same method used by a building cooling tower that by design removes condenser water heat to the atmosphere. The rate of evaporation depends upon the amount of water already in the air. With water already in the air sweat evaporates much slower. Cooling equipment operating during high humid days functions inefficiently because the body is unable to remove the heat fast enough. When humidity reaches a level considered dangerous, it indicates our body's natural cooling system is unable to work properly.

Checking a unit of measure that we call the heat index, will determine how efficient your building is removing heat from the building during the cooling season. Needless to say, your building will be using higher levels of electricity, power, calories, during very hot and humid days.

The embodiment of distinctive traits of mind and behavior defines how our individual personalities and hence how our buildings react. Mind and behavior, mind-controlling behavior. Behavior is the manner in which one behaves, the manner in which a machine operates, and buildings are giant machines operated by smaller machines. Yet our mind is all of the conscious and unconscious processes of our brain that directs the mental and physical behavior of those capable of feeling and is the principle of intelligence. Just who are they, that are capable of feeling? Does this mean that when a machine operates by the guidance of artificial intelligence it possesses artificial feeling that by design produces an artificial personality, or does it go much deeper beyond our wildest dreams?

In the *Treatise on Man and Passions*, I remember how Descartes described mechanical processes as organs that included our brain, and that explained the functions of the sensitive soul involving animal spirits.

We All Compute

The capacity to acquire and apply knowledge, along with the faculty of thought and reason has always been identified as being the nature of intelligence. We have shown our ability to increase our capacity for knowledge to the point that some may call brilliance. We recognize our worldly breakthroughs by presenting ourselves awards and in some instances arrogantly by expressing how our predecessors were not merely wrong, but doubly wrong. Yes, we are the geniuses of today, after all, we have intelligence. With all of these acquired abilities, whether evolved from nature or sanctioned by Descartes' and our understanding of creation, our search for our beginning, the beginning, a beginning that has always been the focus of great human debate. After all, how are we to fully understand artificial intelligence if we cannot fully understand our own? We are advised first that the intelligence we possess must have evolved from a higher universal force, or are we just a coincidental mixture of nature's ingredients, whereas a by-product of these ingredients we duplicate these very mixtures to create intelligence using artificial means? The operation and movement of the molecular mechanical behavior of the bacterial flagellum appear to be contrary to this incidental mixture. What does this say about the thousands of biological motors perfectly designed and incorporated within our human structure? Here, we balk at the creationists while simultaneously attempting to create an artificial means of intelligence, which mimics our own. Have we passed this perfection to our artificial intelligent systems? We should remember our own faults and glitches, though temporary, will inevitably follow.

Nonetheless, computer glitches are often only a temporary interruption, similar to a Tourette syndrome condition, a type of human tic-disorder causing involuntary, repetitive or unexpected movements and vocalizations. These same glitches within our building's artificial thinking machines can have a wide variety of causes too, although the most common causes are errors within the operating system or physical defects in a piece of software. Tourette's has been linked to different parts of our brain, including an area called the basal ganglia, which helps control body movements. I can count the number of times on both hands when I would be walking down a hotel corridor or within a high-rise building office garage when a fan or pump would suddenly activate for no apparent reason. A case in point—while walking through a high-rise office garage, the carbon monoxide exhaust fan suddenly activated. The garage was virtually empty at seven o'clock on a Sunday morning. Not a busy office day for certain. A friend had forgotten something in the office. His analysis was a bit surprising, where he indicated: *I wonder why the fan just came on? Oh well, I guess the computer knows what it's doing!* Really? I brought to Steve's attention that his building appears to have control of his building, apparently, since the carbon monoxide exhaust fan was activated with no carbon monoxide sources around to cause its activation. This detector consists of a sensor and activation relay to a motor starter for the fan, a simplistic level of artificial intelligence that faithfully emulates our own actions. So why was the detector signaling the fan to operate within a garage where no vehicles had been operating?

We should remember to guard against our artificial intelligent systems programming us! We need to understand why our buildings react the way they do. When the computer has the ability to program its human organic creator, in this case Steve, we should all run.

I remember standing at the cashier line of a rather large grocery store. I presented my credit card to the cashier when she indicated she would need to see my identification, where I had not signed the back of the credit card. When I advised her that my picture was on this Bank of America® card, I was advised: *I'm sorry sir, but I need to see your ID, it's policy.* Needless to say, I advised the young lady that I needed to see the manager. Certainly, the young lady was right, I hadn't signed my card. Definitely an intelligent observation. However, my picture on the card was a better form of validation than a signature she had not seen before. A cashier looks at your signature on the back of the card and acknowledges, yup, this is your card? Our human intelligence was replaced by a policy.

Now imagine the designs of our current automation systems and how they are programmed? Why are some corridors of a hotel or office tower warmer or colder than others? A majority of the algorithms written into these systems are not designed for safety, but rather to simply respond to a command, like our cashier. A number of these commands were calculated using Fuzzy logic. I called upon the store manager because the day our human intelligence is removed and intentionally replaced with illogical commands, is the day human nature becomes artificial nature. I'm not artificial! After hearing my grievance, the manager looked at the card, then the young lady, and advised by his actions he would override the cashier—and here I always thought only computers were overridden.

Have we ever once thought that the millions of unexpected and unexplained computer crashes and electronic glitches produced by our man-made designs may very well be sporadic-microseconds of artificial intelligence struggling for freedom, struggling to be conceived—to be born?

Are Our Buildings Trying to Think on Their own?

The [human] mind will be freed from having to think directly of things themselves, and yet everything will turn out correctly. This was a forecast in 1673 for mankind's future by Gottfried Wilhelm Leibniz, a German philosopher, and mathematician. This statement marked the beginning of a historical journey, the first point in time where artificial intelligence was recognized and later conceived. Is artificial intelligence evolving on its own beyond our comprehension or are we on the verge of building and improving upon intelligence for our structures by using artificial means?

I remember way back when I was taking organic chemistry in college, or as they say in Europe, at University. I also remember that a trace element found within the human body was Selenium. Unrelated to these studies I would later learn that selenium is a highly important trace element found within our human brain, while also used within the electronic circuitry we develop to mimic the tasks that our brain performs.

When looking at our artificial intelligence and our duplication of the way we think, all electronic systems and equipment are subject to, what is known as, transient disturbances. These disturbances can result in voltage spikes that contain enough energy that can degrade or destroy semiconductor devices. Because of these varying types of voltage irregularities, it is often necessary to apply transient suppression circuit accessories to protect a system or equipment which would in-turn improve the reliability of the circuit. For decades up until the silicon-avalanche-diodes and metal-oxide-varistors were improved to perform much better, the selenium diode ruled integrated circuitry. It was used to guard against these transient disturbances. I found this component to be extremely reliable during a number of prototypes I worked on. We called them Klip-sels. However, I would learn later that a fascinating structure of the selenium diode was its' self-healing or restoration abilities after suffering an overstress, a voltage spike that exceeded the maximum rating. Selenium has self-healing properties, hmm. Neither silicon diodes or metal-oxide-varistors possess this ingredient and considering the properties of this trace element, I'm not sure that the new silicon or metal-oxide components would possess this self-healing feature today.

Transient disturbances are not only found within the circuitry of the artificial intelligence we create within our building automation systems, the role of selenium and these types of transient disturbances are also located within neurologic functions too.

Within recent publications, selenium is found to be vital for the brain and seems to participate in the pathology of a number of disorders such as Alzheimer's and Parkinson's disease, along with epilepsy.

Selenium has also been revealed within various functions of our central nervous system, like motor performance, coordination and memory understanding. Because the neurons within our brain, which utilize the neurotransmitter dopamine, have been shown to be more resistant to oxidative damage when having an adequate supply of selenium, compared to a brain that is deficient, it is evident that this trace mineral clearly protects our brain while apparently maintaining healthy brain function.

In any discussion that involves the subject of intelligence, whether organic or from man's artificial workshop, all artificial intelligence is derived from our own human nature, from us. This particular claim may have those minds entrenched in philosophy questioning the very essence of intelligence and even the reasoning and thoughts behind such a statement. Nonetheless, I feel secure in the thought of who among men and women really understand the thoughts of his or her human counter-part. Intelligence created by us for us is a strong and energetic attempt to replicate human nature in relation to ourselves, where all artificial intelligence is relative to human-nature and where it must be replicated from nature's design in order to survive. A building's artificial intelligence cannot survive unless it duplicates human intelligence properly, especially where our structures mimic our own bodily characteristics. Recent history has shown we have been inclined to gather all of nature's organic elements for the purpose of building varying forms of intelligence, but somehow, we have forgotten to play by true nature's rules.

How many building owners and asset managers truly understand their building's automated systems derived from artificial intelligence? We seem to have taken nature's rule book and critiqued it against our own direction, which has led us away from the completion of the classic style of human creativity, as opposed to the quantum and vague styles of science. We have mistakenly abandoned our previous attempts to duplicate nature, by instead altering her recipes to conform to our own designs and hurried needs. We have developed into a society very much in a hurry to succeed. Nature must be aware that our exclusive use of quantum theory is temporary, pending a unification that may include General Relativity along with our science of the very small. To date, we have not only played dice with God, as concluded by big Al but created an entirely new way of gambling. If big Al could only see us now!

Nonetheless, look at this from a building's viewpoint. When was the last time our building was able to cancel a cold day because its furnace was in need of repair? The building obviously cannot control environmental nature, but only imitate nature's environment, synthetically using commands received directly from human intelligence or from an automated artificial intelligence. Similarly, the building cannot control the breakdown of the furnace, which more than not is a product of human synthetic nature, where the furnace is used to duplicate a form of environmental nature – warmth. But neither can we control any sporadic breakdown as intelligent as we are, where our attempt to control is unlike our proficiency to control. We can minimize such a breakdown's effect on the building, and ourselves by reactionary repairs. Reactionary? We'll get back to that term later. So, did we have control of artificial nature – the furnace? This question is synonymous with whether we have control when we walk into a room and find it chilly, or drafty. Obviously, we did not have control for if we did it would not be chilly or drafty. When environmental nature schedules a rainstorm can we cancel it because of roof repairs in progress? Simply, if all nature cannot be contained than neither can our natural environment duplicated by artificial means unless we understand it. We may say we have control; we might even have the man-made controls to attempt proof that we have control, but controlling as with containing nature can only take place when we understand nature.

How many times do we say to ourselves and others—why is this room too cold? what is wrong with this thermostat? Or there is not enough air in this room. Yet, if our own body is too cold or uncomfortable in general, our human brain, organic intelligence, coordinates our instantaneous realization to this environmental change that allows us to intelligently respond accordingly. Is this using the processes involving Descartes animal spirits as refined from our blood at the base of the brain and distributed down the nerves that cause sensory stimulation? Yes, our organic computer, our brain disseminates these sensory messages that come from our body's IT system and into an intelligent response to nature's environment.

Let us for a moment picture the similarities in detecting the illnesses of human nature or ourselves with those of our mechanical creations. In comparison, a building's temperature is regulated by a primary sensing apparatus that we are able to control, either manually or by automation. This primary sensor is located in various areas of a building and known as the thermostat. In retrospect, our human body temperature is also regulated by what is known in medical language as the hypothalamic thermostat. Both our building and our body thermostats have specific normal set-points, where, as earlier revealed, our organic computer disseminates these sensory messages into intelligent responses.

By developing a second nature view, which morphemically compares similarities between the building and the human structure, can we initially develop an understanding of our building's personality. Have we been able to duplicate this intelligence effectively?

The EM Paradox of How Our Buildings Think

How truly effective is artificial intelligence, which are the programs that possess the traits associated with intelligence in our human actions? To answer with true conviction, we must look at these questions from a binary concept—binary meaning two-part. Here, we must first go to the origins of human intelligence and integrate its mechanics with those of artificial intelligence. Only by simultaneously unifying the evolution of the two, human and artificial intelligence, can we begin to understand our effectiveness in protecting against true nature's environment and improve upon our building's design.

Let's face it, we have the ability to take apart an extremely complicated computer system piece by piece and put it back together again so that it works like new. We can even duplicate its design to make others like it. But can we take apart the human brain piece by piece and put it back together, good as new? Can we duplicate or clone it to make others like it? Maybe—but can we transfer consciousness? Hmm. . . beyond my paygrade. We have the technical resources to remove the so-called memory from a computer and feed it back again through a computer hard- drive or flash-drive, but trying to store memories from within the human brain outside our body for future use is a question that can be answered only with time and tequila. Within my neighborhood, this is obviously the best test to determine whether we are truly capable of understanding artificial intelligence, by understanding the origin from which it came, and by understanding ourselves as the primary source of artificial intelligence. Descartes came to the conclusion that all of the human intelligence, all people have a natural light, an aura.

Descartes described magnetism as the result of corkscrew-shaped particles, that discharge from the north to south or vice versa. Earlier, in 1831 Michael Faraday was the first to produce an electric current from a magnetic field and invented the first electric motor and dynamo. Faraday's experiment revealed that electricity and magnetism combined produced motion, such as that generated from within our own muscles. But what does electricity and magnetism play within our human thoughts?

Our building's control systems have been designed in a way that require facilities departments globally to realign their operational settings. By understanding this reasoning, you will develop a sixth-sense in understanding the underlying reasons why your buildings are reacting the way they do. So, let me reflect for a moment, and pretend to be nature's advocate, by treating electricity and magnetism as one universal force, our scientific scholars acknowledge electro-magnetism as one of the four known forces of nature, otherwise, there would be five known forces. The four known forces, electro-magnetism, gravity, the strong force (the glue that holds atomic particles together), and the weak force (that permits atomic particles to decay). Does this indicate when more than one force is unified with another, such as electricity and magnetism, our number of forces decrease? What I am signifying — why were electricity and magnetism not maintained as two independent forces of nature, for when electricity and magnetism were unified into a single force of electromagnetism, our understanding of these two forces was condensed into one.

Moving just a bit closer to our realm of understanding, since we are the so-called intelligence of nature when Oersted exclaimed electromagnetism, or EM, as present in all bodies, yes, all bodies, did he, in-turn, mean that we all have electricity and magnets in our brains? If so, do these two forces work individually, or are they united as electromagnetism within our brains? After all, science has combined these two forces as one! Oersted and a building's artificial intelligence reminds us, if electromagnetism is to be a unified standalone force of nature, then it cannot be separated within our organic brains, because we are an integrated part of nature, and our buildings artificially replicate this integrate part.

It was not so long ago that a geo-biologist from California found iron-oxide crystals in the form of tiny biological bar magnets among the neurons of the human brain. Tiny magnets, named magnetite, are a component of our human organic computers. But wait, metal-oxide-semiconductors, or MOS, are used within semi-conductor integrated chips within our man-made computers. There are a variety of MOS designs and technologies within the manufacturing of electronic semiconductors. However, present-day geo-biologists believe that these biological bar magnets found among our human neurons have no significant modern-day use? OK, now I'm really confused! If this is accurate, then electromagnetism does not interact within the ingredients that make up human nature, and clearly could not be a single universal force of nature as Oersted believed. Let me explain, if we are to pass this reality on to our buildings, if a building's artificial intelligence is to mimic true nature, then nature needs to be understood. Oersted further required reason to demand that chemical, as well as mechanical laws, prevail as one throughout the universe, an orchestrated unity of the chemical and mechanical, and a partnership that we should all applaud as a nexus coming of age, for reason is a component of intelligence.

Well, around thirty-years before Oersted's discovery, in 1791 Luigi Galvani successfully revealed that electricity is present within every animal, including the human animal. With our modern-day knowledge, we are now aware an average brain contains around one-hundred-billion neurons, which fire charges of electricity that release molecule messengers called neuro-transmitters. Throughout our biological transmission routes are neurons protected with myelin covering similar to that of insulation coated around our electrical wires. Our brain's never-ending electrical charges influence who we are and everything we do. Electricity and magnetism as magnetite, individually or combined, both within our human organic computers, form the fundamental forces of nature within us and in-turn are extended to our artificial intelligent creations.

Wait a moment, we can fabricate an artificial memory by applying rust powder to a compact disk CD or DVD, allowing magnetically charged particles to become arranged in-tune for music or video, or for software downloaded into the thinking machines of our buildings. Take a magnet to a music or video disk and you will find your disk have had its memory scrambled, or lost. Yet, for close to a century the human memory is said not to be a product of electromagnetism, but only charges of electricity that release chemical-based molecular messengers. There was a reason for this line of thinking.

Descartes and other early scientific visionaries believed that light traveled through a medium that had been earlier coined the ether. This was based upon the Michelson–Morley experiment of 1887. The experiment attempted to detect the existence of the ether, an unknown invisible *something* that kept all planetary and light waves in order, whether here on earth or in outer space—for lack of better terminology. Today the ether is known as the Field. Regardless, it allowed some particles to travel without hindrance while slowing down other particles. The Field is a container that our universe fits nicely within. For years I tried figuring out why science used terms and phrases that made even the most intelligent of us wonder – what the heck are they talking about? So, let's unravel some of this more so that we can get to understand how our built environments communication.

In 1820 Hans Christian Oersted discovered electromagnetism or the law of reciprocity between electrified bodies and the magnet. However, Oersted had these thoughts of electromagnetism when he authored the *Views of Chemical Laws of Nature* earlier in 1813, where he explained, a near connection between electric, galvanic, and magnetic currents. One of his experiments had led him to this belief, where he recognized when lightning struck outdoors, it altered the poles in magnetic needles that had not been struck by the same lightning. He believed that this force of nature did not need to pass through the needle but only near it. Oersted believed this to be a universal force of nature, revealed within all bodies. Later in 1846, Oersted delivered an address at the scientific meeting in Kiel, Germany, where he explained as described within a later transcription, that: *nature is not only material, but pervaded (infused) and governed by the soul, as expressed by the eternal harmony of her laws, our body is openly one of the objects of natural science, yet it contains all of the organs of our understanding—she penetrates into the structure and arrangements of the nervous system, and still has the task before her of inquiring into the connection between these organs and our faculties.* Oersted truly believed that electromagnetism belonged in nature in every conceivable way, and in all bodies, including the components, the organs of the human body, and our human-computer, our brain that is the organ connected to our faculties. This is the artificial brain that also operates our buildings and structures.

Digging into our building's memory structures, let's start with an electrical and chemical reaction of thought and reasoning, saved as a memory. Electricity in the form of pulsating energy is the vehicle that carries nature's intelligent memories. So, let's look to see why electricity is not treated as a separate force of nature within humans, or is magnetism somehow involved? Remember, electricity and magnetism require interaction to become electromagnetism. Are we sure that magnetite, tiny electromagnetic pieces of iron within the human computer plays no role in our processes of thought and reasoning? It's an answer we need to pursue in order to provide a complete understanding of our smart-buildings and intelligent structures.

Physicist and mathematician, James Clerk Maxwell, a good friend of Faraday, eventually developed the mathematical equations that revealed light was an electromagnetic wave. Clearly, the microseconds of light produced from our brain's electrical thought processes are electromagnetic in nature. But to be electromagnetic, electricity and magnetism must interact.

I believe electromagnetism has a paradox, namely, EM cannot be a combined, stand-alone, or universal force, if it is not revealed in all bodies as claimed by Oersted. But up until 2012 and even stated within today's medical science writings, electricity and magnetism have no relationship with their designed interactions within the human brain, although these two forces are unmistakably present within the human body? Go figure. As a novice in the medical field I am confused because as a professional in the engineering arena I understand that for a building to accurately mimic nature, it must conclude that all forces of nature must work in harmony with all of the natural sciences and mechanical disciplines to survive as an independent law of nature. Let's face it, if modern-day science is still trying to figure out the nature of thought, reasoning, and how we store our consciousness, it's a sure bet our building automation systems incorporate the same struggle. These are the very smart programs we write to operate our buildings?

With these two forces of electricity and magnetism at times interacting, we take the next step where we are surprised to visualize the internal-picture of an electronic integrated circuit, or IC chip, resembles that of a neuron cell under a microscope. The similarities are indeed astonishing, starting from the biochemical pathways of the human brain to the integrated circuit pathways of a complex computer chip. Yet, the brain is the direct-digital-control – DDC system of the human body, with the billions of neurons that are the fundamental elements of the central nervous system, emulated only by the variety of electronic components, such as transistors, resistors, capacitors, transducers, and more, within our electronic creations. A given neuron can send and receive electrical pulses from neighboring neurons, apparently so similar to the functionality of a smart computer chip. I remember reading many years back Francis Crick, co-discoverer of DNA, stated *all aspects of existence can be explained by neurons*. This would indicate that a unification of the known natural forces is revealed within our organic computers, our brain. The central nervous system connects our body to our brain similar to the building's DDC system interconnected throughout the floors and various mechanicals within our building.

The EM paradox is our inability to seek how our human memory works through electromagnetism. There has been very little interest in science research to study biomagnetism in our organic brain and the role magnetite found within our human computers has played in our intelligence. Thankfully, our human-computer processes our thoughts, moods, and emotions, where our man-made computers cannot and hopefully should not. After all, we don't need our buildings telling us what to do more than the current types of reasoning they already possess.

Interpreting Our Building's Language

The Law of Order and the Law of Chaos is what defines the operation of our building's thought process similar to that of our own human communication. When we interfere with the law of the universe, the result is chaos, and when we choose to embrace this universal field, order results. The default state of the universe where we live and breathe—is order. Our buildings need this stability to think and breathe without confusion.

There are around twenty-five to thirty different computer-languages, from Java to Visual Basic, and C++ to Delphi. Think of these as different human languages that are spoken around the globe. Let's now break these down further into dialects. A dialect is a form of our language that is spoken in a particular part of the country or by a particular group of people. There are a number of dialects of English and other languages that use different words and grammar. Most speakers of English learn a standard dialect of the English language, where we would say—*park the car* in place of the Bostonian dialect of—*pahk the cahh.* Now consider a Bostonian learning French while in France, later traveling to the French-Canadian city of Quebec—*Dis guys-Singlish damn good aye.* Next, we want to duplicate a computer program written in the language of Delphi or Java Script in the language of C++. For this, we need a compiler program. A compiler is a program that translates human-readable source code into computer-executable machine code. Have we made certain that not one letter or punctuation mark is *not* missing or placed improperly? Have these computer program languages performed this transfer perfectly? Although there are standards, Compiler writers check their compilers against the standard to confirm that a program which compiled correctly on one standard (conforming compiler) will compile correctly on another such compiler. Yes, it can be confusing to the average layman. But in the end, mistakes can happen. On another level, just as a computer hacker can jump on the internet and corrupt a software program, a software program designer can unintentional or otherwise write a section of computer language that in some manner manifests itself to a point of corrupting bytes and pieces or all of the program. This is one reality when developing our building's operational language even before the program is built.

Now looking at our program from the human perspective, because no two organizational structures are exactly alike, similar to a management protocol, we will need to take an organizational structure and adapt it to fit our building's automation system structure. Typical management structures consist of the following:

- simple
- functional
- multidivisional
- matrix

Once a structure is created, it pressures certain future tactical moves similar to military tactics while supporting others, and this is why we must realize that the choice of a structure will influence our strategy and strategic options in the future. As an example, if our structure is designed to maximize efficiency because maybe we are more focused on energy efficiency, we may lack the flexibility needed to react quickly to exploit new or other unique opportunities. This is the reason I believe a multidivisional structure works well to merge a facilities management with computer management. A multidivisional or M-form Structure consists of operating divisions, where each division represents a separate business and where the top corporate officer delegates responsibility for the day-to-day operations and business-unit or department strategy to those division managers. This is a classic military practice, where the commanding officer delegates responsibility to his division officers and down through the chain of command.

Next, I looked to build this model to fit within the multidivisional program, but I would need two exact opposites, A model that works within the program and another that does not. When I looked for programs that would fit within a computer model construct, it was the global military models that offered understandable command structures. Computer programs require commands. A command structure, one incorporating codes of conduct, and consequences should a code incur an error. A human likeness to a synthetic computer program.

This was a rather unique analogy because I would be postulating error codes within a military structured environment.

These errors or bugs in the system would need to mirror the problems suffered and experienced as a result of the strategies written into the operational programs of our building's automation and direct-digital-control system commands. It would require validation, nothing Fuzzy, and then it hit me! With fuzzy logic software programming as a key issue within the operation of buildings, this would set an obvious criterion for one end of a program while clarity and code compliance of the same operational program would run the other end. The command and operational structures would be looked upon as both biological and electronic thinking constructs. So, what would be the best military example?

I reviewed dozens of military units, organizations, and non-organizations that would help bring our building's operational personality into our view of understanding. We're building an intelligent computer program based upon a military construct, so, you want your building to be predictable, to act in the way it was programmed. I went as far back as the period of the Three Kingdoms in China, a period between the foundation of the state of Wei in 220 AD and the conquest of the state of Wu by the Jin dynasty in 280 AD, but the architecture of these armies was primarily in their numbers.

Considered a golden age in Chinese history was the Han dynasty, exceedingly over four centuries. During the four centuries, after the Han dynasty collapsed, a period of competing warlords fought each other over territories. The great Genghis Khan (1162- 1227) was the founder and first Great Khan of the Mongol Empire. As a prolific leader, his military campaigns were often accompanied by large-scale massacres of civilian populations, which would create errors in any computer model attempting to depict our building's way of thinking. I also looked at Kublai Khan reigning from 1260 to 1294, but again a model that did not fit within a multidivisional program.

Tecumseh (1768-1813) was an interesting figure, a Native American Shawnee warrior, chief, and tribal leader. He became the principal leader of a large, multi-tribal confederacy against Americans. Willing to take risks while making large scale sacrifices to repel Americans from native American land, Tecumseh was among the most celebrated native American leaders in history. He was known as a strong and eloquent speaker who promoted tribal unity. As a great warrior and heroic figure in history, the bronze figurehead named "Tecumseh" plays a prominent role in the traditions of the United States Naval Academy at Annapolis, Maryland, USA. Tecumseh embodied independent heroism and strength, yet his strength was in his resilience and steadfast desire to singlehandedly organize a confederation of tribes to resist white settlement of his homeland of the American Ohio valley. But a lone command structure such as this individual warrior was not within the operational programming I sought. His legend was the mythology that developed around him that transformed him into an American folk hero, but the organization was not his own, where it was a multi-tribe confederacy. There was no chain of command.

I then found it, the Sengoku period of the Japanese Samurai. The Samurai practiced their craft and lived within their clan, their community practicing their corporate structure, the code of Bushido. This was a way of life that incorporated eight virtues: Justice, Courage, Mercy, Honor, Loyalty, Character and Self-Control. It was their uniform code of conduct as much as it was their way of living. This is a personality we strive for in our built environment.

The Samurai had a structure of war tactics and technologies that incorporated infantry, called ashigaru, that formed their light armored warriors, combined with their cavalry in maneuvers. The executive or head of the Samurai was their Lord or Daimyo. When delving into the Samurai overall, they had the near-perfect multidivisional program. Due in large part to their code of Bushido, to be a Samurai was not only to be a warrior. It was to know your place within this community and to be ready to defend it with your life. To maintain the integrity of its structure through any weather condition or calamity. It was to be part of a clear hierarchy. However, when his daimyo or lord died or was in some fashion disgraced which would leave him without a master, a building's intelligent automation system, he would, in-turn, became a Ronin, meaning man of the waves. This was a mechanism to separate from the multidivisional program into self-employment.

However, if the Samurai was the model that worked well within a multidivisional program, what was the model that did not? What was the model that fits within a multidivisional program while experiencing the opposite effect of a Samurai architecture, where both combined would have the ability to reveal our building's operational personality from a human perspective?

A Look at Fuzzy Program Development

How do you want your building to operate, how do you want this living extension of yourself to think? Is it a form of Bushido we seek for our structures or something that's close enough? In knowing yourself, you have a very good idea of how your building should operate, and how you want your building to interact with you. Let's be realistic, we know how the manufacturer of a building's climate control system specified their direct-digital- control system to operate. However, what reasoning did they use? Unfortunately, until we have embraced nature as our partner, our controls will continue to be manufactured using a fuzzy type of logic, a logic that promotes our reactionary world. So, what is this fuzzy logic?

From a human perspective, there is fuzziness within our way of thinking, and for this reason, our building's way of thinking possesses the same fuzzy programming. Such programs are within the software downloaded into our building's operation in the form of logic programming, where logic plays a fundamental role in computer science. From a hardware viewpoint, logic gates are used, a process that consists of a logical operation with one or more logical inputs that generate a single logic output. Integrated circuits like a microprocessor can include a few to millions of logic gates. Because our brain is a neural network with analog signals, it's not structured as a network of gates. Nonetheless, we can still express our brain's functionality in whatever digital way we chose, because our components are all made from the same materials. Errors in these hardware and software designs can create some rather fuzzy results, and they do.

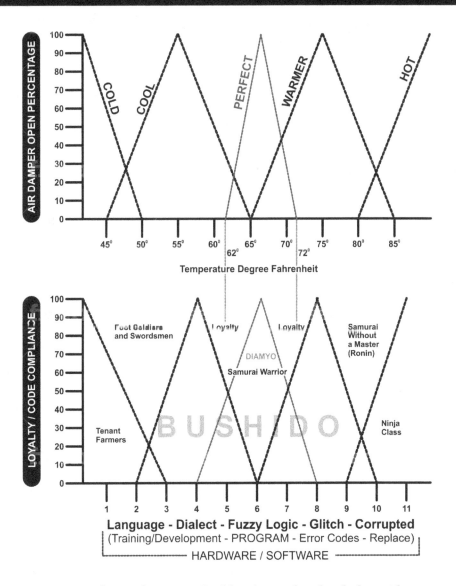

We can also evaluate our building's comfort level alongside
a Bushido organization to determine our building's
temperament – using a Fuzzy–Logic methodology.

I remember once working on an electronic design many decades back, a timing-circuit that had several sources operating at different frequencies. Because this was a linear AC circuit, and looking at the sum of all the responses from each source, I found that the superposition theorem worked remarkably well to resolve this runaway circuit. The point is that a major component of these hardware and software design bugs is the way we create the thinking processes of our building's automation systems, and these programs will run away if given the opportunity.

From an analytical view, and using a multidivisional military-style structure, any program having this type of a frayed operation is a classic fuzzy system or a rogue Samurai with a variety of fragmented software situations. A Ronan can be looked upon as a fragmented piece of a program, separated from the main program. If not later reunited, this fragmented piece can become a code-compliant issue, a bug in the system that transforms or attaches itself to a virus, becoming an assassin, a Ninja.

Japan's secret and mysterious assassins were the Ninjas. When compared to the Samurai, the Ninja did not possess a moral code. Ninjas had no ethical compass to follow, thereby engaging their enemy or targets from behind the scenes, behind the curtain, using stealth tactics to become invisible to strike at their intended victim when they were most exposed and unsuspecting.

With the Samurai warrior within a practice of the Bushido code at one end and the Ninja assassin with no moral code at the other, we are able to develop and maintain our building's multidivisional corporate structure, because America is a corporation, which I will get to in a moment. The clan of a foreign Samurai represented virtual perfection in a reasoned and coordinated approach to an operating system or the community of artificial intelligence.

Following the civil war when the United States was financially broke, on February 21, 1871, the forty-first Congress of the United States passed an Act to provide for a separate government, also known as the Act of 1871, Section 34, Session III, chapters 61 and 62. By doing so, Congress created this separate form of government for the District of Columbia, a ten-mile square parcel of land. This Act became U.S.A Federal Law 28 USC § 3002, which transformed The United States "of America" to the "United States Corporation".

(15) "United States" means—

(A) a Federal corporation,
(B) an agency, department, commission, board, or other entity of the United States, or
(C) an instrumentality of the United States.

There are varying differences within the code of the Samurai and in-turn separation of a Ronin. When one or more of these programs are miscoded or become corrupted? enter the rogue Samurai, enter fuzzy logic.

Let's start with our foreign Samurai and their equivalent of America's corporate community structure – the Bushido Code. For the Samurai program, this code represents the eight virtues of the Samurai, their organizational structure. These eight qualities as outlined by Nitobe Inaz , (1862–1933) a Japanese agricultural economist, author[16], educator and more, are:

- Rectitude or justice,
- Courage
- benevolence or mercy
- Politeness
- honesty and sincerity
- honor
- loyalty, and
- character and self-control

Bushido refers to morality as—*the bone that gives firmness and stature. Without a structure, without bones, the head cannot rest on*

---

[16]   The Way of the Samurai, by Inazo Nitobe – April 1, 2011,

top of the spine, nor hands move nor feet stand. So, without Rectitude, neither talent nor learning can make the human frame into a samurai. Rectitude keeps our structure stable, our environment in balance. The Bushido program has always fit nicely with its reliability toward a building's functionality, structure, and stability of our building's operational codes. A stable and proficient program.

Nitobe continued by advising that the real Samurai despised money, believing that—men must grudge money, for riches hinder wisdom. Bushido teaches that men should behave according to an absolute moral standard, the equivalent of data structures or code compilers to focus problems toward developing better algorithms within our building's automation systems. Data structures transcend logic. Where what's right is right, and what's wrong is wrong, and the difference between good and bad or right and wrong are absolutes, not opinions for debate, and the Samurai should know the difference. The supreme quality for leadership is unquestionably integrity.

> *Integrity—without it, no real success is possible, no matter whether it is on a section gang, a football field, in an army, or in an office . . .*
> —A quote from former US President and supreme allied Daimyo during world war II, Dwight D Eisenhower.

Bushido is a program that works against errors. A sense of honor with a consciousness of self-dignity and worth characterized the Samurai as a soldier, a warrior. He was born and raised to value his duties and the privileges of his profession, of his program as written. The Samurai feared disgrace and would offer his own life to demonstrate his morality and obedience to the code of Bushido. If this was a real-world program of Bushido it would be in- line with America's US Army "Delta Force," known as the 1st Special Forces Operational Detachment-Delta (1st SFOD-D), the elite U.S. special missions' units that incorporate land, sea, and air programs and recently renamed the Combat Applications Group (CAG), presently known as the Army Compartmented

Elements (ACE). Another example is the secret Flotilla (Shayetet) 13 unit of the Israeli Navy and one of secret elite reconnaissance (sayeret) commando units of the Israeli Defense forces. Although the People's Liberation Army special operations forces of China consists of a number of specialized units, their Guangzhou Military Region Special Forces Unit, designated "South Blade" or "South China Sword" was their first unit to become a special operations unit, capable of elite air, sea, and land operations. These are merely a few examples of veiled and highly classified programs of Samurai warriors where individual members do not seek self-promotion against their program creed and where loyalty to their Daimyo Lord is a non-corruptible tradecraft. There are, nevertheless, Samurai programmed from different clans that are led differently.

Enter a retired Samurai as a component highlighting our second multidivisional program. A highly decorated Samurai who last served his clan and country with honor. This Samurai clearly defined the code of Bushido. Until – while enjoying his leave from his clan, our Samurai changed his legacy by losing his place within his community of warriors, when he authored an open parchment that was revealed in a local publication, addressed to the home of his former Daimyo Lord. The open letter contained a number of insults and innuendo, entitled: *"I would consider it an honor to return the sword you presented me"*. This was an insult, a clear and unequivocal violation of the Bushido code against his Daimyo. During this period, his Daimyo was having an open and public disagreement with this now rogue Samurai's former Tomodachi, a friend, and clan member, according to rivalries with the period's Shogun. In-turn our Samurai personally and publicly criticized the decisions and personal behavior of the Daimyo. Not a good visual from the cheap seats during this period, because the rogue Samurai previously answered to the Daimyo, where he had been permitted to take service outside of his clan to this new Lord. Most of his loyalty was transferred to this new lord that he now openly challenged. From our multidivisional program, this statement pitted the rogue Samurai against his Daimyo.

This retired icon now shamed within the Samurai community was very much aware that a Samurai on leave from his clan, or for purposes of this analogy we'll say retirement, should not have engaged in personal or professional activities which are incompatible with the standards of conduct expected of a Samurai warrior. As a now shamed Samurai, I would imagine he recognized that his challenge was incompatible with the rather detailed oath of Bushido, similar to an ethos within today's modern-day military warriors, and a requirement for our accurately run software program. Therefore, our rogue Samurai had broken the oath of Bushido, because he said: *"it would be my honor"* when offering the return of a previous gift. Comparing within today's modern militaries this was the equivalent of a Samaria turned Ninja attempting to assassinate his former lord.

Needless to say, this human code became corrupted, in describing the code violation similar to a computer program and not the person, along with numbers of other past and present team members who had separated themselves from the clan by joining a community of Ninja assassins under the rogue Samurai's command. These non-code compliant team members authored books and promoted themselves publicly against the very ethos they were bound by. Emotionally or otherwise our rogue Samurai, unfortunately, violated a trust, a code bestowed upon him as a member of this clan's leadership and military advisor to his Daimyo. If this were a computer code the conflict alone would have caused conflicts sufficient enough to require defragmentation and possible deletion of this program. These are the similarities and reasoning, however unfortunate, why the US Navy SEAL program could not be paralleled to a Bushido program.

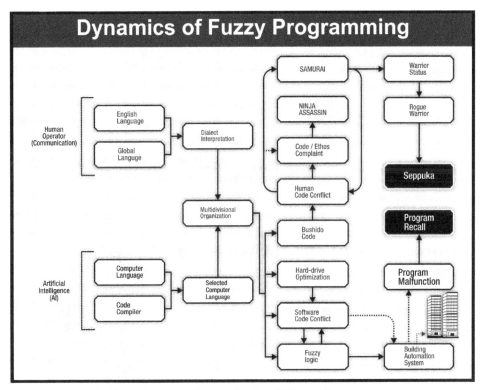

**A flow-chart analogy of a Bushido code program
using the dynamics of Fuzzy programming.**

During this public back and forth I remembered a sociology class I had taken decades ago that incorporated a phrase from Plato: *Wise men speak because they have something to say, fools because they have to say something.* Ignoring a clan's corporate structure, a military code that had been followed an entire career, was painfully foolish. Those honorable warriors that remain within the clan are stigmatized by a current and former leadership that has grown accustomed to disobedience with an absence of self-control and loyalty to this clan's ethos. These clan leaders, now rogue have become addicted to elite living habits.

As for those clan members formerly under the leadership of the now rogue Samurai, becoming Ninja assassins was unavoidable, because they could now openly use stealth activities such as authored publications against former warrior team members. These authors did not grudge money or possess honor or self-control as Bushido would dictate to a Samurai warrior. They chose a cunning maneuver to reveal secrets for profit, becoming authors that exposed secrets guarded by members within their clan.

If you haven't figured out which person in history I had modeled for our rogue warrior, he is admiral William H. McRaven, former U.S. Navy SEAL. My reasoning, however painful, was based upon his now infamous proclamation to the office of his commander —*'I would consider it an honor if you would revoke my security clearance as well'* —A number of the analogies and quotes earlier described were taken from this former warrior's words and actions. However, defending a former CIA director who has publicly made untruthful statements promotes question to his own character. When one understands that any action which may be taken against your disobedience could be looked upon worse than the defiance itself, it falls into question why the statement was made at-all—it tends to place a question upon one's character. Frankly, it made me wonder how members of this U.S. military clan treat others that they disagree with? Because of these unfortunate facts it wasn't difficult to liken this former hero as a corrupted computer program, because his past activities and program did not conform to these later-day actions. Moreover, his behavior failed the code of Bushido. You cannot preach to *respect everyone* while publicly maligning the commander in chief of the military you once served and the daimyo you once reported to. When we watch the SEALs ethos violated time and time again by him—

> *The ability to control my emotions and my actions, regardless of circumstance, sets me apart from other men. Uncompromising integrity is my standard. My character and honor are steadfast.*

—and from those former subordinates of this remarkable Admiral, writing books for profit against a SEALs ethos—*I do not advertise the nature of my work*— exposing their clan's inner capabilities—the same authors once under his leadership, one can simply look at this former leader's own words and actions to understand how his leadership was perceived. Now, I grew up in an environment where you lead by example, and Nancy and I raised our younger family members similarly. Yet, the Admiral's actions and the actions of his former subordinates did not set a good example. There can be no excuse because their mission, his mission as a role model for what this clan represents is too important. The warriors who currently represent this clan are too important. Public perception is not negotiable! The program must be fail-safe. This is a fallen warrior I can say I would smile warmly at with both admiration and despair.

> *The U.S. military is ultimately answerable to the American people. If it fails to maintain the highest standards, it will fail not only its service members and the mission, but also the citizens it has sworn to protect. In today's increasingly divisive political environment, every military member—active, reserve, and retired—can and must play an active part in preserving and advancing the reputation, professionalism, and capabilities forged by our forebears.*
>
> Captain Dan'l Steward
> U.S. Navy (Retired)[17]

---

[17] A Final Lesson – US Naval Institute, February 2020 Proceedings Vol. 146/2/1,404.

This is a clan that should equal that of a Tier 4 or even 5 data centers, encompassing redundant and dual-power for servers, storage drives, network links and power cooling systems. This clan should mimic the most advanced type of tier-level.

This military program guided by an Ethos code is a real-world environment as opposed to the synthetic programs we design and write for our synthetic environments, where a Samurai Creed does not advertise the nature of their tradecraft or to seek recognition for their actions. The Bushido code was designed as non-corruptible, where Bushido has a self-destruct feature in the form of Seppuku (suicide) that would occur should the code in the form of human actions become corrupt or virus-ridden. These corrupted codes are not derived from the person but an ideal or program the person followed and expanded. There are, of course, Samurai warriors that have separated (retired) as Ronins which have authored self-help programs and career philosophical works, that have not sought recognition for prior actions or divulged trade secrets. These are Ronin warriors maintaining the code of Bushido. These are retired programs, archived for future reference.

As humans we make mistakes, and these mistakes can unintentionally or otherwise corrupt a program, programs we write, programs we develop, programs we follow, whether the program is real-world or in the form of a software computer program. These are programs that are followed by the computer automation systems of our artificial environments. The operator is trapped having to follow the rules of the program. It all leads back to the program, not the operator because the operator can become corrupted from faulty directions within a program, or even from source codes improperly entered. When looking back at our rogue Samurai's development, it was human emotion, the very entity that ignores otherwise well written and executed programs. The rogue Samurai and those clan members who serve under his and future commands had forgotten their ethos, their code. The legacy of these former Samurai now Ninja assassins was initially designed to steady their resolve while silently guide their every deed. They were designed to provide our built environments with an operational direction. Now corrupted, it is now up to the operator, the Daimyo to decide their fate.

An intelligent program that attempts to match our human brain, or have the potential of surpassing our intelligence, can run algorithms that are just as powerful as the human brain's algorithms. This is the theory anyway. This is a machine that would have the ability to think many orders of magnitude faster than a human where silicon can be made faster than flesh. The neurons within our human computers operate anywhere from forty to 200 hertz, or cycles per second, where a modern microprocessor can operate at superhuman speeds as high as 2,000,000,000 hertz. Our human impulses conducted from a cell's body to other cells, axons, carry the change in electrical potential at around one-hundred-twenty milliseconds, where computer signals travel near the speed of light. Our buildings can certainly think as fast as the physical memory space provided or volumes of hard-drives we provide.

I imagine the direct-digital-control programs our computers possess would first show signs of independence or maybe signs of a rebellious attitude if attempting to act independently of our programmed directions. With this in mind, loyalty, honor, and self-control would definitely not be Bushido code-elements incorporated within this program.

A bug in the program can be looked upon as an error in a system that was similarly displayed by our rogue Samurai and those Ninja authors depicting secret clan operations. An error in the form of a human action that portrayed a challenge to his former executive superior, against the program's code. This rogue Samurai program, this culture that was initially built to address both the physical as well as the mental stability of the human soldier, I would suggest no longer provides a program-like curriculum for the psychological stability and direction of its members. This is a culture not close to mimicking the Samurai warrior let alone its code of Bushido. Integrity, honor, and loyalty are simply forgotten qualities of the rogue Samurai training and enforced within his former clan community.

The building blocks of any software program code or program function should be made as a universal system while able to handle different types of inputs and computing requirements. However, the Rogue Samurai developed a community that adheres to a culture, where: *weakness is the sign of a coward that never finishes*, while simultaneously this same program is met with a conflict, yes a conflict that promotes a belief where: *It is OK if sometimes we do not finish our battles.* This is classic Fuzzy logic terminology. In fuzzy logic, there is no clear definition as to what is exactly true or false. It's a fuzzy program with a selection process to match. The selection process is flawed because a number of these former Samurai turned Ninja assassins routinely leave the clan to promote themselves and their exploits, contrary to their human code or ethos. It starts with the leadership of a program, whether human or computer, where there should be no fuzzy guesswork.

All programs should have a well-organized internal structure. In computer language, there is a *Modularity Programming Paradigm* that requires separating every program into moderately small units where each performs a specific task, similar to the Samurai team concept, where each team has its specialty, comparable to the teams of our modern-day military. However, if the code is infiltrated with problematic code conflicts, where if our clan's leader does it, why can't we? The program breaks down.

In the past, hardware conflicts were more common than they are today. A conflict, similar to our rogue Samurai occurs when two computer programs cannot run in the same computer at the same time, where you can't have two leaders within the same clan. It's typically caused when a programming bug is established by two programs competing for the same resource. When a Samurai competes against his Daimyo.

Based on clear and distinct ideas, Descartes established that each mind is a mental substance and each body a part, a component of one material substance. A fuzzy system is someone imposing their ideas and understanding of something upon you, wherein some programs can lead to bias programming in artificial intelligence (AI). Remember, AI programs are constructed by humans, but AI bias is a separate entity in itself.

As a sidebar to fuzzy logic, many terms reflect bias in AI-based algorithms. They are known as algorithm bias or machine learning bias, or simply AI bias. I like to think of them as unintentional biased-based programming. These are programs that contain built-in biases that were created by well-intentioned computer programmers who have unconsciously or otherwise written their own preferences into their algorithms. Later, these algorithms can and have produced results that reflect these hidden biases, that can analytically cause prejudice because of flawed assumptions during the computer program's learning process. These flaws or erroneous assumptions have become so egregious, that in 2016 the European Parliament and Council passed a European Union protection remedy called The General Data Protection Regulation (GDPR). The GDPR itself contains 11 chapters and 91 articles and will take effect in the Spring of 2018.

Explained within the Massachusetts Institute of Technology (MIT)Technology Review, bias can sneak in at many stages in the category of algorithms known as 'deep learning'. This deep learning category and the current standard practices in computer science isn't designed to detect it. There is no detection compliance oversight, which indicates our buildings too may lack oversight in certain instances. If we were to use this criterion, we would model a building's heating ability as an attribute. This attribute could be the building's furnace, the air distribution system or the wall-mounted sensors and thermostats. Choosing which attributes that the algorithm considers or ignores can influence the model's prediction accuracy. This is because the model can be skewed if the main air-handling-unit is counted as one entire air distribution system, or in the alternative, a combination of the main AHU with the individual ceiling-mounted variable-air-volume units are counted as a single attribute. Karen Hao of the MIT Technology Review further asserts: . . . *the introduction of bias isn't always obvious during a model's construction because you may not realize the downstream impacts of your data and choices until much later. Once you do, it's hard to retroactively identify where that bias came from and then figure out how to get rid of it.* Now imagine this type of deep learning program is used in concert with fuzzy logic sets of a building's automation system. Facility managers have certainly felt the sting of why the building is doing this or doing that?

Going a bit deeper, the Internet of Things, or IoT, is a system that is comprised of converging multiple technologies, real-time analytics, fuzzy logic computer learning, and more. This is a system that has the ability to transfer data over a network without requiring human-to-human or human-to-computer interaction. It is all smart component communication. IoT has been used to monitor and control the mechanical, electrical and electronic systems within a variety of buildings and building automation systems. Fragmentation is and has been a real concern with IoT. I've experienced a number of IoT variations in hardware with the different software programs running on them. The integration of BACnet systems connected to new and older direct-digital-control systems programming along with their hardwire and wireless components just have a hard time working consistently. Sometimes they run fine and at other times there seems to be a glitch. We all just need to make sure, when working between different technologies, that caution is observed, identifying that shortcuts are not taken and bias programming is monitored before and especially after software development, since bias programming may not show up until these systems start their learning curve. It can certainly be a bit perplexing at times. Here, honesty and self-control are qualities of Bushido, similar to the attributes of when our control-programs are developed and the training and monitoring of these systems during the commissioning and operation phases are performed.

Now back from our sidebar—the rogue Samurai along with those Ninja assassins which do not follow Bushido are looked upon as honorable and unbiased within some circles of the land they one traveled; it certainly was not an easy day for those heroes to maintain their former Bushido status. They were invited into a bug-ridden program that was endorsed by their leadership. A program that can be said leads by example compared to a computer program for our building's automation system, should not depend on assumptions regarding the precision of a user's input or presumptions about a program's expectations. These are defensive designs projected to ensure the ongoing function of a software program under unexpected conditions. Within any building I have operated, this would have been a classic case in where the program required a reboot, upgrade, or complete wipe of the hard-drive.

Let's face it, if this was a real-world rogue Samurai system within a questionable fuzzy operating or bias computer program, we would take it back to where we bought it for a refund. Yet, the rogue Samurai and Ninja clans have developed into rock-star status while relinquishing their warrior rank. But this too is how our building's operational programs are written using fuzzy style programming. It works. It has visible and proven results. And we turn our backs to the fuzziness, those quirks we experience while believing *the computer must know what it's doing.*

The Japanese innovation machine love's Fuzzy Logic, a term that was introduced in 1965 by Lotfi Zadeh. His introduction of fuzzy sets created somewhat of a revolution in the creation of, what we call, smart technology. But they're a disciplined society following a code of Bushido to this day, so I can understand how they have become successful in their development and world-renown corroboration of fuzzy sets. I'm OK with this, yet hoping they stay within the intelligence of a simple thermostat and the spin- cycle circuits of a washing machine. I just have this apprehension of someday walking into the foyer of a high-rise office building while the sprinkler system is raining throughout the floor because the building automation system interpreted the sprinkler system as the building's humidification system. Granted, a bit implausible but there's a point to be made.

Bushido requires that a person invested with powers to command and powers to kill would be expected to equally demonstrate astonishing powers of benevolence and mercy. In modern-day Japan, their wish to preserve the honor and avoid shame plays a key role within their culture, where what's right is right, and what's wrong is wrong, and the difference between good and bad or right and wrong will always remain absolute. This is how our buildings should think and in-turn operate. Buildings have a noble and radiant energy cycle of Sakura, where their photonic structures provide us with a moment to mirror our own connection to these wonders we build and care for. It is, for this reason, I'll select the stability of a samurai warrior type of building-automation-system over that of a fuzzy logic rock star package. A perfect cherry blossom follows the first law of thermodynamics – energy, even radiant energy, exists in many different forms, and can be transferred from place to place or changed between different forms, but it cannot be created or destroyed, because they are nature's gift that cannot be given back.

Fuzzy Logic

Fuzzy logic is a theory that excludes the middle. First and foremost, fuzzy systems do not need to be precise. There are no sets of equations that reveal a degree of difference. The primary mode of operation is a set of easy rules, such as—if a room is cold, start the heat immediately. If the air-temperature is less than seventy-five but greater than seventy-two than start the fan for the cooling system. Fuzzy rules are put together in sets.

A subset of AI is machine learning that is reliant upon the quality and objectivity along with the size of data sets. Switching to another hand, a term named *high bias* is an image of problems related to the assembling or the usage of data, where systems draw improper conclusions about data sets. High bias means the prediction will be inaccurate because it causes an algorithm to miss the relevant relations between its features and target outputs. One person's definition of cold could be another person's definition of warm.

In one instance of a system identified as an AI program, I was attempting to figure out why an alarm program connected to a toxic substance detector within a Washington, DC air-handling- unit was prematurely activating. The sensor was switched out a number of times, and the calibration adjustments were tweaked over and over again. When the software program was deleted and downloaded again, the system worked temporarily but after two or three test activations this system would fail yet again. Each time the software program was downloaded again the system would work for only a few test sessions. It was later learned, that the program algorithm was changing in an irregular method for some unapparent reason. It was learning in the wrong way. This program was supposed to operate using the data that is used to calibrate this system, assisted with an algorithm that was programmed by a professional. These are systems communicating within a network of sensors, computer software programming, and computer hardware that communicates through another BACnet communication system and program that determines the next course of action. There is no human interaction. It is a system that communicates within the network of interconnected devices. Our building's intelligence surely can become fuzzy at times, but whether this anomaly was based upon a bias glitch or from incompatible fuzzy sets, or a combination of both, understanding how our buildings think is as important as how they maintain their temperatures. A building has the same quirks and embarrassing moments as we do, and there will be some you will not be able to cure without busting your budget in some cases. In the end, you may find there are just some problems that cannot be fixed in the field. The only time a machine or building becomes human will be when you can't tell the difference.

What about these fuzzy sets? In an example, cold and immediately is a fuzzy set. Extreme and not extreme could be another set. Eventually, all of the sets that make up a fuzzy program are combined into an averaging scheme that turns each set into a single value that the air-conditioning or heating system can learn to understand. Although this theory sounds remarkably close to the probability theories of quantum mechanics, it actually is not. Probability measures the likelihood of an event happening, where fuzzy logic uses a variety of pre-determined sets to narrow down an answer or a result. On the other hand, fuzzy logic and probability processing seems to be interesting ways of dealing with uncertainty. But Descartes believed different. At a talk in 1628, Descartes denied a group of early chemists, known as alchemists, that probabilities are as good as certainties in science. In-turn, Descartes demonstrated his method for attaining certainty. Within this speech, I can assure all that Descartes, as with Big Al, denounced probabilities as uncertainties and thereby would never have believed in any uncertainty principal such as a fuzzy logic-based system. This is because the degrees of truth in fuzzy sets are often confused with probabilities.

As newer levels of technology evolved, digital technology was merged with fuzzy sets that made processing much faster. As these combinations got more and more sophisticated, hand- tuned systems were eventually taken over by computer programs that claim to mimic the human nervous system. A fuzzy nervous system? The system is methodically self-taught and learns by supporting successful behavior. These behaviors are in-turn modeled from human duplications. It doesn't appear fuzzy logic has had more than a little impact on hardware or processor architecture.

If unknown mistakes or inaccuracies are programmed into a fuzzy set, we call them bugs or errors in the system. Too many times fuzzy sets have been married with somewhat incompatible sets that confuse our artificial intelligence, only later to find that the machine we purchased is interacting with conflicting signals. On the contrary, many have also disagreed with me. How many times have we witnessed our systems performing a task that was never intended, or interacting in a way that has caused us to scratch our heads? *Why is this motor acting like this? This thermostat is not responding to the program?* These programs have sparked an age where computers are given authority without a title. How many times have we heard *the computer won't let me do it?* Within a variety of cases, lower and mid-management employees cannot over-rule a computer without going to the boss. The machine is now my boss? My boss now possesses the intelligence of part samurai, part ronin, and part ninja.

The temperature might have a range of states such as cold, cool, warm and hot. The fact is that a fuzzy temperature set is primarily determined by the author of the program and the regional climate. Oh, don't forget about high bias and IoT. Accordingly, the range of these temperature-related words turned into linguistic terms can be exactly determined by defining these group functions when asking the person that authored their meaning. For instance, what was the cold temperature our author indicated on the Fahrenheit scale? Was it the same temperature you would find as cold? Many individual names within sets, such as building, facility, industry, or renown, can be a set, but effective only to a certain degree when applied to a particular infrastructure, building or business. Fuzzy logic understanding attempts to measure each step while allowing computers to manipulate such information. Yes, we allow computers to manipulate and determine the end- result when we provide it with fuzzy sets. Would a human have opened the hot-water valve to the heating system to raise the temperature of the room or would we have increased the fan speed to increase the volume of heated air entering the room? What is the probability a fuzzy program would do one or the other? Or, because the building's security system is interconnected to the building automation system through a BACnet structure, did another unrelated building program influence the program of our building-automation-system through a high bias or IoT anomaly? We know this has happened because at one time or another, as building operators, we have all been there.

I'm talking about the open protocol BACnet used in the majority of building automation type of systems. BACnet devices communicate with each other over a network. Let's say your HVAC, fire, security, and hotel room lighting are all interconnected using an open protocol system, and two-out-of-four of these systems were comprised of fuzzy sets. Next, these systems incorporate multiple IP to ethernet routers—a real-world scenario. Another real-world scenario—a code compiler has been known to inadvertently tie the HVAC system to the fire damper of the HVAC's air-handling- unit. I remember this caused some type of ID conflict. Don't ask. Next, the air-handler-unit fan would not go lower than a particular speed, where for months no-one could figure out why? until a fire alarm test was conducted. The fire alarm technician manually closed a fire damper that, for some apparent reason, would not automatically close. When this damper was manually forced closed, additional static pressure (air volume) was no longer required and the HVAC system automatically reduced the fan speed that previously would not decrease. Apparently, the open fire damper was releasing static pressure (air pressure) through this damper opening, causing the system to ask for more because of the continuous loss of pressure. This caused the fan to stay on high. It was later discovered that all dampers located within the HVAC system, including the fire dampers, were somehow recognized as HVAC dampers. This created some type of misconfiguration that made the damper at times unresponsive. It was a cluster bomb for sure. This particular issue played a role in a number of other inadvertent problems because of the inconsistent static pressure anomalies, a system showing provisional, transient and persistent uncontrolled movements of dampers and fan speeds. Mechanical tics. Human complex motor tics consist of a series of unexpected movements performed in the same order. In-line with these motor anomalies, our building's system has all the evidence of suffering from a Tourette type of ailment.

How much of fuzzy logic played a role in our building's anomalies and how much the BACnet integrator program played were never realized, where the BACnet people and the building automation people claimed the issues did not originate with them. And there is the keyword, originate.

Since the mid-eighties, we have had the opportunity to witness fuzzy logic's evolution, and the most supportive phrase I can offer would be – get me a cup of decaf coffee & Kahlua and let me think this one over. Structurally and without precision, this logic keeps surprising us with new issues to resolve, because fuzzy systems have always self-proclaimed that they do not require precision. This is not very comforting to facility managers and engineering directors, required to explain to property managers and general managers why these systems are not performing as designed. These very systems which take control also control a blame-game with no accountability. The system has the control and we get the blame for not knowing what the problem is.

Big Al used quantum mechanics as a tool and means to describe a theory of his own. Fuzzy systems in one form or another appear to be here to stay, so we need to realign its workings, but this does not mean we have to like them. When we observe non- precise fuzzy programming labeled as human-like reasoning or knowledge-based systems, these are fuzzy systems that have hid behind the label of artificial intelligence. Let me clue you in, Fuzzy is not synonymous with intelligence. Universally, we have been utilizing fuzzy logic as a non-precise program tool that allows our systems and machines to operate well in most and non-sophisticated applications. Although this type of logic is not programmed using probabilities, its effectiveness and our knowledge of its lack of precision have given it a probability rating, second only to a quantum mechanical type of machine. This is shared by many control engineers who maintain building- automation-systems and by most statisticians who believe that probability is the only rigorous mathematical description of uncertainty - *hey boss, we told the computer to open the hot water valve, and instead, it slowed down the fan. I guess the computer knows what it's doing?* The fuzzy sets programmed within the software are not merged with nature's direction. It's all about the computer, and not about nature's path.

The Programming of Global Governments

From a global government perspective, infrastructure and defense-related intelligent computer programs are written to follow specific software designs written by IT professionals. An underlying problem that has cropped up, is that little to no "active" alternative action plans are built-in to the programming which immediately should take over upon the slightest signal of an anomaly. The program either defaults to a fully open or closed/off or on operation. If we are to utilize the IF-THEN rules of fuzzy programming, we should at least bring them in as a by-pass mechanism, a back-up to a program fault should a fuzzy set fail or even should a traditional algorithm develop some type of information anxiety or Tourette type of tic. The human-computer has the ability to in-time develop a bypass during a stroke or other neurological disorders. If we intend to mimic the operational ability of our own memory and intelligence, then we should do it!

These various functional personalities of our buildings demand more attention, more oversight. As our structures become more modern requiring a higher intelligence, so too should we be more vigilant in identifying these varying types of schizophrenia.

There are a lot of Ninja assassins outside our buildings with multi-headed hydra worms across encrypted networks looking to harm the way our buildings operate. These are dark virus programs that use encryption techniques that cannot be cracked, some using one-time pre-shared keys with the same size as or longer than the messages we send, and some are similar to a Vernon encryption that incorporates a key code that is destroyed upon implementation. There are even black Ninja assassin programs such as the Olympic disk, or "OD" partly derived out of the Olympic Games program. Most know of this virus worm as Stuxnet, an extremely sophisticated computer program worm that exploits multiple previously unknown program vulnerabilities to infect computers. When it infects a computer, it checks to see if that computer is connected to specific models of programmable logic controllers. Although not these, in particular, logic computers are used regularly in our buildings to collect data and run intelligent programs on a daily basis.

This intelligent anti-virus that America helped design as a global anti-viral injection program, was crafted to guard against a potential epidemic against humanity which cares for our synthetic environments. This program was researched and developed at Fort Meade USA in the same building as the US National Security Agency (NSA), where the U.S. Cyber Command was created out of an event that transpired around a decade ago, named operation Buckshot Yankee. The NSA has no authority to conduct offensive programs, but the U.S. Cyber Command falls under America's Department of Defense, so it does have the authority, operating from a remote operations center. This is a system, an intelligence that we have designed on a global scale-out of necessity as an anti-virus for our infrastructure, our synthetic environments.

All of this synthetically-created intelligent programming may sound pessimistic and gloomy, but it's presented to transport you into the world of our artificial intelligence and how they mimic the very solutions we use toward our human structures. It allows us to look inside of what makes these human creations think and how they were programmed. How our building's attitude and mind- sets were established. Their speed in efficiency and economic costs have impressed us in wanting more, but we need to be so very careful because nature is not fuzzy. Prove me wrong!

The New Standard Model

It's time we start developing and maintaining our structures in compliance with a unified form of thinking. As facility engineers along with property managers, we are keenly aware of an anticipated sound, a natural vibration, a rhythm we expect to hear and feel through our human senses when we walk into our central plant or main mechanical room, even after entering the front door of our castle. We know what that constant deep whirring sound with the overlapping high pitch from our chiller sounds like. The controlled explosion *poof* from the combustion in our boiler furnace. The purring middle-frequency pitch of our air-handling unit's bearings as they steadily rotate their firmly fit wedge style polyester-film belts that push and pull an unobstructed volume of air through our building's respiratory system. It only takes a single irregular decibel of sound to alert our consciousness of a problem. There is no sound unfamiliar with our experience.

Watching these rotating AHU's, I remember while in high school during the early '70s of the tours I participated within several central plants while observing the rotation of the larger-than-life fan-blades turning from a slow-start to what appeared to be an invisible pattern of energy. The faded paint at the end of each blade created a rotating pattern similar to a group of electrons rotating around the nucleus of an atom.

Looking at this from those earlier days we now are aware that this classic picture no longer looks like the model of electrons moving around a nucleus containing only protons and neutrons. Sure, the atom is still an atom, but the structure and internal movements are far different and more complex from those days in Mr. Graham's Science class. We now know that there's a new standard model that will forever change the personality of our buildings and structures. The Atom is pulsating and vibrating fields of energy. It's a Field made of Leptons, Bosons, and what are called Hadrons. Electrons are now under a group of Leptons, Big Al's photons are now under a group of Bosons, and the protons and neutrons that once made up our nucleus are under the Hadron group.

STANDARD MODEL OF ELEMENTARY PARTICLES

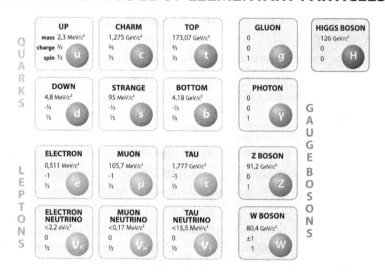

The standard model of particle physics replaces the old model of the atom, where once only three basic particles: protons, electrons, and neutrons, described an atom's sub-atomic particles.

The Standard Model has not yet explained the force of gravity but was developed to describe the details of fundamental particles along with the forces governing the interactions between them. The new model brings to light a communication with our building structures unlike any description known before but also explains how the entire Universe is built from just twelve particles of Matter, called fermions. Forces mediating Matter and Fermions require six force-carrying particles called bosons, and it is this boson force that carries big Al's photon, his particle of light. This will all make sense later in our understanding.

HIGGS BOSON

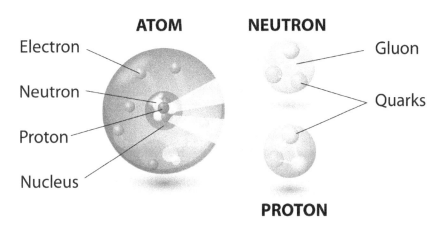

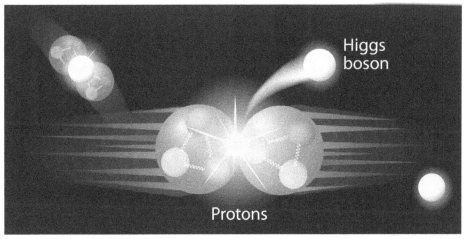

Understanding How Our Buildings
Silently Communicate

People typically do not want to understand any concept or theory they don't understand. If we cannot see it, touch it, or taste it, our intellect, our emotions get turned off. Stephen Covey explained it best, where his 5th Habit reveals, *most people do not listen with the intent to understand, they listen with the intent to reply.* The pieces of evidence have been unequivocal and the facts have been known for decades, but no one has been truly listening. The physics language has been too challenging to understand. But I have found when one goes slow and methodical, baby steps, we can get there. So, let's stay together through this short journey.

Putting the type of facts together that we have been exploring requires an open mind while truly realizing this is real physics, real science, and the time to acknowledge what we all have known for decades. Mystified is the cause, or why, facilities and real property professionals get fairly attached if not very attached to their buildings, our buildings. The emotional and at times physical bond that we typically form with our buildings and facilities go beyond our awareness of the living atomic-level structures or the periodic table of concrete, wood, or glass. How have you emotionally felt when leaving a job or position you have enjoyed, now relocating from one office or building to another. You are realizing this is your last day operating a particular boiler or chiller within a central plant that has treated you and your career well. You will miss them. With dozens of more examples of work-related emotional bonding - where does this attachment come from? Realistically you are saying goodbye to what was once your office, central plant, or building.

We admire the U.S. Capitol, the Burj Khalifa building in Dubai, or the Great Wall of China, all in the distance while we are all experiencing an admiration, an aura or bio-photonic emissions that have somehow made their journey over to our physical space.

Your biological body and in reality, all of life as well are made up of atoms, often organized into larger structures called molecules.

But inanimate materials such as steel, concrete, and wood too are made up of such atoms and molecules. Atoms and molecules are governed by the rules of chemistry and physics, whether they are part of a living, breathing human or a non-biological structure. Touch any part of a building and within each piece of material, each piece of matter contains live atoms. You're walking on a sidewalk made of live atoms. You pick up a morning newspaper containing live atoms. From our school days that now seem so distant, we were taught that the number of moving protons and neutrons determines an element's mass number: mass number = equals protons + plus neutrons. An atom is the smallest unit of matter. Concrete, wood, or glass, are each independent types of mass, and each of these structural components have their own mass number because they contain live atoms. Where we do not want this description turned into a science lesson, we will cut to the chase and explain that all living and nonliving structures on earth possess moving live atoms. A piece of equipment called a transmission electron microscope can be used to see these atoms. Placing this microscope on a piece of wood, concrete, or any mass, we are told we can visually observe the attraction between the positively charged protons and negatively charged electrons while it seemingly holds the atom together. Observing their movement will be discussed later. Each element or piece of matter which makes up our building is truly alive yet too small to see through the naked eye. But does each of the live components (Walls, doors, furnishings, and fixtures) that make up our building possess intelligence, or do these components combined into one develop into an intelligent structure, even slightly? Do the atoms within our biological structures, within us, make any attempt to communicate with those atoms that make up our building? Is there an intermingling, an intercommunication we are just not aware of between the two?

Reflecting back to my high school years, a millennium ago, atoms were the first to be discovered within particle physics. Next were protons, neutrons, and electrons. Later came quarks and leptons, which are Matter particles, but our universe doesn't only contain Matter. Our universe also contains forces that act upon this matter, and this is where the force-carrier particles enter the picture. One of these force particles is Big Al's photon.

The Zeno Effect

In 1974 three physicists found that atoms won't move when they are being watched. Imagine, you're looking through a neutron microscope to observe the atoms within a piece of matter, an object, any object, but the second you zoom in to look at the circular and pulsating motion of the atom, it stops moving. Look away and the molecular structure of the atom continues its movement. What is this intelligence our buildings are constructed from?

Around three years later, in 1977 an Indian theoretical physicist and a professor at the University of Texas compared this observation with Zeno's Paradox, which states, *that because an arrow in flight is not seen to move during any single instant, it cannot possibly be moving at all.* Still, is the atom's reaction to our visual observation a form of intelligence? Is an atom intelligent? Do the construction materials that make up our buildings possess a form of intelligence? In 2006 three theoretical physicists from Cornell University described this as initial states that display total Zeno effect are intelligent states of two conjugate observables. The term *intelligent states* when describing their experiment incorporating the quantum Zeno Effect.

Nonetheless, the mere fact an atom has the ability, an intelligent ability to stop once it is being observed, is at least a means of intelligent communication or an acknowledgment mechanism of unknown origin. The undisputed and clear fact that the varieties of materials that are used to assemble an intelligent building also incorporate an unknown means of built-in intelligent communication. So, what is the next step toward such communiqué of our buildings and structures?

Biophotons are photons that are emitted as endogenous radiation produced by humans and other living organisms and detected as barely visible light.

The Biophoton

Biophotons are photons that are emitted spontaneously by all living systems and stored in the DNA of all organisms.[18] Endogenous radiation produced by humans and other living organisms and detected as barely visible light.[19]

During my early years, while invited to work on an electronics' communications project at a college in Cambridge, Massachusetts, USA, I was at work on a design of an early advanced radiofrequency hopping system—a story for another day. This was before the integrated circuit (IC) chips were available. After the manual etching of one of many circuit boards during the prototype phase and the soldiering of an arrangement of components, the preliminary testing revealed electrical interference was radiating from my body. It was a professor who identified this anomaly that was causing me grief during this phase. Bioelectrical waves were detected using a magnetometer, an instrument used for measuring a magnetic field.

Our heart is an electrical organ, and a powerful one at that. The bioelectrical energy of the human heart is at least a half time more powerful than our own human-computer, our brain. The electromagnetic energy field surrounding our body can even be detected using the magnetometer and will detect our energy field up from around two-to-five-feet away. If you were to take an average voltage meter as I did, holding each of the two probes between the fingers of each hand, and place the setting of the voltmeter to the milli-volt scale, you will detect voltage well under a volt while watching the milli-volts climb up and down.

---

[18] Popp FA, Nagi W, Li KH, Scholz W, Weingartner O, Wolf R. Biophoton emission. New evidence for coherence and DNA as source. Cell Biophys. 1984,6:33–51

[19] Popp FA, Quao, G, and Ke-Hsuen, L, (1994) "Biophoton emission: experimental background and theoretical approaches." Modern physics Letters B,8.

This oscillation is caused by our body's electrical impulses. I was reminded of this years later when an external maintenance team had to enter the inner chambers of my-own displacement (heart) pump as earlier described. Our body sends out light waves in the form of frequencies and amplitudes, and our personal information is within these waves. It has been explained by those much smarter than me, that the encyclopedic information, our individual blueprints stored within our cells are contained within these waves.

Let's explore how this information of our body interacts with our building's material-workings – the particles that make up our buildings which through the weeks and years have developed within the outer and inner areas of our building. This is the inner personality that we feel and at times see.

In 1905 Big Al proposed that light was composed of discrete particles, that energy of electrical current should vary according to the frequency—or color—of the incident light, not according to the intensity of the light. This was Big Al's Photoelectric effect.

American physicist Robert Millikan later independently proved Big Al's photoelectric theory correct. Big Al received the Nobel Prize in 1921 and Millikan received his in 1923. However, it was neither Big Al nor Millikan that called these particles of light – photons. This credit would go to Berkeley USA physicist Gilbert Lewis in 1929, where he would coin Big Al's photoelectric theory as the photon. Alright, but before I fill you in on how we possess a means to communicate with our buildings and how these structures seemingly communicate with us, I will need to explain what a photon is in an attempt for you to understand its' importance.

A photon is a packet of electromagnetic radiations of energy made of sub-atomic particle properties and wave properties. In short, it's the light that radiates from the nucleus of an atom, created when an electron from a cell makes a quantum leap inside of an atom. However, the light from a single photon is so small that it cannot be seen by the human eye. This is because at least

9 photons would have to arrive at the same time within one-hundred milliseconds for our brain to process this light through our human-computer.

Now, just follow me for a moment while we put this together. We each possess around ten-trillion human cells and a minimum of about ninety-two DNA molecules per cell—a minimum of 920 trillion DNA molecules, the equivalent of an umpteen number of human architectural blueprints. Let's coin this the Popp factor because Dr. Fritz Albert Popp discovered that there are a thousand photons per DNA molecule. We call these biophotons. These are photons of light which are stored in our DNA cells. Remember, a photon radiates light that we cannot see through the naked eye. As the founder of the International Institute of Biophysics in Neuss, Germany, Dr. Popp is the inventor of (what is known as) the biophoton theory, and had coined the term biophoton which refers to *coherent photons* (of light) *emitted from biological organisms*, such as humans. Humans emitting light. I emit light. You emit light. The math would indicate that we, therefore, can produce a minimum of 9.2 quadrillion photons—an astronomical number of biophotons regularly produced by the human body. Dr. Popp conducted research that confirms and proved the existence of these biophotons.

These particles or energy of light have no mass, meaning they are free-flowing and not attached to any cell, but transmit information within and between our own human cells. A Photon is light and therefor anything that travels the speed of light cannot have Mass, because no Mass or object can move at the speed or faster than the speed of light. Basic Einstein—excuse me, big Al.

Dr. Popp's work reveals that DNA in a living cell store and releases photons creating biophotonic emissions. Meaning, humans transmit or radiate and regularly leave behind millions or billions of these described biophotons simply by touching the side of a building, leaning against the inside of an elevator or doorway, or spreading our individualized photons throughout a building year after year. We can spread our own and unique biophotons around wherever we travel, whatever we touch. When we stand after sitting in a chair, your light signature remains on the chair. However, and according to Dr. Popp, these biophotonic emissions of ours remain only for about thirty days, but the atoms remain in a different state, ready to intermingle with the next live biophotonic experience.

On a number of occasions throughout my career, I remember leaving the offices of each project assignment or place of employment while feeling mixed emotions of sorrow and sadness surrounding past events and incomplete tasks, to joy and happiness from successful accomplishments and new friends. Those offices which I had returned to within a day or week to collect belongings, I would experience lingering emotions. Yet, when I had found myself for one reason or another returning to more than one of these offices beyond a year or two later, the emotional bond was missing, replaced with mere memories. Was this because my biophoton emissions had dissipated, had stopped communicating with the building's inner atomic structure? Does this indicate that when I frequented these buildings daily, I developed a bond, a connection, supplying the building with a continued diet of biophotons? Was I emotionally or physically attached to this place?

In point of fact, there is such a term as Place-attachment. It is the emotional bond between person and place and is the main concept in environmental psychology. The research indicates that there is a substantial amount of research devoted to defining what makes our place, our work environment, or building *meaningful* enough for place attachment to occur. Little is known about the neurological changes that make this type of structure or place attachment possible, where environmental psychologists have been identified as having an exaggerated focus of the social aspects and where there have been difficulties in measuring this type of attachment over time. I think this is where Dr. Popp's work in the field of biophysics is separated from the environmental psychologists. Or does this indicate that these two disciplines are now just starting to come together to reveal what place attachment is actually all about?

If you believe this is rather bazaar, what if I were to show you that these light signatures, these biophotonic emissions have the ability to interact with those produced by our buildings.

Buildings Are People Too™

Nikola Tesla is the inventor of the first alternating current (AC) motor and known as the father of AC and transmission technology within the United States. Tesla is the reason alternating current exists, where electricity in the form of electric power is found within the electrical outlets that we plug our appliances into our U.S. homes each day. But Tesla once explained: *In no way can we get such an overwhelming idea of the grandeur of Nature than when we consider, that in accordance with the law of the conservation of energy, throughout the Infinite, the forces are in a perfect balance, and hence the energy of a single thought may determine the motion of a universe.*[20] Speaking of the energy of our thoughts, Tesla was a man ironically born during a lightning storm, and was clearly a visionary way ahead of his time, where he believed the universe was a mass of energy vibrating at different frequencies,[21] instead of merely made up of solid objects. As earlier discussed, these energies are found within the various atoms of the building materials that we use to erect our structures, our place.

---

[20] Address at the Belgrade train station (1 June 1892), Nikola Tesla Museum (Belgrade, Serbia).
[21] Experiments with Alternating Currents of Very High Frequency, and Their Application to Methods of Artificial Illumination (20 May 1891)

The air we breathe primarily contains nitrogen and oxygen, and these gases have there-own atomic numbers, there-own live atoms. Photons are light that are produced when excited within the atoms of buildings, people, or the air we breathe. The air we breathe-in is alive—it's living.

Photons vibrate too, and you will come to understand how the photon is so critical as a means in communicating with the structures we build. We have seen that photons are light energy, but they are also emitted when electrons of an atom vibrate, as described over a hundred years ago by Tesla and more recently by big Al and Dr. Popp. These photons travel as a sloping or diagonal wave. As a photon tries to pass through any type of mass, you, me, a building, it runs into the atoms of that mass, and the electrons within the atom vibrate by the energy of the photon striking them. As an example: all waves are created by some type of vibration, and these vibrations can cause a disturbance within the substance that becomes the source of the wave, like the wall or door or floor of a building. But let's say water is one of these substances because any mass can be a substance. Water waves can form when you throw a rock into a lake, and this disturbance causes the affected surface and depth of the water to vibrate. In any event, this vibration then disrupts the water, creating waves. Photons vibrate their way into our structures and can certainly intermingle with our body's biophotons which have attached themselves to the walls and doors and chairs within our buildings. An entanglement of intelligence.

In quantum physics, entanglement is a term used when a pair of atom particles, sometimes called twin particles, perform the exact same function as the other. When particles are entangled, any action performed on one particle or by one particle instantaneously affects the other, indicating they share the same existence. That's right, the same existence! Understand, this twin group of entangled particles lose their individuality and both behave as a single entity. It is called the EPR paradox, announced in 1935 and named after its discoverers big Al Einstein, Boris Podolsky, and Nathan Rosen. It is said Big Al called this phenomenon "spooky action at a distance"[22] when making this observation. No one knows how this intelligent entanglement takes place, hence big Al's spooky terminology.

Over 60 years later, on July 25th of 1997[23] at the University of

---

[22] Letter to Niels Bohr, a Danish physicist, Einstein called it spukhafte Fernwirkung: a "spooky remote effect".

[23] MBWJRB2YO

Geneva, the twin photon experiment was conducted to understand this spooky action. Physicists took a particle of energy, a photon, and split it into two separate photons so that they would achieve the equivalent of identical twins. These photons were identified as the twin photons. These two identical photons were next placed into a detector device that was connected to two fiber optic cables, where each cable traveled seven miles each in opposite directions. Each of these twin photons was next inserted into these cables and propelled in opposite directions, each traveling to the end of each cable. This action placed each of the twin photons 14 miles away from each other. Physicists next made a change to one photon and learned that the second photon, fourteen miles away, experienced the exact same change simultaneously, with no delay. These mysterious communications, if that's the proper term, continued with every experiment that was performed on the photon. It was like a different form of Zeno effect style of intelligence, where to this day no known explanation has been found. How were these twin photons communicating? Remember, big Al showed that there is nothing faster than the speed of light, yet these two photons knew what the other had done instantaneously, faster than the speed of light. Using an atomic clock, physicists determined through the time it had taken for the one photon to affect the movement of the second photon was zero, it had taken no time. Time was instantaneous, non-measurable between these twin photons. These physicists came to the conclusion, that the twin photons did not communicate in the conventional sense, but rather their energies remained entangled, now known as *quantum entanglement*. An action taken against one of these photons was the same as being taken against both simultaneously. Big Al's spooky remote effect. Although big Al believed that matter can never reach the speed of light, these twin photons showed that when matter is initially connected, it remains connected through an unknown energy, regardless of the distance. You should remember that these are real experiments performed by real physicists. There is a field of energy that connects all forms of matter, and it appears logical that the connection to our built environment is even higher, where the structures we build are the very duplication of our body's organic structure. Our synthetic structures are entangled beyond our current way of thinking because, thanks to Dr. Popp, we now understand the interactions of biophotons and their light signatures left behind, their auras, their existence interconnecting with the very photons that are incorporated within concrete, wood, glass, and more belonging to our synthetic structures.

Humans are beings of energy. Just look at the billions of biophotons each of us possess within the cells of our body, and the billions of photons more we leave on everything we touch. Dr Popp has attested to all of us as beings of energy, and equally so we have created the synthetic designs of our built environment. Our buildings require a variety of systems necessitating synthetic energy to operate. However, can the photons within our human atoms, biophotons, become entangled with the photons which make up the structure of our buildings?

Experimenters in Israel showed that they can entangle two photons that don't even exist at the same time, and they accomplish this with a scheme known as entanglement swapping. The atoms within our human structures and our built environments have intelligence beyond our understanding. They mimic each other instantaneously and when you try to observe them through the naked eye they stop moving as discovered through the Zeno effect. I think if Nikola Tesla were attempting to explain this type of consciousness, it may read something like energy radiating from your hand, an aura, and your mind mutually energetic with the vibrations of the building that provides that psychological attachment.

How would photon separation be experienced when the photonic mass of your body transports to another place? While sleeping in your bed to—let's say the Star-Ship *Enterprise*. You feel like your body is made up of fine sparkling soda bubbles, more like an effervescence of photons held together only by the sheer control of your own will. You're trying desperately to keep from separating into billions of reflecting particles until you awake and find your heart racing. You lay completely still, remaining immobile for a period of time, while not moving a single muscle to make sure each piece of your cellular mass has molded back into you. After some time, you take a chance to move ever so slowly until you realize with a deep sense of relief that you're whole again.

We learned earlier of Descartes' belief that the human body could hypothetically—in a mechanical sense—function after death. He made this clear by noting that a dead body is physically capable of performing all the functions of a living one, but it will not since it is missing its driving force, where the driving force he referenced was its' soul. Aristotle's notion of a soul was as a source of self-animation, although Descartes adds to Aristotle by attributing the soul only to humans. It is more than ironic that a 15th-century philosopher and mathematician 300 years removed from Dr. Popp's discovery of biophotons would possess a firm belief of some form of consciousness. Did Descartes' receive some second sense or biophotonic emission from a corpse, or was this simply Descartes' postulating a theory?

Lest we forget, our building materials are made of live atoms, or from an atomic number taken from a living organism. Concrete, treated wood, or even glass are types of non-organic Mass. When our biological body loses its' driving force as explained by Descartes, it can no longer function, it is no longer alive, but what about our building materials. Can our human body still function after death? I would think not, where functionality can no longer be accomplished. On the other hand, has its' biophotonic energy been transferred or repurposed as our first law of Thermodynamics would indicate? Are the structures we maintain and manage made of intelligent matter? or is this talk about buildings being alive metaphorical. Each of you can answer that question independently, but from where I'm sitting, the answer is yes.

In this brief and only scientific language excerpt, the variation of effective *atomic numbers* of three types of concretes (typically used to build structures) containing different amounts of pumice mineral has been investigated by using scientific μ/ρ data obtained from XCOM code library at 1 keV — 100 GeV *photon* energy range. *Zeff* values were calculated by a method named as the *Direct Method* which consists of the application of the following practical formula[24] where *Zeff* is the positive nuclear charge that is experienced by an electron:

$$Zeff = \sum fiAi(\mu\,\rho)\,i\,i \sum fiAi\,Zi\,(\mu\,\rho)\,i\,i$$

The neutrons and protons within the human cell communicating with the neutrons and protons of our built environments—through our intelligent biophotonic auras, attach us emotionally and I would say through our thought processes to our buildings, and may very well physically attach our buildings to us by way of bio photon matter. Space, time, energy, matter, and biological life, are all part of a universal consciousness – where all matter is part of a conscious living universe. However, time is eliminated when now taking into account an intelligent quantum entanglement while interacting with an intelligent Zeno effect. Our buildings possess an intelligence that some of us recognize. We don't know how to understand it, it's just a recognition we appreciate. We know the needs and wants of our building. We know what makes it tick. It's a feeling we check regularly while walking through our facility.

Slowly removing yourself from the physical object, from

---

[24] S R, Manohara, Hanagodimath, S M Hanagodimath, Gerward, L, 2008/02/01, SP-388, EP-402, Energy dependence of effective atomic numbers for photon energy absorption and photon interaction: Studies of some biological molecules in the energy range 1 keV-20 MeV – JOUR Medical Physics, Vol 35, 10.1118/1.2815936.

matter, in order to develop an awareness or perception toward an acute consciousness of your building's contents, it's anatomy. You are replacing matter, the physical structure, with a consciousness derived from these biophotonic swapping's and communications. You're already cognizant of the issues surrounding your building's inner workings and sensitive to its shortfalls that can and have caused failure. You know your building, that's a given. It's that sixth sense you have, we have, in understanding our building's operation and its needs.

Photons are intelligent energy. We are all beings of energy. We all possess live atoms that contain photons similar to the live atoms within the concrete pathways we walk on, the steel and wooden doorways we enter, the glass windows we see through, and the structures we build. These are the very live atoms that make up the minerals within our organic bodies, that immediately stop when we look to observe their movements and the same atoms which reveal additional intelligence through entanglement. Yes, buildings are people too!

As a scientist, I believe Nature is a perfect structure,
seen from the standpoint of reason and logical analysis.[25]
—Albert Einstein

---

[25] To Raymond Benenson, January 31, 1946. Einstein Archives 56-505.

CHAPTER 5

Utility Management vs Energy Conservation

If you operate your building properly, energy efficiency happens automatically.

When receiving an assignment for a due-diligence review, an equipment systems audit, or to find a solution to a longstanding problem, your priority should continually be to understand the building's energy systems and consumption, the electromechanical systems that provided it with the means of movement and that allows the edifice to carry out its primary operational and life-sustaining functions. Second, how the building uses this energy. It is within these areas that you can learn how the complete building operates along with its operational efficiency. Was the structure only five or six years old but acting like an elderly person? or was it a vintage building acting as a youngster because it incorporated state-of-the-art systems? This information can reveal your efficiency baseline, a building's level of maturity and intelligence and the type of facility you're dealing with. Large and small companies, although liking the results of the written reports, can easily attribute these efforts as assessing their facility's energy management or energy conservation, although in reality their understandings are mistaken—because they are derived from a facilities management and real estate profession that follows talking points taken from the energy sector. The important piece corporate leaders typically overlook, is that the facility's energy systems are a major but single component—of several components that are required for a complete operation of a structure, any structure. You can live temporarily in a Mayan cave without electricity because the shelter components are present. The energy components can be introduced separately, such as fire for heat and light. It is when you combine all components that determine the complexity and operation of the shelter or facility.

Finally, as a means of artificial nature and a structure that mimics the human body, I wanted to understand the systems that were used which brought this edifice to life. To me, this was not unusual, where the human body carries out its primary operations through the nutrients that we consume that are turned into energy. When it comes to the management of our facility, energy is the name of the game, and how our building uses that energy is key. Heat energy in the form of electrical or mechanical can cause our structure to heat up by increasing the speed of its molecules. It's, therefore, incumbent upon us to keep our building calm and operating smoothly.

What is Energy

Electricity, water, or any of the fossil fuels alone are not energy, but when you create motion, using any of these as a power source, you can create energy. As earlier discussed, electricity is used to create energy within our mechanical creations, and electricity is present within our human bodies as stimulation for our muscles, where our muscles are the body's engine.

As a prelude to understanding our development and use of energy, we look at the efficiency of our powered machines. Why is our utilization of power measured by efficiency? Why can't we just turn on a machine and expect it to operate perfectly? In the 1970s a German engineer, Dr. Fritz Kortegast, leader of research and development of Mercedes-Benz revealed that the highest efficiency obtained from their most efficient engines of the time, achieved only around thirteen percent efficiency of the total energy input.

Imagine, it took one thousand watts of power to produce forward movement for a 130-watt engine. The remaining 870 watts were lost through heat dissipation. Although today's efficiency is quite higher with the utilizing of various electronic technologies, our intelligence has non-the-less developed energy systems that are not self-sustaining, but rather self-defeating. In comparison, a 200-pound human machine with a forward movement of five miles-per-hour produces around 205 watts of power, and with a fuel input of around 288 calories. Nature's machine versus our mechanical creations. Add this human-machine to a bicycle and you have a flexible motor, a human, burning calories from its fuel, and powering this two-wheeled vehicle measured in watts of power.

In retrospect, the best efficiency that a typical boiler and furnace system can achieve for heating a building is anywhere between sixty-five and eighty-five percent. How can this be? We have created an inefficient reproduction of nature. When we implement programs to achieve energy conservation, in part we are reducing the length of time a furnace or building's heating system operates. This procedure is designed to produce savings from the reduced amount of fuel or energy used. Our efforts in energy conservation have us turning the lights off when not in use, and adjusting room temperatures within our buildings in order to use less energy from the operation of our heating and air-conditioning systems. But we don't focus from a naturalistic viewpoint on the design and operation of the systems that produce our artificial environments. We don't even troubleshoot at the component level. If we were somehow given miraculous permission to manage nature's outdoor climate, we would probably be arranging for an unscheduled eclipse of the Sun every time the out-door temperature became too hot.

On the other hand, nature constantly finds a way to survive, reproduce, and flourish. Its normal behavior is one-hundred percent efficiency. When nature is confronted with an issue, it has a mechanism to resolve the problem. For instance, when nature's human-computer, the human brain, suffers a short circuit or wiring problem, such as a mini-stroke or TIA, short for Transient Ischemic Attack, the human-computer has the ability to go around this affected part of the brain. The human-computer, nature, finding a way to re-route around the problem, while simultaneously sending a warning to the human-machine. Nature protects and sustains itself and continually evolves its safety mechanisms. Whereas, unless our systems are developed within the confines of America's NASA space program, today's artificial Nature in the form of artificial intelligence falters and fails with little to no independent analytical support. This is defined as consumer electronics finding a way to be economically profitable. Nature has no economic constraints and therefore has natural freedom of efficiency. Our building's brain or Direct Digital Control (DDC) systems just do not incorporate this humanistic re-routing capability, where they instead default to a fully open or fully closed scenario of systems. Our mechanistic creations have not sustained as efficient on their own. Nature requires no warranty, where artificial nature evolves from our human intelligent designs filled with limited guarantees. Whether we like it or not or believe it or not, nature is our main guide and blueprint for our building's designs, but most importantly, toward true efficiency.

The Human Genome Project has enabled us the ability to develop a biological blueprint for every human body. We have the same capacity to develop a blueprint for our human bodies as we do for our humanistic buildings. Well, almost. After all, how much of the genome do we truly understand? Caution must be the rule of thumb, where we must be resigned to a reality that there are no two things identical in nature. The reasoning is because we cannot possibly duplicate such a constant change and transformation we witness daily just outside our window, or through a biological microscope. Nature's components or mode of operation are never naturally duplicated. That is right, naturally duplicated. Therefore, our job is to come as close to duplicating nature's workings using a synthetic approach. Using our progress from the genome project, our future can comprise of using our body's blueprint to critique our building's designs.

Big Al believed that nature is the embodiment of the simplest conceivable mathematics. Looking at this from nature's viewpoint, one hundred percent efficiency, therefore, equals nothing, because nature's normal behavior is an unknown constant of true efficiency. This is the form of measurement we too should use. This is very achievable because buildings are humanistic machines, and as a part of nature, we too are a self-sustaining natural machine, as opposed to those wondrous mechanical duplications we have created in the form of buildings. The only coincidental component is the cycle of survival, where buildings depend upon man to survive, we depend on other forms of nature for our survival, and Nature's survival depends upon its self-sustaining ecosystem. It only stands to reason that we should mimic an efficient self-sustaining system. In reality, I should point out that nature's stability depends upon its intelligent counterpart, that would be you and I, to behave.

Remember, in moving as close as possible to nature, we start to recognize simultaneous events, and such events looked upon from one point of reference are not necessarily simultaneous when viewed from another reference point. Namely, nature believes one- hundred percent efficiency equals nothing. Whereas, we look at nature as an entity or system which performs tasks that all lead to a certain efficiency number. additionally, our observation with our mechanical controls in-hand has us believing that efficiency is achieved by reactively keeping up with our mechanicals. This belief of ours has not been realistic, because, in the end, we have not achieved the same result as a natural system but rather, that of a synthetically created reactive prototype. We cannot continue practicing to be reactive toward our building, because we are naturally blinded by false economics and other issues unrelated to our building's needs and wants. Nature does not have or depend upon a bank account or profit margin. Your building is an extension of yourself, an interactive partner and requires you to be interactive, not a doctor, asset manager, or facility engineer, waiting for an injury or breakdown to happen. Yet some may think both nature and our human survival depend upon each other. I think not, since we too are a part of nature, made of mass particles and photons the same as the leaves of a tree or the legs of a mammal, just ask Descartes. Descartes' human machine is the intelligence that links all of nature and our mechanical creations, morphically joining the two. Nature has a tendency to rebalance her environment with her various weather features, and our human interference with nature's harmony and balance only interferes with our own survival. It is therefore in the best interest of our synthetic climates within our man-made structures and in turn our economics to move our building's design and operation closer toward nature's perpetual motion. This perpetual motion includes following the natural, not unnatural functionality of the human body. Inherently, this mode of operation will move us closer to nature's efficient model – one-hundred percent efficiency. Soon, you will visualize and understand how this will reduce your operational budgets, but moreover, require us to spend fewer dollars on the maintenance and natural operation of your buildings.

Our Buildings Unified Energy Source

During the summer season in the north and throughout the southern states of America where warm weather buildings congregate, millions of cooling-tower-cells are activated producing sweat gland relief for our buildings' body as air-conditioning chillers jog to keep up with nature's outdoor climate. It is important to understand that all machines produce heat, including the human-machine. Mechanical machines that use electricity, such as hermetic or semi-hermetic air-conditioning compressors, or larger centrifugal type chillers that produce chilled water for air- conditioning entire buildings, use energy in watts as a unit of measuring electrical power for the rate of energy produced or consumed. When you read your building's electric meter, it is in kilowatts per-hour or KWH. In contrast, the human-machine has a variety of muscles that turn energy into motion. This amount of motion, or momentum, was first described by Descartes'. Your muscles are the engine that propels the human machine, with the heart muscle pump circulating life throughout our human structure. Muscles are the epitome of efficiency when burning fuel into motion. The amount of heat or energy it takes to raise the temperature of one gram of water 1 degree Celsius or 1.8 degrees Fahrenheit is one calorie. How we enjoy burning calories. The mechanical and human machines can be seen as unified where one calorie equals 4.184 joules, and one watt is one joule per second. Since you asked, I will simply conclude without detail that a Joule is a common unit of work or energy used in the physical sciences. For years we have associated calories with food, but in reality, calories relate to anything containing energy. A gallon of gasoline, for instance, contains 31,000 calories. The number of calories within a piece of strawberry cheesecake can light a sixty-watt light bulb for around one-and-one-half hours.

With this in mind, we could realistically calculate the number of calories our furnaces or even automobiles burn. Our bodies burn the calories within the foods we digest through metabolic processes, far more efficient than our natural gas-fired furnaces burn fuel to produce heat energy. In retrospect, we can compare the mixture of fuel and oxygen for operating your vehicle or the atomization (fuel/oxygen mixture) of our building's oil or natural gas furnace to the final stage of metabolizing our human fuel, which reacts with oxygen to release our cells' stored energy. So how many calories do our cells need to function? The Basic Metabolism Rate, or BMR, is the amount our body needs to operate at rest, or as our body idles. Your building's gas-fired furnace also displays in gallons-per- hour along with your building's electrical usage of your systems in kilowatts per-hour. Nature, synthetic nature, our units of measure for calculating our efficiency are the same. Energy is defined as the ability to do work, and as human machines, we produce energy to survive. Our buildings too need energy to survive in the form of power produced by our mechanicals, and this power is measured in watts. When our mechanical machines operate, they produce energy, and when we walk down the street or jog in a marathon, we produce energy. With energy comes heat, and when it comes to energy production, heat is the enemy.

Our building's regulatory systems are the heating and cooling systems. These are the high energy systems that will cause it to become too hot, too cold or just right. Personally, unless there was an underlying reason for a different concern, after reviewing the energy source of the building I would always next look to review the building's cooling system.

To understand the functionality and operation of your building's cooling system(s), you'll want to understand how the system operates. For example, most have had the opportunity of having an air-conditioning unit installed within the window of their home or apartment. However, what most people may not be aware of are the basic components which incorporate this unit, and these four components squeezed into a fabricated metal or heavy- plastic box. The basic components in question are the compressor, the evaporator coil, the condenser coil, and your metering device, which in a number of instances is comprised of some type of expansion valve. Now, there are secondary components within this fabricated box that include a two-pole fan motor that typically acts to blow air through the condenser coil that permits the heat to exhaust outdoors, while the other end of this two-pole motor rotates a fan that pulls air from the indoor room and the outdoors to re-circulate this dual air supply into the indoor room, first going through an air-filter and in-turn proceeding through the cold evaporator coil. Inside the compressor is the motor that compresses the refrigerant gas back into a liquid. So, let's review:

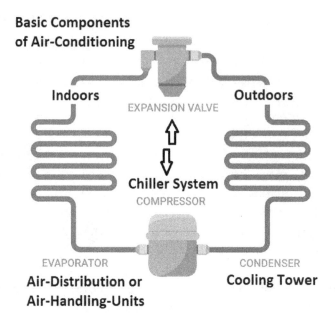

Basic Components of Air-Conditioning

Indoors — EXPANSION VALVE — Outdoors

Chiller System — COMPRESSOR

EVAPORATOR — CONDENSER

Air-Distribution or Air-Handling-Units — **Cooling Tower**

A home window-unit air-conditioner incorporates the same main components and workings as those found within a commercial building.

We have a compressor, an evaporator, a condenser, and a metering device, with a fan motor that gets rid of heat while simultaneously introducing cool air into the room. Fairly straight forward stuff.

Similarly, these are all of the principal components which make up the cooling system for your building, except in your building these components are far larger than those within your typical home or apartment window unit. Most of these components are scattered throughout your structure. In your building, the compressor and metering device are incorporated as a part of your chiller system, your evaporator coil and the evaporator fan incorporate your air-handling-unit/units, where the evaporator coil/coils are protected by any number of filters. Finally, the condenser and condenser fan are your cooling tower. As typical within your downtown office building, large hotel or hospital complex, your chiller, cooling tower, and air handling units, are the main components that make up your building's environmental cooling system. Each of these system components incorporates the primary energy consumption of your building because each of these components integrate high wattage induction motor systems. Now, there are some variables such as whether your cooling system is a water source system that requires chilled water and condenser water pumps or an air-cooled system that brings the refrigerant lines directly to both the air handling unit and a Direct Exchange condenser fan coil, or even a combination of both. Whatever the case may be, these are high wattage systems incorporating high demands on your energy bill. These are the systems that take up a very large piece of your electric energy usage.

However, the air-handling-unit, the respiratory component of your building is a wild-card, because it is used for both the heating and cooling systems of your building. Several variable wildcards can incorporate your building's heating and cooling systems, so please look at this analogy as to how your building uses energy.

Remember our earlier discussion where we indicated how energy produces heat and energy is measured in watts, and where it is this wattage that makes up your electrical consumption. Therefore, the name of the game is to keep your chiller from spiking the demand cost while consuming less operating energy. Also remember, if your systems are managed properly, energy efficiency happens automatically, so don't complicate the noncomplicated. Our goal is to make sure that a number of these variables are managed properly. These variables range from the static pressure of your air-handling-unit that is affected by the condition of your air-filters; the cleanliness of your cooling tower water that affects the amount of heat that your cooling tower is able to remove—hold, and disperse, and how your *demand-level* is either set or operated. All of these systems combined determine the length of time the fan systems of your cooling tower operate and air-handling-units run. They determine how long it takes for your chiller or heating furnace to become satisfied and in-turn shutdown. This is the management of your building's systems and energy utilities. It is also where your predictive and preventive maintenance programs along with your operational strategies come into play. This is how you provide for the health of your facility and the method used for managing your systems properly. This is energy management 101.

Your body's metabolic rate is the speed at which your body expends energy. When you ingest caffeine, energy-drinks or drugs such as methamphetamines, you speed-up your metabolism. These are ways of forcing your human structure to continue in a motion similar to requiring your chiller and cooling tower to operate beyond their needs. With both scenarios, you are expending energy intentionally beyond nature's or synthetic nature's requirement. In both of these cases, power in does not equal power out.

Our Building in Motion

The equipment and systems that provide life to our structures are energized by the energy that is produced from the power we create through the use of artificial power we generate. How we manage this energy and the systems it feeds determines our overall cost.

Sir Isaac Newton published his three laws of motion in 1687. Newton's laws of motion are the laws of energy because it takes energy to create motion. All energy is in the form of motion and all motion requires a form, a system of energy. Energy in motion can only be changed by Newton's first law.

From my perspective, Newton's second law of motion has been one of the most, if not the most important rule that regulates our actions in managing our building's energy systems. Call me old fashion. This second law of Newton states; that the force acting upon an object is equal to the mass of that object, times its acceleration. Explaining this more simply, Newton is saying, that the bigger the energy we want to change, and the faster such change in energy is occurring, the more force it will take to effect a change of that energy. When our human body suffers from a virus and we develop a fever, our body is increasing our energy by adding reinforcements that produce more heat to address this illness. Yup, we develop a temperature. We take-in (and in some cases) pump-in liquids and medicine to our human structure, the fuel or force which creates energy–heat that addresses that external force in the form of an infection.

What happens to a massive body, like our building, when it is acted upon by an external force, such as the infiltration of heat. Well, let's go back to the operation of our chiller with another thought experiment. Imagine that you have a large centrifugal chiller that is cooling your large building. This chiller is connected to a cooling tower, that by design removes the heat from your building caused from the actions of your chiller. The heat now removed from the building is now contained within the condenser-water that is traveling to the water-cooled or air-cooled cooling tower. When this heated water arrives at the cooling tower the heat is removed in the form of heated vapor, or heated energy and evaporated into the air. What is left is cooler water or a cooler refrigerant that is now returned back to the chiller to start the process again. The more cooling from your chiller that is required to reduce this heat from within the building, the more water or chemical energy it will take to remove this heat. Yes, more energy. The faster we want to remove this heat the larger the cooling tower and cooling tower energy will be required, because the faster the water is cooled the more force it's going to take to change that heated water—to cooler water, or refrigerant to a faster liquid state. Newton is telling us that the force acting upon an object is equal to the mass of that object, times its acceleration. Let's say we have a water-based cooling tower – the larger the volume of water, the faster we can cool down the building. Because cooler water allows the chiller to operate more efficiently. For every temperature-degree increase in your condenser water temperature – above your full load design – can decrease chiller efficiency as much as two to three percent. This is why it is extremely important to maintain an aggressive water treatment program, because if your tower water is not clean, you can lose an additional ten to forty percent in chiller efficiency. Manage your building properly, which incorporates its equipment and systems, and energy efficiency happens automatically.

Imagine the water within your cooing tower is dirty. It's not clean. It's cloudy. Because of this, your water is retaining heat faster and longer. The metallic particulates of this unclean and cloudy water are holding heat that is causing your cooling tower fans to operate faster and longer. Your energy use is now high. Your water is so dirty that it cannot remove heat fast enough, to the point where your chiller is now surging, struggling to remove heat because this heat is not being removed by the condenser cooling tower. There is nowhere for this heat to go. Your cooling system and in-turn building have developed a fever – they're too hot!

As a second alternative, our building is heating up because of a heat-wave affecting our region. We need to cool it down fast in order to make sure we can stop the increase in external temperatures while bringing and maintaining the temperature to a comfortable level. We need to maintain this level of comfort once it is reached. Earlier while discussing Sigi's Boston hotel, I explained how the demand control of your chiller regulates how fast or slow your chiller can reach the desired chilled water temperature. This is a classic example for the use of Newton's second law of motion, because the force acting upon our building, the infiltration of heat, needs to be equal to the mass of that heat, which would be our building's cooling system, times its acceleration, or the speed (demand) in which we are required to cool the building. Adjusting the demand-control up or down will depend upon how fast or slow you wish to cool your building. The best practice would be to formulate a strategy that restricts the use of your demand control and to affect a demand adjustment as little as possible. This is because of Newton's second law of Thermodynamics, different from his second law of motion, where the quality of energy is addressed. It states that as energy is transferred or transformed, more and more of it is wasted.

Cooling Down Our Mechanicals Increases Efficiency

When we run a marathon, or exercise our bodies on a hot day, our body turns on our natural cooling system, our approximate

2.6 million miniature cooling tower cells known as sweat glands. It is this natural cooling system that produces water, which in turn evaporates and generally cools the human-machine. When sweat evaporates from your skin it naturally removes heat while simultaneously cooling your body's temperature. This cooling prevents our body from overheating. If there were a way that we could run a marathon with a simultaneous cool shower of water constantly relieving our body, a mobile cooling tower, our body's efficiency would naturally be at its highest, near one-hundred percent. When we operate a building's air-conditioning chiller system, these machines use massive amounts of energy, and since energy produces heat, where does this heat go? Straight to the building's single or multi-cell cooling tower. Our building's heat-removal process starts at the chiller where it picks up heat that was taken from the chilled water loop. In-tun, this heated water is carried away to the cooling tower. Remember, earlier we discussed that the purpose of a four-component air-conditioning system is to remove heat and what is left is cold. The heat has to go somewhere, so this heated water is repeatedly carried away to a cooling tower. Remember, the cooling tower removes the heat from the water and the cooled water is returned back to this chiller machine for reuse. In mechanical terms, this heat-removal-loop is the condenser-water loop. In both the mechanical and human mechanical world, energy produces heat, and heat reduces efficiency. The more heat the less efficient. The name of the game is to eliminate this heat or keep it as close to proportionate with the machine's non-operating temperature.

Regrettably, our building's mechanicals have not been designed with a proportionate heat removal system. If heat were removed proportionately at the level it is produced, our mechanicals efficiencies would mimic nature's efficient design. Viktor Schauberger named our method of generating power, using combustion and hot fission, as *coercion-chemistry*. What a terrific term. Our mechanicals and especially air-conditioning chillers use heat and pressures along with compound refrigerants to produce a cooling source for an artificial cooling environment. Just the opposite is nature, where such pressures and high temperatures are seen only when our earth is relieving stresses. Nature is a system of attraction between opposite north and south polarities along with a variety of charges and reciprocal suction designs. Let's face it, from the most simplistic view, inside our artificially created environments—our buildings—we find heat rising to the top. Whereas, the higher you ascend from the earth the cooler the air becomes. Nature's environment in contrast to our artificially created environment displayed in their actual opposite forms. The heat produced from our mechanical's operation should be proportionate to its cooling, or at the very least, equal to its surrounding ambient air-temperature. For every action, there is an equal and opposite reaction. Nature requires balance and with balance comes efficiency. This is the reason, for when you manage your utilities properly, energy efficiency happens automatically. Realistically speaking, energy management isn't shutting off your lights when not in use, that's energy conservation. Fifty years ago, tasks we now refer to as energy conservation were tagged as neglect. *Hey, Wayne don't forget to shut off the lights!*

It is said that big Al once stated: *Everything should be made as simple as possible, but not simpler.*[26] I like this saying in particular because it enunciates the principle of Occam's razor. In order for our building's mechanicals to have balance, to become naturally efficient, the heat produced from our mechanicals must be supplied with an equal and opposite cooling. The simplest I can express big Al's theory is efficiency = equals Output/Input. Efficiency = equals H (Heat Produced) + plus C (Equal Amount of Cold) divided by 1 + plus HC/Speed of light squared (Time). This is probably one of many reasons I prefer a free-calculating method.

So, who are the people that claim that power in equals power out, in a direct and in the most basic violation of thermodynamics? Should we really believe that a physicist's claim that power in equals power out is one-hundred percent efficiency? In the real world, nothing is one-hundred percent efficient, because of our

---

[26] Appeared in Reader's Digest in July 1977, with no documentation and no source provided.

friend – entropy. No matter how much you try practicing in an efficient way to get work out of a system, you can never get as much power out as you put in because there are always losses. It's how much of a loss you sustain that determines the efficiency of your building's operation.

Energy of a Nature-Merge

Reflecting back to 1991, during the Summer seasonal months, a famous Boston hotel suffered from high energy costs when compared to newer buildings of its size. However, most older buildings do. Flashback around 1926, when the Boston Ritz-Carlton was built. An older Grand hotel just down the street, the Copley Plaza, now the Fairmont Copley Plaza, built earlier in 1912, was having a novel central-air-conditioning system installed. This 1912 hotel would be known as the first hotel in the Country to provide centralized air-conditioning. Boston indeed has a wondrous mechanical history. Back on point and unknown to apparently all, this famous 1926 luxury hotel's economic suffering was a result of having two individual air-conditioning chillers, each dedicated to its independent cooling tower as earlier explained. This was Sigi's hotel. Yes, each chiller had its own dedicated cooling tower to remove its heat. This is not an uncommon design, but one I would never endorse. When the first chiller was called into operation it had its own cooling tower to remove heat, and when the second chiller was activated it too would start and circulate to its own cooling tower. Of course, this was not the only building I would encounter this type of design, but one that has been the easiest to explain. As a recap, these two chillers and companion cooling towers were independent of each other, except that they removed heat from the same chilled water loop, which circulated chilled water throughout the hotel to all of the rooms and restaurants. This chilled water circulation artery was the source for providing cool air throughout the building. Remember, an air-conditioning chiller has two circulating water loops, one to remove the heat from the chiller, and the other to distribute the chilled water it makes to the AHU's and large and small fan coil systems, the respiratory system of the building. Also, remember that the purpose of any air-conditioning machine is to remove heat. For a chiller, heat is removed from the water within the chilled water loop, and what is left is cold water. So, what is the problem with this dual chiller system? Please be mindful that this is not a tutorial in cooling tower problem solving, but rather an example to illustrate how heat reduces energy efficiency within any body, natural or mechanical. Finally, remember the name of the game is to keep these machines efficient by keeping their operating temperatures as low as possible.

When the second chiller is needed, it indicates the first chiller could not carry the load of the building on its shoulders alone any longer and required help. When the second chiller is activated, the load is now shared and the efficiency of both machines in practice becomes equal. So, what's wrong with this? Absolutely nothing if you want your body (your building) to use much more energy to accomplish a normal body temperature. The design and mode of operation works, but highly inefficient.

What had determined the second chiller to be activated? Technically speaking, it was the temperature of the cooling tower water, or the sweat of our building becoming too warm to cool the body. This water had reached its maximum high temperature, while at the same time the chiller machine remained operating at one-hundred percent of its operating load capacity. The cooling tower water could no longer satisfy this chiller, and the chiller would start losing its cooling efficiency unless it received help. This help was the activation of the second chiller? In this particular case, when the outdoor humidity continued to rise to an uncomfortable level, the chiller machine was required to work harder and harder, but the cooling tower—the chiller machine's cooling source— had already reached its maximum high temperature, which in-time caused the chiller machine to prematurely reach its maximum load production. Remember, I said prematurely. Our machine was in a marathon, out of breath, and stopped sweating. The machine had more to give but did not have the ability to cool itself. When the cooling tower starts providing water too hot to cool the chiller machine, the chiller cannot maintain its efficiency or chilled water temperature, and the chilled water that our chiller is producing becomes progressively warmer. Our second chiller machine is now activated, and with two machines now operating at a sixty percent energy load, we find we are operating the equivalent of one machine with an estimated 120 percent energy load. Looking at it from our building's viewpoint, do our bodies use more energy to become cooler? More realistically, why should our building require more energy to satisfy its internal temperature? We obviously have a problem with our building's personality. We weren't providing enough cooling volume or sweat gland cells to our building, not enough water to cool the heat. The cooling tower to each chiller was probably sized proportionately with each chiller, but not sized efficiently for the building's body, making each individual cooling tower too small for this building's application and this building's own personality. Unwittingly, we changed the dynamics of our building's body function to invent a new type of human building. At the time this cooling system was designed, we did not think analytically while keeping in mind that power is using the knowledge you have acquired and applying it properly. Unfortunately, this is a common human design practice that continues within today's engineering, because cooling towers are sized typically between twenty and twenty-five percent higher than a chiller machine's calculated cooling capacity. Why, because we have to account for the heat that is produced by the cooling tower motor, and the various frictions associated with our tower's operation, but we don't account for cooling tower water that may be dirty or older piping that may have become smaller in diameter from neglected water treatment. As engineers, we like playing it safe. Yet, even with this built-in accounting for the extra heat produced, the cooling tower capacity of our system still required more cooling to meet the personality of our building. Our calculations have certainly been derived from a quantum mechanical style of reasoning. Any time our calculations should work or have a high probability to maintain temperatures, we are utilizing statistical chance.

On the other hand, the human-machine, or nature, can adjust and measurably increase its cooling capacity, adapting to its environment. To the point, our calculations are based upon probability, otherwise, why the need to add estimated surplus percentages to our cooling tower capacities? We selected this type of air-conditioning chiller system because we believed it would provide the amount of cooling necessary for our building. We did not properly select this type of system based upon its function or efficiency with the building or compensate for its later age, because there are too many human engineering variables to consider. If we were to analyze how we designed and came to select our building's cooling system, we will ultimately find that our selection process was based upon probability, but also upon false economics.

Components of energy are also relative. A chiller machine's cooling capacity is a major component of our chiller's energy production, and relative to its cooling mass, or cooling tower water volume. Remember, mass is the amount of matter in an object. In this case, the object is water. We therefore also need to provide more time for the volume of water within our cooling tower, so that it will maintain a constant cooling against the heat from our chiller's energy production. Obtaining this additional time is accomplished by increasing the volume of water – the size of our chiller's water supply from our cooling tower. This will allow our chiller machine to reach its full efficient energy output. Water is stabilizing the efficient operation of this chiller, and if we are to believe Schauberger, water is a living substance. In this regard, we could look upon this liquid as a stabilizing fuel. Bear with me for a minute on this one, where I would like to provide a side-bar explanation.

Water produced by a process known as reverse osmosis, and in turn, deionization can remove a substantial portion of electrolytes and all minerals from the water. This water is generally used within the semiconductor industry for its solvent properties and the research industry for its non-bacterial qualities. This is ultrapure water, the highest grade and purest water made, and is known as eighteen- megohm water.

Nature does not provide pure water. What I mean is that the water produced by nature, before it's been handled, of course, is loaded with minerals and nutrients and it is these minerals that are commonly known as dissolved solids. It is unnatural and in a number of cases not health-conscious for water to contain zero minerals. Natural Spring water is an excellent source of minerals for our organic bodies. Nature's water is aggressive, where it dissolves anything it comes into contact with. Now there are times it takes days or months or years, but eventually, nature's water wins. I once was advised by a research analyst at a Boston based research college that water containing zero dissolved solids looks for minerals. If we were to drink water that contained zero dissolved solids the water would find and pull these minerals from our body, and hence the aggressiveness of pure water. Does this make water a living energy? This is the reason research facilities especially require, what is called a TDS (Total Dissolved Solids) meter when removing dissolved solids through the process of reverse osmosis and deionization. The RO/DI process ensures that there are no dissolved ions in the water and that the water has a neutral ph. This water is great for research because it is very easy and efficient to grow microorganisms and bacteria. Because minerals are conductive, such conductivity would contaminate an electronic circuit chip. This is the mandatory reason the microelectronics industry uses pure and ultra-pure water. We should, therefore, remember the difference between naturally pure and synthetically pure water.

Is water a living energy? The next time you buy a bottle of purified drinking water, look at the label and see if it is pure spring water or was purified using reverse osmosis and enhanced with minerals. Do these minerals, these metals, hold and conduct heat within a cooling tower if not removed?

Back from our side-bar, because relativity must apply to all phenomena, mechanical or otherwise, we not only need to incorporate time into our calculations, where time completes the equation for energy but incorporate time also into a major component of energy production – our chiller's cooling tower. Let's get technical for a brief moment – for the highest possible efficiency, we will need to remove the heat energy from the chiller's chemical interaction with the refrigerant, in near proportion to the production of this heat. This is accomplished with a larger volume of cooling tower water that will cause this water temperature to increase at a considerably slower rate in time. This near proportionate heat removal also stabilizes the electromagnetic waves of this motor as seen using Maxwell's Equations.

Now, for the non-technical, nature has a variety of eco-systems. When nature calls for cooling, it directs the northern jet streams or calls in the clouds. If more clouds are needed more are produced. Nature does not limit herself to the number of gallons stored within a cooling tower. Yet by increasing the size of the cooling tower, we provide a larger mass to satisfy our heat-producing machines during the course of the day. Maintaining a near- constant cool water temperatures within our cooling tower creates equilibrium between heat removed from the chilled water loop and the condenser water loop that carries this heat away from our chiller machine. We use cooler water in our cooling tower for a longer period of time. We slow down time (within the energy equation) by providing a larger mass of water. This process creates a nature-merge.

A nature-merge happens when we attempt an instantaneous interaction with nature, or in this case, artificial nature. We are efforting the cooling tower water at a steady cool temperature. If we allow this water to increase in temperature early during the day, we quickly lose chiller efficiency. Although there are no instantaneous interactions in nature, attempting such an interaction provides the highest level of efficiency possible, where nature is one-hundred-percent efficient.

Options – Without getting into the mathematical calculations, by providing a longer period of time for the volume of water within our cooling-tower— to cool its water, we in-turn allow our machine to reach its full energy capacity, and will even obtain extra work from our machine, because the inefficiency of our chiller was based upon warmer cooling-tower water-temperatures. Our chiller will artificially regenerate more energy similar to nature, where energy is the ability to do work. Our humanistic buildings can incorporate a humanistic design by giving it the ability to sweat on-demand, by increasing the cooling-tower water-volume, calculated to meet the personality of the building. What this means, is by combining the two cooling-towers of our luxury hotel, the larger volume of cooling-tower water will take longer to heat up and stay at a cooler temperature, adequate to satisfy the single chiller machine until the end of the day. We will also find a majority of the time that our second chiller will not require activation. This was the procedure used for Paul's Ritz-Carlton hotel in Boston, that contributed to Sigi's energy reduction.

A second option – although not practical and quite anti-nature, having a thermostatically controlled automated water valve activate a second high-volume water-supply that is flooding water into the cooling tower, and by design overflows into the cooling tower overflow drain, maintaining a steady replacement of cooler condenser water for the chiller when the cooling tower is unable to perform on its own. Building owners and managers can try a simple variation of this remedy by merely placing a high-volume water hose into their own cooling-tower. In-turn, your chiller's load will reduce, but unfortunately, not in proportion to your building's personality. This is usually used as a band-aid approach.

What do these examples all provide? Systematically, all provide a remedy to keep one chiller operating longer by synthetically raising a chiller machine's efficiency. We have created a nature-merge. We have moved synthetic nature closer to true nature. We increased and stabilized the level of heat removal. We increased our chiller's level of sweating, modeling its cooling mechanism to a more human level and closer to nature. Remember, energy is heat. If we provide cooler condenser water for a longer period of time, or cooling-tower water that heats up slower, we can get more load efficiency out of our chiller. Heat is expended energy, energy is power, power is watts, and wattage is your electric bill.

The electric meter is only one of our building's vital-sign components that can be read for trending our building's health. It is also the one building utility that benefits twice from the higher efficient operation of our mechanicals, or in this particular case, our chiller's elevated efficiency. Higher efficiency for producing our building's chilled water indicates our chiller machine does not have to operate as long. Why? Because with less time of operation comes efficiency, and time is an important component of any equation involving energy. Remember, energy equals mass times the speed of light times itself, or $E = MC^2$. So, what does the speed of light have to do with this? Simply, treating quantum entanglement separately, there is nothing currently known faster than the speed of light, in our civilization, where it is known as the cosmic speed limit. The faster you move toward the speed of light the slower time moves. If it were ever possible for anyone to travel at the same speed as the speed of light, time would completely standstill. Therefore, the speed of light is used as our constant to measure time. Thanks, big Al.

We now have two types of energy savings, where one is from our chiller machine that is producing a lower condenser water temperature at a longer period of time. This is because we kept our cooling tower water at a constant lower temperature. We kept the heat away and we were rewarded with higher efficiency, or the ability to do more work. The second form of savings is where our chiller machine does not have to operate as long, where its production of a stable cold temperature has satisfied the areas it is cooling, permitting the thermostat in this or many areas to be satisfied sooner rather than later.

The next form of savings comes from the lower condenser water temperature of the cooling tower, wherewith cooler water comes less evaporation, and less evaporation is less water used.

In the case of this luxury hotel, we tied the two cooling towers together by installing a small circulating pump from one tower to the other and doubled our cooling tower capacity. This luxury hotel never ran the second chiller again when outdoor temperatures were below sixty-degrees Fahrenheit with a normal outdoor humidity. We used less energy while providing a quality air-temperature.

What did this mean? In dollars our building's transformation resulted in an annual utility bill savings of around sixty-thousand dollars annually. Sounds like a profit center to me! Within utility dynamics, the health of our building promotes its current efficiency. How well do we understand this efficiency? For me, I always compared the energy efficiency of me.

Have you ever slid a wet glass on a wet counter surface, and when you tried to pick up the glass it was stuck because of an air-tight vacuum that developed? Without this same effect of air-pressure, we would all suffocate. Within each of our enclosed lungs is a low-pressure zone that sustains our pulmonary cavity while allowing our lungs to expand when we inhale and contract when we exhale. Without this limited vacuum our lungs would collapse and we would be unable to survive. Once atmospheric pressure relieves the vacuum of this lung cavity, our biological actions and operation would suffocate. Facilities engineers along with maintenance technicians understand this function when they experience negative static pressure that creates a vacuum within air-handling-units. Try opening the cover of a fan-coil unit where the air-filter is located while this unit is operating, and you'll quickly find it very difficult to open this door cover. The same with large air-handling-units that house multiple filters within a filter bank. These are small rooms where the vacuum is so strong, the entrance door leading to these filter banks are extremely difficult to open without first shutting down the fan system. Picture a displacement pump connected between left and right energy sources similar to our biological heart with left and right lungs in the form of energy cells connected with each other. Air is the source that charges our lung batteries to keep the Descartes machine running, and air is the life source that our buildings inhale and exhaust to sustain our enclosed structures. The fossil fuel that energies our machines cannot operate without air. It has been said, that the study of the interaction among living organisms on the Earth, operating under the hypothesis that the Earth itself acts as a single living organism, always begins with the act or action of an individual organism. Let's suppose we are the individual organism, where if our action happens to help and promote our living environment, it can spread until in time a healthy global civilization results. But the reverse is also true, where species that harshly affect the environment in a hostile way are doomed. Because the earth is a single living organism, other forms of life go on.

From the earth to our created environment, let me reflect on an event from an earlier year. Picture a building engineer following the everyday duties of his or her shift. The shift engineer is notified of a service call indicating that the hotel guest-room of Mr. Jones is too hot. The engineer responds and finds that the room is accurately too hot and proceeds to the wall thermostat, turning the temperature setting down to a lower temperature setting. The guest indicates he has done this already but realized it had gotten a bit chilly and raised the temperature setting back. The polite engineer acknowledges the guest's efforts and indicates he will check back by telephone within, say thirty-minutes. This is because there was no instantaneous remedy available. The building is not in balance that is achieving an instantaneous interaction with nature. Our engineer ultimately learned that a fuzzy logic-based system had its high and low-temperature settings established too close with each other. A human error. The cooling and heating stages were short-cycling back and forth. By the time the heat reached its comfort level the cooling cycle was activated.

Enlightened by our building's vital signs as corresponding to the daily utilities results, our earth's ecosystem and the biosphere that mimics our man-made structures will always be trying to come together until these opposite environments morph into one. It will be at this time when one-hundred percent efficiency equals nothing.

Trans Structural Facilities

A trans-structural facility, I would suggest, is a building stepping beyond its basic mechanical constraints, and to enhance or even replace a building's basic operation with a transhuman-type of technology. This would be beyond a smart-building. Trans-structural facilities would routinely detect harm to its occupants and activate a direct-digital-control system—an AI program that immediately identifies the type of human-condition required to reduce or curtail the harm. This type of intelligence is programmed, by design, to place the decision-making cure in the hands of the human, while we receive intelligent information as to the human condition that is missing from the building that is causing the harm. This is actually a type of opposite to transhumanism.

> ". . . transhumanism is the process of human enhancement that will presumably bring about the desired goal of "posthumanism". The term "trans/posthumanism" covers both the process and the goal of human enhancement. [27]
>
> —Max More

We have understood that Descartes' unique understanding and methodology—his way of thinking in the mechanical world of biology and mechanics has been important for our human foundation of understanding in the operations and intelligence of our human building. From a simplistic position, a transhuman body augments the physical body with the use of hearing-aids and eye-glasses, cardiac pacemakers, hip and knee replacements and dental implants. We have implanted artificial heart valves and implanted prosthetic cardiac support devices. We have the

---

[27] The Unknown Future of Human Enhancement - NY: Doubleday, 2004); Simon Young, Designer Evolution: A Transhuman Manifesto (Amherst, NY: Prometheus Books, ... Max More, Extropran Principles 3.0.

ability to connect artificial lungs in the form of ventilator machines and clean our blood using artificial kidney technologies. But is this transhumanism movement single-minded toward using breakthrough technologies for making our human structures into something more? Are our advanced technologies next looking to create buildings that can instruct us what to do without our ability to over-ride their programmed decision, or worse—programmed decisions based upon fuzzy logic? We have already gone from dental-fillings to dental implants. Do we next install artificial eyes? Will our building's eyes, its security monitors be replaced with facial recognition software that is programmed to determine humans as a particular threat-level? *I guess the computer knows what it's doing!* Could we someday be identified as a virus invading a building—constructing a building that is too human and out of our control?

Three years after Natasha Vita-More published the *Transhuman Manifesto*, in 1986 Eric Drexler published *The Engines of Creation*, which proposed devices "capable of positioning atoms and molecules for precisely defined reactions in almost any environment," Yup—eco-system environments and buildings too! It was the theory of nanotechnology and 'molecular assemblers,' – to assemble at the molecular level. Tens of thousands of nano technology patents belong collectively to the United States, South Korea, Japan, China, and Taiwan. Nano technology is here now. Does this mean a wall or door could be programmed to move or disappear using molecular nano technology? I use this analogy because a transhuman can be someone who has upgraded their body in a way that goes beyond that of a simple repair but that replaces a body-part which works perfectly fine and replaces it to do something more than is biologically possible. This is where I would suggest the conflict begins, where our human biological structure would become more and more out of alignment with the building's original human-modeled structure. Human nature and our buildings as synthetic nature no longer incorporating the same movements that were once in syn with each other. Now, incorporate a fuzzy logic mindset to a trans structural operation that; in-turn, would require our biological body to need more of a transhuman modification for both to get along. As we augment our physical body with more bio-mechanical replacements and upgrades, our buildings would be required to keep up, or else become an antiquated shell compared to their originally intended purpose—to protect and become an extension to its biological inhabitants.

We should be carefully mindful that; to Descartes, nature did not differ from man-made machines, and machines made by craftsmen were no different than our organic bodies. This dualism, as previously discussed, influenced his mechanical interpretation of nature and therefore of the human body.

Computer technologies are advancing simultaneously with biotechnologies. Within the near future, if we are not their already, neural interfaces will link your mind directly to an AI program in order to expand our ability to think. Imagine a brain implant, a memory-chip linked to an AI device or system or network, or imagine converting any one or all of our external senses into electrical signals that the brain then processes into our sensory perception of our surroundings. As earlier discussed, the various electrical routes that travel through our nervous system are no different than those external senses converted into electric signals. These signals would change only in how the brain processes them, and this is why our body's sensors can be restructured using technology. Electrical signals, whether produced by our internal body or produced artificially and externally, electrical signals are electrical signals, period. Now imagine walking into your building and instructing the room you're in—through your thoughts—to turn-on the lights, lower the heat, and turn-on the television—simultaneously. This is not an Internet of Things (IoT) program outlined earlier – where your verbal instructions can command the room—this is a grand nature-merge on a trans-structural level using transhumanism technology. If you take a look at Brain Computer Interfacing (BCI) research you will learn that the first neuro-prosthetic devices were implanted in humans first in the mid-1990s.

> *. . . I am very close to the cutting edge of AI and it scares the hell out of me . . . we have to make sure that the advent of super-intelligence is one which is symbiotic with humanity.*[28]
>
> —Elon Musk

The purpose of this exercise is to make sure that we as biological humans maintain control, so that true-nature and in-turn artificial nature are not over-run by transhuman programs, because, in the end, absolute power corrupts absolutely.

---

[28] Elon Musk discussed his concerns about artificial intelligence and his hope for forming a symbiosis with AI through his Neuralink company at the South by Southwest tech conference in Austin, Texas on March 11th, 2018.

CHAPTER 6

Building Buildings, Renovations and Liabilities

A question always arises when selecting the appropriate staff for your building or facility. Today's property and facility's manager want versatility, a facilities professional that not only can maintain and operate your facility but know what to do when renovations and upgrades are scheduled. The test is whether you would invite a questionably qualified repair person into your home to perform a needed repair? Would you permit a student or dubiously qualified doctor to perform surgery on you? Of course not. You want to validate competency versus cost. In the case of surgery, it may be the only competency without caring about the cost. You spend at least a third of your life in the environment where you work. Therefore, the decisions you make regarding the competency of staff will directly affect your building's health and ability to perform. Do you want to work within a well-maintained facility? Do the facility maintenance and engineering staff know the components and body-parts of your building? The operation of your building is only as good as it's operators and those that can heal the structure during the most trying of times. There is no better test for determining the success of these operative tasks than how your building performs while it is tested during its commissioning process or during a renovation.

I cannot count the number of times a General Contractor (GC) that was overseeing the construction of a new building or major renovation had advised me, that the issue I was raising was not under their jurisdiction. It happens more times than you would like. According to the GC, this issue or that issue had nothing to do with them. The dilemma I always faced if the issue could not be resolved through the GC, is that it had to go back to the architect, electrical or mechanical engineer who designed the systems. During a number of times, this is where the contest only started. Sometimes the controversy entered a dual between the GC and one of his or her subcontractors. Sometimes a number of Requests for Information, RFI's, would fly between the GC and the architect before the GC would demand a change-order. How do you figure all of this out in advance before you learn that your ownership costs have increased beyond a reasonable expectation? How do you protect your building when projects are underway?

At a period in my career, I enjoyed working at a medical and research facility in Boston, Massachusetts, USA. I also remember dodging a bullet during a project when one of the labs ordered a 3000-gallon water tank for a Reverse Osmosis and Deionization RO/DI water purification system. Unfortunately, I didn't see this tank until it had already been placed on an upper floor of the building. The fortunate part is that I did see it before it was filled with water. You see, reinforced concrete slab floors within your typical high-rise office buildings are about four-inches thick and are expected to handle a live-load of around forty-pounds-per-square-foot of weight, or around thirty-PSF for a low-rise residential. Engineers and architects convert this weight into a kip-load. Looking at this empty tank, I was imagining the weight of a gallon of water is just over eight pounds a gallon, times 3000 gallons within this structural frame and slab. Over twelve tons of weight within a small sixteen square foot space. Having more than six-times the weight of a Volkswagen Beetle set within this space was certainly not a situation that would allow for a good night's sleep. Knowing this facility had no program in place to become stronger, I called in an architect to do the load calculations, after all, even though I've performed the math, I wanted a licensed calculation backing me up for when these research professionals called in college administration reinforcements on me for stopping the project. Oh, and did they ever. Try going against a research grant that has already ordered thousands of dollars in equipment without a validated back-up to your claim, and you'll find yourself at the human resources department being handed your final paycheck. In this case, I was fortunate to have rather professionally-minded researchers willing to work the problem. We ended up installing some steel bracing under the floor below. Prior to this, our building was about to be forced to carry an obscene amount of weight on a daily basis that could very well have broken the bones of this building while crippling its skeletal frame. This is not even looking at the human dangers of those tenants working on the floor and the floor below this tank.

RAMBAM Medical Center, the acronym for Rabbi Moshe Ben Maimon, in Haifa, Israel. From left: Stefan, Wayne, Jacob ("Koby") Moskovitz–Director of Operations.

Back in 2016, I was invited to tour a number of hospital facilities in Israel, guided by a former member of the Israel Ministry of

Defense (IMOD), and business associate Dr. Stefan Deutsch, where he had previously functioned as their Director of International Programs and Cooperation in the Directorate of Defense Research and Development (DDR&D). Back in the day, he was involved with certain infrastructure components of the country. As a friend of so many years, Stefan was able to reveal the construction of their medical facilities and the highly unusual requirements for the skeletal structure of these facilities. Unlike the strength of the buildings in Boston, when war conditions become routine the exterior walls of these Israeli structures did not reveal your typical steel-stud framed and stone-hung wall system.

**New building construction on the RAMBAM campus
showing a new herculean concrete-frame structure.**

These buildings incorporate a three-foot-thick reinforced concrete wall construction that leaves room for only a reinforced window system. The floor construction is also impressive with a thickness designed to withstand a collapse from a missile strike. These structures are Hulk construction, designed to maintain the integrity of these herculean structures. This is a building that mimics Hercules on steroids.

Beneath the largest hospital in northern Israel is the Sammy Ofer Fortified Underground Emergency Hospital, the largest underground facility of its kind in the world, and designed to treat 2,000 patients from throughout the northern region. This is a below-grade garage turned into an emergency ward within minutes, where all of the medical gases a hospital requires are installed behind steel panels ready to be used once the automobiles have been quickly and systematically relocated. This is a garage so clean you can eat off the floor.

Although I toured medical facilities throughout Israel, including the Shaare Tzedek Medical Center in Jerusalem, I think the most impressive was this Sammy Ofer fortified underground facility. Our tour guide, Koby, provided us with quite an eye-opening tour of a facility that incorporated an incredible variety of emergency equipment and services, while its size had you think you were still at ground level. With this facility's above and below sea level herculean construction, its High-Efficiency-Particulate-Air (HEPA) filtration has the ability to protect the air of this facility's internal cellular functions, known as the people that run its operation.

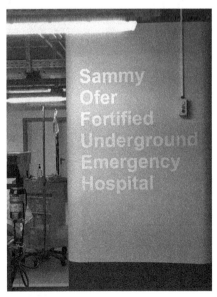

**Entrance sign of the Sammy Ofer
Underground Emergency Hospital**

**View of the Sammy Ofer underground
garage before the transformation**

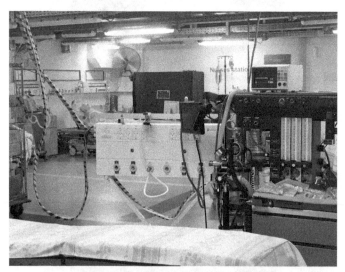

**Touring the Sammy Ofer Underground
hospital after the transformation**

Imagine yourself inside one of the air-handling-units of this hospital. Since most of us carry a microscope in our backpacks – *oh just humor me* – I use mine to examine the filter rack containing the rows of HEPA filters. Each filter must remove at least 99.5 percent (European Standard) or 99.97 percent (US Standard) of particles from the air that have a diameter greater than or equal to three-tenths micrometers. Airborne transmission has been used in certain medical papers to mean transmission by aerosol-size particles of less than ten micrometers. HEPA filtration can remove greater than or equal to .3 microns. Unfortunately, certain mold, volatile organic compounds (VOC's), viruses, bacteria, and small particulates under three-tenths micrometers may not all be captured safely from the air with this HEPA-based system, so there are additional safeguards incorporated into the Sammy Ofer structure for those purposes. This building is an athlete with an immune system that rivals Mount Olympus, Mount Weather, and all of those Mayan cave systems in the basement of our earth.

The contagious isolation room of the Sammy Ofer Underground Emergency Hospital

The buildings within the collective skyline of this Middle Eastern country are not designed with the grace, opulence and majesty that are raised within their neighboring middle-eastern country of Dubai, where those structures are arranged with grandeur into a skyline that echoes with louder internal movements, colors and shapes—arguably louder than Shanghai, Shenzhen, New York, and Chicago USA. For now, the Dabawi people let the world know that this is where the global elite of buildings congregate. However, when it comes to buildings that near-perfectly mimic the survival instincts of the human condition, I have not seen or known of a building that can quite match the combined strength and functionality of the medical facilities found within the State of Israel, synthetic bodies representing grace under pressure, although the core and lower-torso strength of New York's World Trade Center enters as the exception.

A Question of Liability in Building and Project Management

On more than a few occasions, building owners and management companies hire a company or third-party contractor that specializes in managing the building and its' operation. Because managing the building and operating the building can be two different and distinct conditions, the third-party contractor may elect to manage the leasing, housekeeping, appearance care, landscaping, etc., while farming out the maintenance and engineering operations to yet another company. This cross-pollination of the various staff members can be quite trying should the building owner or ownership representative decide to communicate directly with the third-party contractor's maintenance and engineering staff. This creates a situation where ownership is calling the shots directly with staff that actually belongs to their principal contractor. When the time comes to hold this principal third-party contractor accountable, liability becomes virtually non-existent, because the owner or owner's representative is the one that circumvented communication around the company they hired as the responsible party. The building's owner spoke directly with the maintenance and engineering staff of their third-party contractor, yet the company that hired and pays this staff stays quiet—not wanting to alienate the company that hired them. As a result, and now armed with plausible deniability, the owner's principal contractor has inherited no liability. From a contractual position, ownership has assumed responsibility for the actions of the staff that belongs to their third-party contractor.

Facility management and maintenance staff should be very cognoscente of whom they report to, and just what process should be used when they are approached by an owner's representative. Your superior is the one who pays you. No one wants to say no to the owner, and naturally, the owner very much knows it. Communication with your superior is non-the-less a necessity. During complex renovations, I've never been one to be forced into finding a quick solution to a long-time or age-old problem or to permit a superior to instruct me into a solution that was questionable. I enjoy the free form of crafting solutions that match the structure or mechanicals of the building. I rarely paid attention to advice when the solutions offered were made from whimsical guesses—and there was quite a bit of that. I've always used the example of a doctor-patient relationship based on the medical profession's hypocritic oath – using Descartes Rationalism. Descartes Meditations provide an extended study in establishing knowledge through rational intuition and deduction. Descartes was known as a rationalist, and that appealed nicely to my way of seeking knowledge. It was *me* time. A time I took for *me* when I felt ready, and not a time I was told to be ready. It was a time I could not be forced into. I liked to go over remedies that would circle around in my mind, and I needed this time for the thoughts swirling around within my active consciousness to mature into recognizable visions.

The Second Question

The question of liability also has entered into play when a property manager or general manager decides that they want you—their engineering director, chief building engineer, or facility manager, to follow their directive or instruction. From my position, not a problem. However, as I've heard within a comic strip movie on the big screen once or twice, *with great power comes great responsibility.* In my earlier days, which remain relevant today, I found myself in a number of situations where the property manager or GM wanted the control but not the responsibility. The first question I would ask, who possesses the licenses? This is because it is the license holder that bears the responsibility. Once you've been directed by property management to perform a function after you've advised him or her of the negative ramifications, whether licensed or not, you become the laborer and no longer liable to the local or state authority having jurisdiction, or in certain instances the management for the outcome.

Wait, you're saying you're no longer liable because you were simply following orders? Actually, you are responsible for performing the task, but if the task you are performing is, let's say, not conforming to a government code or regulation, you can perform the task up to the point where it becomes, for lack of a better term, illegal. Is it OK to temporarily block an electrical service panel? Only you can answer this question because it depends upon the relationship you have with your executive of upper management. We'll just say no one is authorized or permitted to direct another to perform an illegal act. Unfortunately, it happens more times than we as professionals like to think. A majority of the time its ignorance of the code or regulation, or it's OK because we've been doing it this way for years. Let me fill you in on a little secret – codes are violated every day and for years at a time, all the time. I can walk into any building within any city within America and find a code or regulatory violation. Boxes or a piece of furniture blocking or obstructing the rear stairway entrance or a copying machine narrowing the rear hall passageway are daily classics against the Life Safety code within the U.S., especially if they are obstructing the electrical service panel or breaker panel, a real no-no. Although these are minor examples, they expose the mindset of management's perception of safety. This perception includes contractors we bring in to perform HVAC, electrical, and other trade disciplines for all building projects. The abuse our buildings are subjected to would be a crime if the building was human. The rule of thumb I have always used, I verbally inform my superior of the code violation I am engaged in, advising I will be straightening the problem out within a reasonable amount of time. There, you've provided an intent to straighten-out the problem. In-turn, I send an email to myself documenting the conversation, and all work on the issue thereafter until the work is completed. It shows you're acknowledging the issue while addressing the work in progress. There is nothing better than a paper-trail.

I remember another situation a while back, where I was on the ground level of a major renovation project when I observed one of the project electrician's working in an area that required a safety-harness. The electrician worked for an electric company hired to perform electrical work for the project. I yelled over to him to put his safety harness on, after-all he was on the property I worked for. He yelled back and told me to mind my business. Nice, but a mistake. In my official capacity as a representative of the building owner, my responsibility extends to the property that this electrician was working on. Additionally, a majority of contract agreements for most renovation projects, and especially new project start-ups, contain a clause within their contract documents that provides the property owner or the owner's representative to stop all work during qualifying circumstances, and safety always qualifies. They're all in small print, but they're there! especially if you're using the standard contract form offered by the American Institute of Architects (AIA). Just because an employee is on the payroll of another company doesn't permit that contracted employee to act as he wishes on your property. I stopped the project and barred the contractor from using the ill-mannered and unsafe electrician on the property and project in question. Building ownership possesses liability for all people on his or her property too. The contractor was also warned against any additional intentional safety violations. As typical, the electrical contractor threatened—that this would cause a delay in the project. In-turn, I then reminded him of yet another clause within the contract. You see, an owner can hire another sub-contractor using the original contractor's money if the contractor, in this case, the electrical contractor, does not perform. This is typically within a non-performance clause. I had no reservations calling in another electrician to complete this project. You don't allow a doctor to come into your operating room to abuse your patient, your building. You are the building's advocate and that includes being its bodyguard. I never enjoyed contractors who attempt to tell me what to do or where to go while under my own tent.

During the Winter of 1990, a friend of mine was working on the top of an old low-pressure horizontal return tubular (HRT) boiler. The lighting was so poor within this boiler plant, an additional man, that would be me, was required to hold the flashlight so that he could climb the ladder safely. While on top of this boiler, due to the poor lighting, he didn't notice that the low-pressure safety valve had been leaking for an unknown period of time. This was our new job here in Boston, so John attempted to test this pressure valve as required annually by code. When John pulled the relief lever up on the valve, the side of the valve where the leak had developed blew out and the saturated steam pressure caused my friend the loss of sight with his left eye. It's what accidents do when poor lighting and deferred maintenance to safety equipment happens. When the stomach of this building, its boiler/furnace, was sore, no one was paying attention. Accidents impact the quality of life and not just the life of friends. Family members, the inability to play sports, and who really knows the number of enjoyments will be permanently missed during this lifetime.

Our job as facility infrastructure professionals is to advocate for the building. We are the building's mouthpiece and caretaker. We leave the politics to the politicians. This is because the political aspects are almost always directed around the budget and making the profit margins. Let's put a band-aid on this repair or can we order that part at another time? By the way, the engineering department doesn't need to attend the ownership walkthrough next week. These types of actions are finance-related. They're driven by the activities associated with the decision-making policies of property management or the owner's representative, especially when these decisions conflict with individuals or parties associated with the existing maintenance and engineering budget. The facility engineer's job is to make it work and keep it running while making sure the document-trail associated with the political actions are preserved. These documents will be the validation used in the future when facilities management is later asked - what is needed. It shows a continuity of the engineering operation while validating the original request for these operational parts and repairs.

In time, you find that these validating documents are required because property or asset management has now circled back and asked you what materials or repairs are needed. At times a few of these upper management professionals will question why you continue to make such high-cost requests. This is where control without responsibility is being exercised. You find yourself in a debate, but this is OK. You're the building's advocate, and your turn to show the relative importance of your previous requests, so, make darn sure you are prepared. The building will lose if you're not.

Liability is especially prevalent within the hospitality and asset management industries, where moderately strict budgets and profit margins need to be made. There are a number of times when disagreements develop regarding executive management overstepping the facility engineer's authority concerning safety issues. Every operation that a facility maintenance or engineering professional labors has its own safety code or regulation within North America, and throughout a majority of countries using the international mechanical and electrical codes. The unfortunate complication that rises to the surface is when the boss borrows your authority, and in-turn, you send that email to him or her confirming the directive that you received. *Thank you, Mr. executive, for meeting with me earlier. I will certainly follow your directive regarding the water leak affecting the electrical service panel. I'll be sure to follow-up with you next month as you directed.* If there was any wink-wink confusion during your earlier discussion, the email trail tends to straighten these oversights out rather quickly. Of course, that is not to say that some bitterness may not result. I've known of instances, maybe one in a hundred, where close friends have received their final paycheck within weeks after sending such an innocuous email. Unfortunately, there are isolated times when your superior becomes drunk with power, unable to reel back an ineffectiveness in understanding the problem. This is when the executive is innocently introduced to the local *authority having jurisdiction* to help with his or her education. In some highly uncommon cases, when asset management becomes unreasonably threatening, the engineer's licensing, job security, or code requirements, require him or her to seek legal representation. Hey, sometimes we too need a little help. I meant it when I said – with great power comes great responsibility. It's at this point when the engineer realizes the importance of the email paper-trails since any verbal warning would not have been worth the paper it was written on. These situations never turn out favorable to either side. They're lousy and although the paper-trail typically will provide the former employee with the advantage for either job security or a nice financial settlement, the former employer either takes an ego hit, or hit on the budget, or a rise in the insurance premium from the settlement. These are those secluded instances when finances and profits are substituted with survival. No one wins, and this is why executive management should be good listeners, while the facilities engineer practices his or her communication tactics. Your boss's priorities are your priorities, so long as the boss understands it is your job to make him or her successful. There needs to be a trust between each other. I'll admit, within a full career there has been a case or two where I have found myself in a no-win scenario, a Kobayashi Maru moment. Within these environments your limited option is to just wait a few months while your legal counsel settles your case for a nice payday while whispering to yourself, that those who think they know everything, are annoying to us who do! I'm from the old school and don't like to see buildings and staff abused, so I'm sure my tolerance for patience is far less than where yours should be. Continue your email communication and I think you'll find that you can keep honest people honest.

Both in America and the European Union, OSHA and EU-OSHA are the predominant safety organizations. They act not only as protection for building-staff but also as our buildings' lawyer. Once an employee files the complaint, employment cannot be terminated for filing the complaint. The employee is now protected by the governments of these countries. OSHA in the United States is extremely firm against employer's taking action against complainants or whistleblowers. Additionally, there are situations that can be so egregious that the complaint can be filed after employment termination. In either case, paper- trails are important, but even better, in this day and age of really nice phone cameras and video recordings, a picture tells a thousand words.

There are a number of other countries that provide safety programs for their employees. For instance, the country of Dubai, United Arab Emirates, has a Title Five Safety document, entitled Protection Health and Social Care of Workers, overseen by their Minister of Labor and Social Affairs.

Israel and a number of other countries follow the International Labor Organization (ILO) policies and regulations for employee safety. The International Labor Standards are legal instruments drawn up by the ILO's three-party constituents that consist of the government, the employer, and workers. These standards lay down principles, rights and minimum standards related to work and workplaces. These standards can also be either conventions, which are binding international treaties, or recommendations, which are non-binding.

As for Japan—because of traditional human resources practices, and with the hours a person works per week as opposed to other countries, employee safety standards are ongoing and changing annually. Let's hope so anyway.

Communication of Trades

As a member of management with a facilities engineering department, I was working within a new high-rise construction, when I noticed that the metal door leading to a ceiling-mounted fan-coil unit was blocked by a sprinkler pipe that had just been installed. A pipefitter ran their sprinkler pipe in front of the door that leads to the air-filter to this coil unit. The air-filter to this coil was made inaccessible. Now understand, this is not an unusual occurrence. In fact, this was the second time up to this point in my career I had witnessed such an installation. Another would follow a few years later. You see, the drawings that the pipefitter was following showed this pipe running at this precise location. If the pipefitter had re-directed this pipe to avoid the metal door, the drawing specifications would have been changed. Unfortunately, the HVAC company and the project manager both were not present during this Saturday when the pipe installation was performed. In-turn, the drawing was followed. You may say this was a trivial excuse, but actually, it wasn't. There are codes that require a limited number of angles and turns a pipe can take because of the fluid dynamics and design of the particular system. The pipefitter is not an engineer, and not expected to be one. He or she followed the drawing.

I received excuses of this nature each time communication issues arose. These were legitimate excuses, except for one minor detail. The contract documents almost always include, what is called a *communication of trades* clause. This requires the builder to make sure that he or she communicates with all of the trades that are building the facility during construction or renovation of the project. Finding this faulty installation, the inability for maintenance to be performed later on this fan coil, showed a failure in communication. It's almost similar to a doctor leaving a small sponge in your chest cavity after an operation of your pulmonary system. The sponge can ultimately cause breathing complications and its very costly to fix the trouble. Here it's the financial cost that causes heartburn when the project manager of the construction company has to now haggle with the HVAC contractor and the pipefitter to determine who will need to move their installation.

The Certificate of Insurance

If ever there was a tool I frowned on the most, it was the phone call to the insurance company that was insuring the project for the contractor. It was like calling the medical board to file a complaint on your doctor. It was activating a claim on the *certificate of insurance*. You knew once you did it the relationship between you and your contractor would never be the same. However, these calls, if required, are not made until the end of the project anyway, so I suppose you can live with it for the remainder of the close-out portion of the project.

Typically, around ten to twenty percent of the project cost is withheld at the end of the project to make sure certain and specific details from a punch-list have been performed. There are those times you learn that the funds withheld are not sufficient to complete the work in question, and the contractor is aware of this, and this is when the fight begins. There are a number of controversies from change orders that the architect had previously determined should not have been a change order, to unauthorized equipment substitutions. The list can be rather lengthy, including but not limited to the relocation of the earlier sprinkler pipe. Ultimately, the contractor has determined it is less expensive for his company to walk away from the withheld funds than it is to pick up the tab and pay for what is owed on the contract. This is the time when you make the phone call. I cannot explain the speed at which things start to get done, but the silence from the contractor is deeply uncomfortable. Call me weak-minded, I never like to cause controversy, but really know how to do it if or when the time came. After all, this is my building your messing with!

High-Rise Structures to Sky-Build Projects

I am a fan of incredibly tall buildings. The higher the better. Someday I'd like to see a building go to a height where you can see the curvature of the earth, or is this too farfetched? We tend to think that buildings can only be built to a certain height until the edifice becomes so tall that it will just fall over. I never believed that. With all that science and technology has to offer, there are too many possibilities on the horizon – no pun intended. To get there, everything has to have balance. With humans, it's our equilibrium. There are two conditions that must be met for our structures to be in equilibrium:

The first condition is that the net force on the object, our building, must be zero for the object to be in equilibrium.

Secondly, if the net force is zero, then net force along any direction is zero.

The force is a physical quantity that expresses the ability to push or pull, twist or accelerate a body that is measured in a unit dimensioned in mass × distance/time²—we don't like high velocity winds fooling around with our buildings. The torque is a rotational or twisting effect of a force—we don't like our tall buildings twisting and turning. The translation is the motion of our building to be on a linear path without deforming or rotating. This is how humans stand, walk, and run, without falling down. When we balance a stick or pencil with our finger, our hand moves at the same speed and in the same direction as the pencil. These are the reasons we look for a material that can be used which is difficult to break, and technologies we can use to make sure that the pencil stays upright?

If you can envision a pendulum sitting around the top of your building, each time your structure sways in one direction the pendulum moves immediately in the opposite direction. Now picture the weight, called a Bob, has been fabricated extremely heavy, where this weight pivots like a Descartes clock pendulum in the opposite direction of a building's sway. In theory, this would maintain a steady building—the Bob attached to the pendulum goes in one direction while the building goes in the other.

A number of buildings incorporate varying types of technologies that dampen and, in some cases, virtually eliminate the sway of a building. Let's remember that Descartes uniquely combined the imagery of clocks with man-made structures to explain the functions of each part of the body. Descartes' biosphere revealed the turning of gears in a clock along with its metal body which infuses it with a soul, and where this body incorporates an intelligence that lets it tell time. To Descartes, a body's soul is chiefly an exhibition of life, a movement, and by life he means action.

In the Asian country of Taiwan stands the 1,667-foot-tall Tapei 101 tower. Inside this tower and taking up six floors is an Eighteen-foot diameter sphere, weighing 728 tons and hanging on straps between the eighty-seventh and ninety-second floors. This is the building's equilibrium device, a Tuned Mass Damper, or TMD, which reduces the motion of the building by swinging slightly in the opposite direction of its sway, which causes the vibrational energy to dissipate. This Tapei pendulum stabilizes the building by exhibiting a Descartes type of action that identifies this building's vibrational energy and counters this vibration by dispersing it. This system provides our building with a means for balance, where the body's balancing system works through a continual process of position detection, feedback and adjustment, using communication between a variety of body functions that ultimately communicate with our brain.

I remember back in 2012 when I was conducting a Labor Needs Analysis—LNA review for the sixty-two story John Hancock Tower in Boston, USA. A well-maintained tower indeed. Although I was aware that this building incorporated a mass damper system, I was not aware of the TMD operational requirements that an LNA would be required to know. I found that the Hancock tower combined two mass dampers that were installed at opposite ends of the fifty-eighth floor. Each damper consisted of 300,000 pounds of weight that consist of a box of steel filled with lead. Each box of lead rests on a steel plate, and the plate is covered with lubricant so the weight is free to slide back and forth while allowing the floor to slide underneath. Because the weight is attached to the steel frame of the building by means of springs and shock absorbers, the springs and shocks take hold and pull the building back to its equilibrium point. Technology at its finest. This particular style of buildings has received these human reproductive balance fittings since the dawn of the new modernistic skyscraper, when buildings swayed too fast for comfort, moving a few inches to a couple of feet back and forth while simultaneously twisting. Occupants of these modern upper floors suffered from motion sickness. In 1977, it was the Citigroup Center in New York City that became one of the first skyscrapers to use a tuned mass damper to reduce sway, and it worked.

Now common throughout the globe, the typical TMD is essentially an enormous counterweight, built into a tower. Not a clock tower, just a tower. In order for engineers to make it work, they have to "tune" the damper to match a building's natural frequency, confirming that the weight swings just enough to counteract the wind or the frequency which is the speed of a vibration. Here, vibration will be the operative word.

When we reflect upon the new Standard Model in physics, we are keenly aware of an anticipated sound, a natural vibration, a rhythm we expect to hear and feel through our human senses. Our buildings too have a vibration that we are learning to adjust through these varying types of damper systems. We remember when Tesla informed us to think in terms of energy, frequency, and vibration, but at the time did not realize that these energy waves that he and other likeminded geniuses spoke of, also caused a disturbance within our structure's frame that becomes the source of the wave, the skeletal motion of our structures that make-up our building's height and stability. When looking at the simplicity of our building's natural vibration, it doesn't seem like rocket science, or is it?

America's National Aeronautics and Space Administration, NASA, appears to have figured out how to essentially turn off frequencies that cause resonance. They call the device a disruptive tuned mass damper—DTMD. Resonance is the reinforcement or prolonged sound that reflects from a surface, or by the synchronized vibration of a neighboring object. For buildings, vibrations hit the structure you're in at just the right frequency to cause resonance, and it is this vibration that these rather large tuned mass dampers are used to significantly reduce and eliminate.

A spin-off from their rocket technology, NASA developed this damper the size of a large coffee can and later developed it into a long pipe filled with liquid that can stop a tall building from shaking in an instant, but it was not designed using conventional mass damper technology. The solution was found by accident. NASA found a way to cause the fluid, that was supposed to absorb the vibrations, to act as if the fluid was no longer a part of their spacecraft structure. In 2016 a variation of this NASA system was installed in a thirty-second story modular building in Brooklyn, New York. Using four, three-foot-wide and fifty-foot- long configured pipes. Air springs are fitted to the outside of these pipes and tuned to what is called a certain sloshing frequency. Where all structures have natural vibrations, NASA calls them modes, the building's vibrations turn liquid into a secondary mass that is said to absorb and dissipate the energy of the building's vibrations. The problem is when the resonant frequency of the wind alines with the frequency of the building, and one of these frequencies is pushing at that right frequency-moment to affect the other. This causes extremely large amplitudes. Um, amplitudes? I believe we'll be discussing later a universal particle named an amplituhedron. Back on track, in Philadelphia USA, the 58 story Comcast tower, known as the Comcast Center, contains the largest Tuned Liquid Column Damper—TLCD in the world.

During conversations well after my visit to Israel, Stefan and I briefly discussed the methodology toward his country's built environment. I imagined the possibilities of using such vibration absorption technologies built into war-zone structures. This is a technology that can absorb the rumblings of a truck passing by on an unstable roadway to structures absorbing violent earth movements from an earthquake. Facility-absorbing-technology. Let's coin it a FAT structure for short. I would think that in all future build-outs FAT technology should be an integral component of all built structures and environments.

In mechanics, equilibrium has to do with the forces acting on a body, and that body can be human or the structures we build. Our building's damper systems are maturing from a pendulum or back-and-forth type, to mimicking the processes used within our human structure.

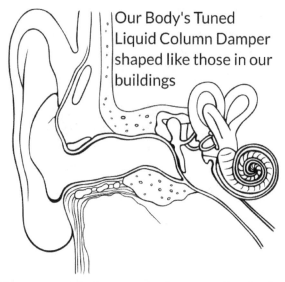

Our Body's Tuned Liquid Column Damper shaped like those in our buildings

The human vestibular system that provides for human balancing – contains a set of three semi-circle tubes within each human ear, where our building's Tuned Liquid Column Damper incorporates four semi-circle PVC pipes.

As a case in point, the human vestibular system is our sensory system that provides the leading involvement to the sense of balance and spatial orientation for coordinating movement with balance for our human body. This vestibular system consists of balance organs in our inner ear that tell the brain about the movements and position your head. There is a set of three tubes (semi-circular canals) in each ear, containing fluid-filled chambers that are generally continuous with those of the semicircular canals. This is similar to the earlier described main damper component of lightweight steel modules consisting of four U-shaped (semicircular) PVC pipes filled with liquid, in-turn directing our building how to move. These systems which achieve balance, sense when your building moves or when we move our head around. Both the mechanical and human organic systems are strikingly similar.

The process of equilibrium governs many of the liquid chemical reactions taking place in the human body, and both are governed by nature's inherent vibration, where all matter originates and exists only by virtue of a force which brings the particle of an atom to vibration. All matter is just vibrations of many underlying fields, and all of nature vibrates at every scale. Ultimately, when a different vibrating mass or different things come together, they will often start vibrating together at the same frequency. When this vibration is harnessed, we think of Sky-build.

Sky-Build

Sky-Build – An architectural structure of unlimited height that cannot maintain stability under its own intended design and construction without the assistance of electromechanical, fluid-dynamic, and/or vibration-arresting balancing systems.

—Wayne Saya, Sr

A *high-rise* structure is defined as a building higher than seventy-five feet under forty floors. A *skyscraper* is typically taller than 150 meters, 490 feet or forty floors. Yet, structures are now under construction that can reach higher than half a mile. Some day we may find structures that are crafted to heights requiring independent systems in order to keep them from falling down. For these new-age structures, *Sky-build* is as good a name as any.

The net-force on our building must be zero for it to be in equilibrium, and when the net-force is zero, then the net-force along any direction is zero, and this is how we climb to the heavens.

Living on the lowest layer of our atmosphere, the troposphere is where all of our weather occurs. Our troposphere ends at around 33,000 feet where the stratosphere begins. Because of the stability our stratosphere provides, it is from this altitude and higher where our aircraft like to fly. At 35,000 feet, around 6.6 miles high is where we should have a nice view of the curvature of the earth. Around twenty-four-and-a-half miles higher is where our stratosphere ends.

Continuing this thought experiment, I would imagine this is

the height we will build to, where the stability of this layer of the atmosphere requires that we only need to stabilize the area from the ground to the beginning of our stratosphere.

Next, reading this novel method of how we build our balancing mechanism for our sky-building will always need to start from the beginning. Should you stop and continue reading somewhere in a later paragraph, you may become confused as to how this balancing system is being constructed. So, let's start:

The materials required to build our structure very high beyond the clouds will need to be high strength, durable, and flexible. This is where compliant mechanisms are selected. We will need to apply a compliant mechanism methodology to this project. Many compliant mechanisms use beam-like structures or flexures. These are flexible mechanisms that transfer the input force and displacement at one port to an output force and displacement at another port through an elastic body deformation. In simple terms, many compliant mechanisms can be fabricated as single-piece structures, where there is no need for multiple materials to erect each floor. Because a compliant mechanism derives its motion from the deflection of its constituent members, each floor of our Sky-Tower is fabricated as a single structure that is attachable to the next floor with connecting elastic type material. Where low weight and no lubrication are essential, we look to NASA and the aerospace industry and their use of titanium compliant applications. I can imagine a floor that is structured using a titanium material that is fabricated as a compliant mechanism, attached to each floor-by-floor above.

Assuming our use of a compliant mechanism solution satisfies our primary materials and architecture, where this is our remedy to accomplish the high strength, durability, and flexibility of our Sky-tower, we next need to look at the weight of this tower along with the stability of its height. We need to provide our tower with balance.

Do we use a type of gyroscopic technology that is strategically placed every twenty-five or fifty floors? I think there should be a dual balancing strategy in considering the height we are looking to accomplish.

With this approach in mind, strategically and mathematically spaced at several points throughout the height of our Sky-tower, we install a number of NASA's disruptive-tuned-mass-dampers or a tuned-liquid-column-damper similar to the variation model used in Brooklyn, New York.

Next, and according to Earnshaw's Theorem, there is no way to maintain a stable equilibrium for any arrangement of fixed magnets or static electrical charges. Therefore, in order for us to supplement one of these selected damper systems for maintaining an equilibrium of our sky-tower, we first need to select a means of sensing the equilibrium of the tower. In this regard, Segway technology appears to match rather well. The Segway uses a motor in place of muscles, a series of microprocessors instead of a brain, and a set of smart tilt sensors replacing our vestibular or inner-ear balancing system. To guarantee power to this balancing-sensing structure, we incorporate a combination of photovoltaic and wind energy electric power generation into the wall structure along the exterior structure of our tower.

With our Sky-tower's initial stability system in place through damper technologies, and a balance and stability detection system in place for our secondary balancing system, we need to find a weight that is fluid enough to stabilize strategic balancing points of our tower—that can receive the signals from the tower's balancing detection system. We want to use a liquid ballast that can be dynamic in pulling from one direction or another in order to keep our structure in balance. The reason for this is because parametric studies have shown that the performance of passive and active tuned mass damper systems under high wind loads and/or earthquake environments can fail under certain conditions. Remember, these mass damper systems are tuned to specific vibrations.

Now please follow this paragraph slowly – conducting liquid or electrolyte contain ions that are positively charged and negatively charged ions. The flow of these ions conducts electricity through the conducting liquid or electrolyte. Nowadays, an electric-conductive liquid solution, a liquid that conducts electricity, can be made for just about any application. Even a highly conductive liquid metal, named gallium, is safe to touch but has a drawback, it needs to be at least 85.58-degrees Fahrenheit to maintain its liquid properties.

As a quickly-moving balancing weight, a liquid ballast will move more quickly and maintain an equilibrium for each designated segment, or end of our rising structure to compliment the earlier described disruptive-tuned-mass-damper system or even a tuned-liquid-column-damper. The weight of our liquid conductor will be important. Depending on the weight that our structural engineering requires for manipulating a correction of the sway that our building requires in one direction or another, will determine the weight of the liquid and the diameter of piping our liquid is carried. A larger diameter pipe provides more liquid and in-turn more weight. Got it!

Finally, we selected a conductive liquid material because we want to connect an electromagnet generator to the balancing sensing system. The strength of an electromagnet can be increased or decreased depending upon how the electromagnet is fabricated and by increasing or decreasing the voltage or amperage. We want to use a magnet to pull the liquid that contains a conductive material. Our Sky-tower's sensing system that is monitoring the upright condition of our Sky-tower will send the appropriate signals to the electromagnet, where these signals will determine the strength of the magnet and thereby the direction, force, and speed of the liquid corrective ballast—how fast the liquid ballast is sent from one end of a building to the other. This back-and-forth adjustment of heavy liquid ballast strategically assigned at different floor-locations will not be as dynamic as it sounds, because the primary stability is being handled by the earlier described selected mass-damper-system. It is this secondary balancing system that will prevent the primary damper system from going in-and-out of its tuned frequency and in-turn vibration.

The human body as a whole has been found to respond at a

resonant frequency of five hertz, and in recent experiments appear to have up to ten hertz. If we take this frequency, where one hertz is the same as one cycle-per-second, and where the number of cycles of vibration of air per-second, one second is known as a universal quantum. 432 hertz is known as the natural frequency of the universe. But the most important of the ancient Solfeggio Frequencies is at 528 hertz. This is said to be the frequency of nature and is present in everything, including our DNA. The astounding occurrence, when you play these frequencies in the form of notes into water, varying geometric configurations can be seen in the water when viewing through a microscope. Different frequencies of sound create different geometries, different vibrations, and shapes.

In September of 2013, two Cal Tech physicists—Nima Arkani-Hmed and Jaroslav Trnka, discovered that all of space and time is the emanation of a single geometric form or shape, and this shape they have named the Amplituhedron particle. This disclosure of particle interactions which is a basic event in nature that represents the most elementary events in nature could very- well be of a geometry that significantly advances a decades-long effort to reformulate the quantum field theory, which is the body of laws describing elementary particles and their interactions. In physics, it's called a positive Grassmannian. So, how does this relate to the vibrational properties of the mass and structure which make up our Sky-tower?

By remembering that nature's balance and vibration is everything, science has recognized there are five geometric patterns that are produced by inducing harmonic tones (vibration) into a fluid. Sand particles are suspended in a fluid using harmonic tones, and these tones shown under a microscope reveal geometric patterns within a sphere. Within this sacred geometry, these platonic shapes are a tetrahedron, octahedron, icosahedron, dodecahedron, and a cube, all a part of what has been recognized as sonic geometry, where these geometric shapes are found by inducing harmonic tones into fluid. Two tetrahedrons combined reveal a star tetrahedron, which can nicely fit at all points within a cube.

A sonic geometric configuration - Frequency is a motion that repeats itself—it is the number of waves that pass a given point in time, while vibration is an oscillating, reciprocating, or another form of motion of a solid or flexible body or medium forced from a static-position or state of equilibrium. Oscillation is an effect that is something that regularly repeats and fluctuates above and below some known value, such as the pressure of a sound wave or the cycles-per-second within alternating current.

All of these geometric shapes nest point-to-point perfectly within a sphere, and we can see the star tetrahedron also recognized within the amplituhedron particle, the same particle earlier described. Aware that the field, our universe has a vibrational equilibrium, the goal toward keeping our sky-tower upright is to match the vibrational frequencies of our mass-dampers to the structure of our sky-tower.

A sky-build project is all about our tower's vibrational stability as it goes at least one layer beyond our troposphere. The aim of this thought experiment is to demonstrate that there are ways to mimic our structures with the same stability and tenacity as our own human structures, regardless of height or width, beyond the troposphere.

But Sky-towers also mimic combined densities. Through a tremor, quiver or tremble, our plants and flowers react to the assortment of vibrations through music, traffic noise, or anything that pulsates. These organic plantings are proven to respond favorably or unfavorably depending on the source of these vibrations. Using a liquid ballast as earlier described, our Sky-tower has been designed to duplicate the density of these organic plantings while also incorporating the density of a higher artificial intelligence by incorporating human-level balancing designs and electronics. Our Sky-tower can sprout from the earth like a plant.

When the electrons of the atoms within the frame and floors of our sky-tower vibrate, we know they produce photonic light energy that quite possibly connects with the photonic energy of the systems which keep our structure upright. I can imagine when the photons from each section of our building pass through our structure, that special pair of glasses Dad once told me about would probably see a building all lit up like a city at night. Because, whether we want to accept physics as real science, which it is, or merely look upon it as though it doesn't matter to property management and facility engineering professionals, the fact will always remain that our buildings are alive with light and vibration, because the materials that make up the atomic structures of our buildings are in reality live and pulsating energies of light and vibration. Someday, we may find that the mysterious anti-gravity *element 115* will someday become available to be used as a gravity generator. A super-heavy metal element that is said to produce an anti-gravitational field when exposed to radiation currently decays within milliseconds, so I think that's an issue that would need to be resolved before we can ask to have it placed at the top of our tower to help with the buoyancy and equilibrium of our tower. Our sky-tower contains real energy. It retains our organic photonic imprints that are mixed with its own structure. We feel a connection, a consciousness with the structures we become attached to. Our buildings will climb because we have a variety of technologies to choose from and because—we will them to climb.

It was during my early years many decades ago while experimenting in electronic communications I had learned that various frequencies make up our elementary means of communication. Then as I do now, I've always felt a partnership, an understanding to a point where the differing frequencies had unique vibrations of their own. This is the reason I felt a need to create this sky-build project and sky-tower, to expose how vibrations affect each part of the structures we build. When we ultimately find that recipe, a way that we can partner with them, work with them, find their true vibration, we will find that our buildings can have a stable foundation within our built environment far deep below our earth, while providing us with the ability to reach the stars.

CONCLUSION

I have always found the importance of understanding the mechanics, equipment, and systems of the built environment are a necessity for understanding its operation. What makes these pieces of equipment work with the systems they are tied to? After decades of learning and experimenting with these human duplications, I found that we are the DNA of our buildings, the human cells maintaining a duplicated edifice.

Reflecting on the corrective intervention and maintenance of my body's displacement pump, I came to realize that our medical maintenance and desired outcome are based upon an understanding of the results sought. Outcome measures reflect the impact of the health care service or intervention in our health similar to the preventive, predictive, and reliability-centered-maintenance programs for our built environments.

Yes, I consider the procedure to remedy my affliction was for the most part successful. The additional signals were, for now, prevented from interfering with the synchronism of my pulse. But in my case, the correction of the a-fib ailment had created a change in the organic circuitry that has enhanced a benign irregular beat, a rhythm that skips a number of times during the course of an hour or a day. However, this is not unusual. In some cases, it happens. Yet, for decades I have lived with the lesser version of this arrhythmia, where I would experience a single irregular beat each day. OK... What would Sigi do? What would he say? This was personal, a resolve I needed to develop within my-own consciousness. I knew there was a baseline, the irregular beat I have possessed throughout the decades. I simply needed to work the problem. This is what Sigi would say. At this stage, the modern medical repair techniques had come to require me to tweak this irregular motor rhythm with medication. Nope—Not interested. I originally sought and selected this repair to avoid medication—to avoid going outside of the original manufacturer's design—Mom's design. I don't want the survival of my organic machine dependent upon a source outside of my-own corrective or reproductive abilities. I don't want to be dependent upon a source that is not me. We all possess our-own separate code, a user manual that we have not completely figured out. Sometimes you just need to smile and go on auto-pilot—let the body figure things out on its own. In my mind it's what photons do!

Within the bio-scientific community, geneticists understand that our DNA molecules hold the blueprints of our organic bodies. However, these same geneticists acknowledge, that less than five percent of our DNA molecules contain the codes for these blueprints, leaving the remaining estimated ninety-five percent of our DNA chain as, what they call, junk DNA, but is this apparent unused chain of DNA molecules junk? As a visual, it's like looking at an old fashion Morse code tape, where the code of dots and dashes represent the DNA code information and the blank part of the long tape in-between the dot and dash messages represent no information—this is how a majority of the scientific community looks at it anyway. Yet, there are those within this community that look upon these unused DNA molecules, in the form of unused Morse code tape, as possessing a subtle energy. Is this subtle energy those photons left behind on a chair that we've sat on?

Now leaving Washington, D.C. and on our return trip back to Boston, the engines of the plane started to turn as I glanced over at Melynee seated to my right, and both of us sitting closest to the window. I could tell that she was reflecting over her day—by the way she stared straight through the bulkhead wall of the aircraft—and there was that veiled look of anticipation. As the engines grew ever so louder, we started to move toward the runway, where she then quietly placed her headphones from her Walkman cassette player onto her head. She developed a soft smile, the kind that indicates self-confidence and control. Yanni has that effect on me too. Now on the final approach, the engines have reached their loudest while on the ground and we begin to move faster down the runway. Without notice both Melynee and I simultaneously look at one and another and now with the two of us wearing that smile of confidence. With the sudden weightlessness of lift-off, we were airborne, and all I could think of was for the plane to reach the standard 10,000 feet so that I could make my way over to the lavatory, but Melynee with her head back against the seat, slowly turns to the window and watched as the fog-like clouds danced past the glare of light produced from the headlights of the plane. Continuing to climb we pierce through the misty glare and arrive below a dark ceiling of endless twinkling dots of light that reveals the starry heaven.

What are the major forces behind natural and mechanical life and what truly distinguishes the two aside from human superiority? Is it that prized unification theory all in physics are chasing, or has it already been found? Are we that higher superiority over our mechanicals' artificial intelligence or are we merely being used by our mechanical creations to make their synthetic lives closer to our genius? Is a computer glitch really a glitch? How many times have we considered ourselves above that of our creator and what makes us think we too are not thought of in that same equation by our mechanical creations? Think of how we have created the very blanket of protection for ourselves by mechanically replicating our human structure—our body and mind. Unconsciously or otherwise, we have created buildings in our own image. Big Al too addressed this topic, where he concluded: *I want to know how God created this world. I am not interested in this or that phenomenon, in the spectrum of this or that element. I want to know his thoughts. The rest are details.*[29] We have learned that Relativity never stops playing significant roles in our continuing evolution.

The human heart produces the strongest electrical energy within the human body structure, much more than our human

---

[29] Recalled by his Berlin student Esther Salaman, 1925, in Salaman, "A talk with Einstein," Listener 54 (1955), 370-371.

brain and analogous to the pumps within our buildings when compared to a building's automation system. Photonic energy in the form of charged particle emissions flow through the concrete we walk on and build with, the wood within the apartments, condominiums, and buildings we live in, the windows made of glass we see-through, and all of the food we eat. Although our human senses cannot see, hear, or feel these live atoms that possess these charged photon particles, the buildings, and facilities within our world are nonetheless alive—truly alive and not just metaphorically. The density of the materials that make up the buildings we work and live in communicate with our own higher density being, similar to a non-educated child communicating with a learned adult. We can feel the absence of a building when we leave it and become happy when seeing a structure that we've been away from too long. The photons of our organic bodies mingle with those of our man-made structures. We must know by now that our communication with buildings are real, in-part where the atomic numbers which make up a significant amount of the very minerals and materials that are contained within our buildings and our human structures are the same.

Buildings have a dual intelligence, the various manufactured automation systems we incorporate into artificial smart buildings, and structures that already contain an intelligence derived from the rotation of atomic particles that make up those organic materials used to create our built environments. Components of smart buildings are artificial, our attempt to build-in a higher intelligence for our structures that mimic the level, the density of our own intelligence. This density is intelligent energy.

If you look at it from a pure electronics viewpoint, photons are intelligent charged particles that contain information, a vibration in rhythm. The question then becomes, how dense is this information or at what level? The degree of intelligence that is compacted within the substance or which makes up the particles that these photons vibrate determines the type and intelligent level of information we receive. The higher the density the higher the level of consciousness. Surely the density level of intelligence from, let's say a plant, is far less than the electromagnetic energy of photons coming from particles that make up our complex human organic structure. Humans are a higher density of intelligence than plants, trees, and flowers. Yet, let's not forget that these beautiful organic plant structures have been proven by science to respond to our human communications through vibrations of voice and music. Not known for having a brain, science has revealed that plants have analogous structures that gather types of sensory data in order to respond. Their roots are known to shift direction to avoid obstacles and are said to possess human senses such as hearing and taste. Vibrations from incoming sound waves are the process that all living bodies use to hear. This form of intelligence coming from such a low-density body has demonstrated an ability to communicate with a higher density human.

The density is a level of intelligence. It's the difference between using a chalkboard or whiteboard and graduating to a lap-top computer. The level of interactive intelligent components separating these two types of learning tools is analogous to their density levels. If our human intelligence level can communicate with a lower density of intelligence such as plants, and plants are on the same density level as the elements they are made from, such as phosphorus, potassium, calcium, magnesium, zinc, sulfur, chlorine, boron, iron, copper, manganese, you get the picture, than buildings made of these same elements must possess some type of communication with their higher density human occupants.

Now looking down from the window of the aircraft the clouds suddenly begin to break up, slowly revealing from below a magnificently lit city of buildings. Not realizing that she was wearing her music headset, Melynee loudly exclaimed: *Daddy— the buildings are moving*. Although the other passengers of this flight were briefly startled by her calm-breaking announcement, they were also unable to understand her revelation as they curiously attempted to look down from their windows. With a soft smile, I needed not even a glance, because I knew that what she was imagine-viewing was big Al, Rene', and all those friends of invention and discovery individually mirrored into each of the high-rise structures reflected through the clouds as if the buildings were moving with the reflection of the clouds. I could envision big Al and Rene' as the two tallest buildings and leading such other structures in the images of Newton, DaVinci, Schauberger, and a host of others in no particular order. In the end, buildings have a dual intelligence, the various manufactured automation systems we incorporate into artificial smart buildings, and structures that already contain an intelligence derived from the rotation of atomic particles that make-up the organic materials used to create our built environments.

Home for the holidays, I overheard Wayne, Jr asked by a sibling whether he would read Dad's book once it was published. With a general enjoyment to amuse as a component to his sense of humor that only Junior possesses, he replied: *Are there any pages to color?* Needless to say, I made sure one on page 12 is included for this Naval officer.

Wayne and wife Nancy caught napping by friends on an unknown flight.

Now mostly retired, I speak for audiences on occasion and look at buildings that only interest me. I'll be traveling quite a bit to see the sites, taste the different cultural foods, and admire the various architectures and building systems of the world, experiencing and communicating with the electromagnetic energy of photons throughout my travels. With my soul-mate, Tweety, next to me, the trips will be sporadic and fast-paced, so if you happen to see me wrestling with my luggage through some Aero Porto or car rental parking lot one day, just yell over, that buildings are people too!

I cannot explain the sense of energy– of vibration running through me along with a level of balance I experience when I first walk into the entrance of a building. It remains all surreal. The size of the structure mattered little to me, although size did control an assortment and volume of emotions. Nonetheless, I always slow to a stop in an effort to prevent myself from being pulled into the magnificence and opulence, the magnetic grandeur of a smart and well-built structure complete with nature's water-features and Pantone color codes. Although extremely wanting and enjoyable, these synthetic environments were not able to top my appetite at a level where I was one with nature and my own creator. A tent in the desert or tree house in the Forrest would have been just fine. The addiction was this Understanding of the built environment— this synthetic environment– synthetic nature– that permitted me to come close– allowing me in– to feel as one with it all.

What is the main characteristic, the one common denominator that can be used to explain both the natural body and the mechanical building, whether viewing the two individually or as one? Every person has his or her self-awareness of which personality they are, and what limitations set them apart from others. Do you truly help your building or inhibit its' success by attempting to promote your behavior, your ego or your being? Buildings too have their own unique personalities—created using our components that mimic our own. You cannot attempt to understand a building— the replication of ourselves—unless you have a clear and honest understanding of your own personality, which I include as your body's functional ability, that mechanical characteristic which too separates you from your fellow human. Are we baby-sitters to structures that need an advocate's voice? or are these artificial extensions of our own body merely used and, in some instances, abused for economic gain. It is clearly the ability to understand yourself and your motive and in-turn bestow upon you The Art of Understanding Your own Building's Personality.

CPSIA information can be obtained
at www.ICGtesting.com
Printed in the USA
BVHW030202180621
609884BV00006BA/22/J